He Said, She Said:

The Spokane

River Killer

By Jon Keehner
Edited by Nancy J. Teppler

Corvus Latrans Publishing
Jonkeehner.com

© 2017 by Jon Keehner. All rights reserved.

No part of this book may be reproduced, photocopied, or transmitted in any form without the express written permission of the author, except for quotations embodied in articles about or reviews of the book.

> Cover photo concept:
> Chris Peltier
> Blood Diamond Ink

ISBN-13: 978-1497575592
ISBN-10: 1497575591

First published September 15, 2017.

Available from Amazon.com and other retail outlets.
Printed by CreateSpace

> Corvus Latrans Publishing
> corvuslatrans@gmail.com

Contents

Preface
Dedication
Foreword
Author's Note to paperback readers

Part 1: Along the Okanogan River 1

1 Pogue Flat 3
2 The Clock on the Wall 21
3 The Smell of Gun Oil 40
4 In Small Town America 57
5 Will Run With Blood 62
6 A Rotting Carcass 74
7 Bits of Broken Glass 86
8 Other Parts of the Town 101
9 Suffer the Beautiful Girl 111
10 A Violent and Frequently Labile Woman 124
11 State Of Unkemptness 135
12 Full Range of Psychiatric Unit Activities 154
13 Once Bristled With Apple Trees 164

Part II: Clairann 179

14 Weed Infested Alleys 180
15 A Night He Would Never Forget 192
16 The Chaos and Carnivale 203
17 The Darkness and Frigid Air 214
18 Swirling Pools of Splashing Green Water 227
19 A Single Story Brick Warehouse 236

20   Brilliance Overwhelmed 246
21   Lace Ruffles So Perfectly White 255

Part III: As the Bodies Pile Up ....…............... 267

22   Princess ....….......... 268
23   Advanced States of Decomposition 276
24   A Gender Psychosis Disorder 285
25   Unencumbered By Her Past 296
26   Fingernail Clippings and a Vaginal Smear 304
27   Yolanda, Nickie and Kathleen 318
28   Final Thoughts ....…. 324

More books by Jon Keehner
Social media connections
The Snake River Killer
Acknowledgments

Preface

This book is based upon factual research, which includes extensive review of public records and court files as well as detailed interviews with persons knowledgeable about the subject of this book, the murders of Yolanda Sapp, Nickie Lowe and Kathleen Brisbois. Douglas (aka Donna) Perry was not interviewed for this book.

While this book is based upon true events, the narrative includes fictionalized accounts of the thoughts, discussion, statements and motivations of Doug (aka Donna) Perry and other persons interviewed for this book. These accounts flow from my research and reflect my best OPINION as to what transpired based upon facts of record. In many instances names have been changed.

In addition, this book includes fictionalized dialogue and thoughts which were added to facilitate the telling of this story. Many of the situations presented in this text are of an extremely graphic, violent and sexual nature intended for adult audiences only. Great care was taken to ensure that the dialogue only adds to the reader's understanding of the personality and mannerisms of the characters involved and makes every attempt not to influence the facts of the story.

Thoughts, dialogue and situations also include a context which may seem disrespectful to the victims and others involved in the story. However, in order to fully understand the plight of many of the people involved in this story, this is necessary. When characters in the story were interviewed by police, the dialogue was taken directly from statements included in the case file. On many occasions, characters use incomplete sentences, confusing wording, and the like. Many of the statements are in direct conflict with other witnesses' perspectives. These errors were intentionally left in, as my goal in this writing was to communicate my opinion of what happened, in story form, while preserving as much of the written record as possible.

The text has been edited by a very qualified editor; however, my writing voice lends itself to some unique wording and phrasing. Save for requested name changes, the grammar, spelling, and other inconsistencies in italicized court transcriptions have been left as they appear in official public records, unaltered and unedited.

For Yolanda, Nickie and Kathleen:

Your time on this Earth was far too short, but your lives mattered too many whether you knew so or not. You will not be forgotten.

"In a situation in a community in which he feels more cornered, Mr. Perry's behavior might be more unpredictable."
Dr. Timothy Keller
May 12, 1988

Foreword

Love, once found, is like a living and breathing entity.
A gift.
It lifts souls upward and makes them better. Greater than the sum of its parts. The sun is brighter, the sounds of a rushing river are sweeter and time away becomes eternal.

But when love is lost, like any living and breathing creature, the malodorous corpse rots silently away into the ground. Forgotten. Putrid and foul. When love turns away and laughs at you, it can leave you destitute and swollen with hatred. Unafraid and empowered to reign in again what once was, and shall be again. Nothing can counter its power, stamina and fortitude to justify its resurrection. At any cost.

It runs, it laughs and it mocks.

And for a sick mind, this truth thunders through the empty heart a thousand fold. Twisted acts of sadness and evil pour forth as simple expressions of love; true and justified. As the mortal flesh of joy, hope and kindness melt away into the soil, only the eternal bones of desperation, bitterness and resolute clarity remain to be discovered.

If there ever was a story to be told about the senseless murders of three women which took place in Spokane, Washington during the winter and spring of 1990, then it is a story of mangled love, sick minds and a distorted sense of redemption.

Or no love at all.

These women had families who loved them, friends who miss them, and dreams that escaped them. Scattered amongst the daily shit of life on Sprague Avenue, they experienced joy, hope and kindness- like all of us have.

And like a putrefied corpse with no identity, this joy, hope and kindness can only be speculated upon. Recreated from the calcified remains of desperation and violence by those who simply want to understand. With no picture or likeness to refer to, the blood, tissue and skin are mere reflections. Reflections of sad, fractured minds which might never be fully understood.

Morose, moribund and mundane.

When the desecrated flesh of love lost in this story is finally washed away and sent down the drain of lost memories, it winds its way through the lush rain forests of the Olympic Peninsula, into the bowels of Seattle and Tacoma, and ends up in the tiny town of Omak, Washington, a hundred miles to the northwest of Spokane; twenty-five years before anyone had any idea, how far broken, this love would become…

*Authors note for paperback readers:

A complete collection of photos and a link to an interactive Google MAP that shows locations and photos of key events and points of interest from the book are available on the He Said, She Said: The Spokane River Killer Facebook page.

Simply go to your Facebook home page and search spokaneriverkiller to find our Facebook page. Please feel free to ask questions and leave comments as well!

Jon Keehner

Part I:

Along the Okanogan River

He Said, She Said: The Spokane River Killer

1
Pogue Flat

May 13, 1987.

It hadn't rained for days.

Maybe even a week. The late spring of 1987 was unseasonably hot in the Okanogan River Valley of north-central Washington.

Every few minutes an easterly breeze sent the sweltering heat from the rocks above cascading downward onto the flat below. Like a flash flood, the arid torrent ripped through the bleached gray tree trunks and shattered branches of the once flourishing apple orchard. What used to be a lush, green oasis, sat dry and decaying.

Ugly.

Starlings and robins fluttered from branch to branch, screeching and chirping as they searched for even a single apple. None of the birds stayed for long. Nearly a third of the trees were dead. Neglected and malnourished, the living ones barely produced leaves, let alone fruit.

Above the aging orchard, the surrounding ridge lines were nothing more than residual volcanic rock and sedimentary deposits left over from a time long ago, when the high-desert scablands served a more natural purpose. Now, washed and eroded, the rocky hillsides sat dormant and dry, scattered with bunch grasses and sprawling desert shrubs. Rising to the north and west of the orchard the rugged terrain was quilled with Ponderosa pines and Douglas fir. The dusty hills streaked upwards toward the blue of the skyline. A pair of mule deer browsed in the shade, while a red-tailed hawk circled high overhead.

Nearly 75 years earlier, man-made irrigation had turned the valley into a productive agricultural enterprise: apple trees, cherry trees, a sea of sweet green.

But the life-giving water was long gone.

Now, the dust and dirt that had returned to lay claim to the valley swirled through the remaining trees and caked into a thick, arid clay. Only a few miles or so west of the town of Omak, Washington, this collection of dying orchards, run-down farms, and hardscrabble ranches was known to the locals as Pogue Flat.

To him, it was *perfect*.

He could move from one end to the other—in or out and through the remains of the orchard—without making a sound. Once he got close to whatever prey he might be stalking, he could wait for the surging, hot wind to rustle the leaves and cover any noise he might make. With his dad's Makarov pistol by his side, he felt he had nothing to fear.

The mangled fruit trees and surrounding pasture along with the adjoining farmlands, corrals, and outbuildings gave him a sense of security. From the south side of the orchard he could look across the pasture a few hundred feet further to the south and see his house, his father's workshop, and the junked out cars and equipment that were slowly losing their color as they rusted and rotted back into the parched soil.

Reaching down to his belt, he unclipped his canteen. Crouching next to one of the trees, he quickly smacked the back of his neck where a horsefly had lit and bitten him. For a few seconds he stared at the mixture of his blood and the splattered remains of what was left of the black insect on the palm of his hand. His stomach relaxed for just a moment.

He giggled.

A wry smile crept across his face and quickly vanished as though he were worried someone might see the delight he relished in killing the creature. Even though he was safely immersed in the confines of his family's land, one could never be too careful about who might be watching.

Discipline and control.

He did not like surprises.

With deliberate purpose he twisted the lid off of the canteen and lifted the water toward his mouth— he stopped and tilted his head just a little to the right.

The robins and starlings had disappeared.

He could usually hear the motion of the leaves, but the high desert silence was giving way to a low, droning roar, *barely audible* in the distance. For a second, confusion slipped across his face. The canteen hovered in his hand, suspended and frozen straight out in front of him.

A tractor?

What the hell is a tractor doing on *our land?*

Without taking a drink, he quickly spun the cap onto the canteen and flipped his canvas knapsack back over his shoulder. Quickly, he dove through a couple of trees away from the access road along the orchard to hide.

Carefully, he listened.

He flipped his long pony-tail of matted brown hair to the shoulder opposite of the knapsack and pushed his heavy glasses back up the bridge of his nose.

His mother had picked the glasses out for him.

He hated them.

But she insisted.

He crouched down behind a decades old apple tree, gnarled and disfigured. He pulled the tie from his hair releasing the pony tail and let it fall across his shoulders.

He strained to listen…

He Said, She Said: The Spokane River Killer

Unmistakably, a tractor was crawling its way down the middle of the access road. The engine whined and groaned as it made its way through the washouts and potholes of the seldom-used path. Its timbre rose and fell with each rut as it drew closer. The bucket of the tractor squeaked and clanked like the tracks of the German tanks he watched in World War II movies.

Once again, a sick smile wrinkled his face.

He was fascinated with World War II.

His father had fought against the Germans. The basement of the old farmhouse he lived in was packed full of WW II era pistols and rifles in various states of assembly and disrepair. Underneath the dimly lit single bulb fixture which hung in the exact center of his bedroom, books, magazines, and other military trinkets lay scattered about as though he simply dropped them wherever he happened to be at the time the particular item's novelty or usefulness wore off. Segregated collections of related junk coagulated into piles where he had started some project and then lost interest. But he knew what every pile was for and what he was working on at the time.

And that was all that mattered.

His mother, like all mothers, would nag at him to clean up his room and the adjoining basement.

Like she ever came downstairs.

He giggled to himself again.

She was way too fat.

The sudden screeching of a robin snapped him back to the present. In the scattered shade of the grove, his olive-green fatigue pants and black t-shirt should keep him hidden. He hated people. He hated interacting with them, and he hated it when, no matter what he said or did, they teased him.

They teased him about his hair.

They teased him about his mother.

He ran the fingers of his left hand along the top of his ear pulling his wiry locks behind it as he strained to listen. Without any warning or control, he burped.

It tasted like his mother's beef-barley soup.

The woman can cook.

Statuesque and motionless he held his breath for just a moment. A few hundred yards away the engine sat idling.

It had stopped getting closer.

Without another thought, he dashed across the trail in between two perfectly uniform rows of apple trees. He dove forward, extending his arms as he tucked and rolled. He nearly ripped the skin off of his forearm as he scraped along one of the old sprinkler heads hidden in the dirt. As smooth as a tumbling gymnast, he rolled into a tactical position behind the largest tree in the row. Flat on his rear-end with his back to the trunk, he peered over his left shoulder in the direction he last heard the tractor and rubbed his forearm. A few drops of blood trickled across his skin. He raised his arm to his mouth and licked some the blood off his salty arm.

The injury only added to his fantasy.

He imagined he was trapped, deep in the Black Forest of war-torn Europe, 1945. His tongue pressed against his bottom lip in a childlike smile.

German tank platoon. Six o'clock.

His hand slid down to the worn, leather holster strapped to his right thigh. His fingers slid under the stiff flap and unsnapped the cover. Touching the handgrip of the pistol sent a shiver up his spine. His mother always told him not to take the pistol into the orchard… that he was "gonna find trouble with the damn thing." Once she even caught him leaving the house with one of his father's old German pistols, so he stashed this one out in the workshop. This way if she ever caught him leaving the house with one of the pistols again, he would have one waiting.

He was smarter than she was.

He Said, She Said: The Spokane River Killer

He was smarter than most everybody he had contact with.

And he loved his guns. Never would one of his guns laugh at his failure to keep his hair neatly trimmed like his mother wanted.

They were always there to protect him. His friends and family came and went like the unpredictable weather of north-central Washington. His guns didn't.

Without them, he was vulnerable.

Naked as a baby coddled in its crib, for as long as he was able to hold them in his frail fingers, he fondled them, disassembled, and reassembled them. Each one was as familiar to him as the shape of his hands and feet. In the darkness of his bedroom he would lie in bed and caress whichever one had grabbed his attention for the moment. He knew every curve and line from the grip to the trigger to the barrel. Sometimes he would reach out across his bed to the shelf where he kept them and grab one in the dark and see if he could guess which one it was before he flicked the pole switch on the wall above his headboard to see if he had guessed correctly. He even learned to grip the light switch tightly so as not wake his mother when it clicked on.

Routine. Never break the routine.

The little game was more of a habit now than anything else. He knew which was which every single time. It wasn't even a fun game anymore.

His mother gave up trying to keep them out of his bedroom; it was a losing battle. She could barely manage her own daily affairs, let alone care for her son. And now that she never came downstairs anymore?

GGGRRRUMMPHH.

Grinding back to life, the engine of the tractor roared back into motion, snapping him out of his daydream.

Krauts are trying to find me. I have to circle back.

He snapped the leather flap back into place on the holster and darted across the pathway. He figured the Krauts were now two or three hundred yards away from his position. As thick as the orchard was, it offered him little protection from being seen, as the open pathways between the parallel trees opened up to the road.

As they drew closer to his position, he could hear two men speaking back and forth to each other in Spanish. He pretended they were speaking German and that they were the last remnants of a Panzer Division trying to escape to the east.

As another rush of sweltering wind ripped through the orchard, he took off between the rows at a dead run. He hoped they would be paying attention to their task at hand and not even notice the imminent death coming toward them. As he approached the iron monster, rattling its way up the dirt access road, he dove again for cover. As he did, the tractor jerked to a stop a mere 15 feet to his left.

The voices were much louder now. The tractor sat idling.

He was *too close.*

His heart began to race.

For a minute or two he strained to listen. But the conversation had ended. Nothing but the clanking engine of the tractor. He had to look around the tree and see what they were doing.

He took a couple of deep breaths and whirled his head around his right shoulder beyond the tree trunk.

No one was there. *Where had they* --

"HEY! Chica!" one of the men laughed a few feet to his left.

Startled, he spun around and there were the two men not more than 10 feet away uncoiling some black plastic piping. They both looked at him curiously and laughed while saying something to each other in Spanish. They dropped the coil and walked slowly toward him.

"Wha-chu doing here?" one of the men asked, in as good English as he could muster. His Spanish accent was thick and robust.

He began breathing very heavily and nearly hyperventilated himself. He just sat there, motionless.

The men stopped and stared at him.

"Hey— lit-tle, senorita— chu cannot be here, no?" the man asked again.

He stood up and faced the two men. His right leg began trembling ever so slightly.

Senorita?

One of them flipped his hand toward him, pointing in the direction of his house, "Chu go on now. Thees is meester Char-ez land, now. Go! Go!"

How dare they. Fucking spicks.

Conversation was not his strong suit. He hated it. Most of the time his sentences were choppy and staccato-like. People laughed at how he talked.

Both of them began laughing.

With that, his anger began to boil over. He reached down and unsnapped the holster to his pistol. The older of the two men saw what was happening and stepped right up into him, not more than a few inches from his face. His knee was visibly shaking.

"What? Chu wanna be a big man now, little chica? Chu gonna pull a gun? A gun on us?" the man yelled at him; he was furious now.

The other man stepped toward him and the looks on both men's faces became even more serious and aggressive.

"Leave me... leave me alone," he quietly muttered and deliberately turned his back toward the men as he started through the orchard back toward his fence.

He could hear them muttering to each other in Spanish as he walked.

He was incensed. They had no right to run him off. That land had been in his family since before he was born.

Inside his head, he saw scenarios of rage playing out before him. He visualized putting his Makarov right up to their heads and killing both of those dirty Mexicans.

Right there.

They would never talk like that to him again.

Ever.

Or maybe a pitch fork—right into their chests. They would bleed, scream, and double over in a fit of death like the neighbor's stupid dog.

He turned and marched away from the stupid stupids. The hike through the orchard and over the barbed-wire fence seemed like a blur. With every step toward his basement his blood got hotter and hotter. His usual long and drawn out thoughts were becoming choppy bits of delusion and anger.

His breathing, heavy and labored, he could barely keep the saliva in his mouth from running down onto his chin. His arms shook, his knees trembled, and he could hardly control the tremoring of his hand as he turned the door latch to the shop in the barn. He reached above the bench top for his stack of empty coffee cans. In his hurry, the cans tipped and fell about the dirt floor of the shop. He quickly gathered as many as he could from the floor and cradled them into his arms.

No matter what... he would *show them*.

*   *   *

Tucked away behind a large grove of pear trees, a few hundred yards away, the neighboring Charles house could have graced the cover of a modern day "Little House on the Prairie" novel. The navy blue trim bracketed the brilliant white paint of the house like frosting on a vanilla ice cream cake. Well manicured and tightly cut, the lawn surrounding the house was such a lush, deep green it seemed to make the air surrounding the home smell fresh and sweet. The wind chimes on the porch lightly strummed a tune while the sprinklers in the background kept rhythm and time. Even the barn, the workshop, and the other outbuildings were meticulously painted to match the main house.

Toward the rear of the house, an older woman balanced herself on a rickety wooden ladder. Carefully, she was hanging hummingbird feeders along the eaves in front of her kitchen window. She had meticulously measured the distance between the hooks but the look on her face indicated they were not quite right.

Not just yet.

Across the gravel turnaround from the house, her husband, an older gentleman, and clearly a man of larger carriage, wrestled with a massive, sliding barn door. He wore dark blue denim coveralls, a perfectly laundered white t-shirt and navy blue work gloves. His thinning white hair was nearly the same color as the house and outbuildings.

"I need some stronger arms?!" the woman yelled toward her husband.

The grinding of the slider wheels on the bottom of the barn door masked her voice so he did not hear her. Mr. Charles leaned toward the half-opened door and gave it another huge push.

She sighed and slipped down from the ladder.

With a loud thump, the door slammed to a stop and the squealing of the slider wheels on the iron track fell silent.

"There," Mr. Charles muttered to himself. He didn't hear his wife approaching.

"I need stronger hands," she said quietly and with a big smile. Startled, he jumped back and laughed.

"Oh... you *scared me*," he said as he clasped his fists to his chest and chuckled.

His wife stood in front of him and softly smiled while she removed the gloves from her hands.

"And you know," she started, pointing toward the corner of the barn, "one of those yard cats has had a litter again. I thought we had gotten them all— but— sheesh! I don't know?"

"I'll take care of it," he replied.

"Just do it in a humane —"

"I will. I always have," he reassured his wife.

She knew he would. He was a good man.

Mr. Charles stood there trying to catch his breath. Over the years, he had sworn he was going to change the tracks out on that old door. But for some reason, he just never got around to it. Despite the perfect yard, beautiful house, and wonderful life he and his wife had built, some things just seemed to slip through the cracks.

"Well, when you get a chance, I need those hooks for the hummingbird feeders turned in a little tighter. I just can't seem to get them in all the way," his wife requested as she made her way back toward the house.

"I will," he said, finally having caught his breath.

The sound of the gunshots caught him a little by surprise.

Crack!...Crack!... Pop! Pop! Pop!

He turned and looked out across the orchard toward the sound of the gun fire. Shooting was nothing out of the ordinary up on Pogue Flat. Bird hunters, deer hunters, and even target shooters were commonplace in the surrounding hills.

But he knew right where these shots were coming from.

And it *wasn't* the surrounding hills.

"What the heck?!" his wife hollered at him.

Mr. Charles just began shaking his head and slipped his gloves off.

"Never you mind," he hollered back at his wife, "I'll go see."

With a steady but reserved pace, he lumbered down the dirt pathway between the rows of fruit trees. His newly hired laborers, Nicanor and Estevon, had probably heard the shots as well. No more than 100 feet into the orchard he could hear the tractor drawing closer through the trees.

He stopped to catch his breath.

He Said, She Said: The Spokane River Killer

Boom!... Crack! Crack!... zzzziiiinnnng.....
He dove to the ground.
Bullets were flying right over his head and into the branches beyond him.
A few yards ahead of him the tractor, now moving in high gear, barreled around the corner of the road and into his view. Nicanor was driving; the horrified look on his face said it all. Estevon had pulled his cap from his head and was hanging on to the fender of the tractor and looking back over his shoulder. Mr. Charles stood and began waving his arms wildly. Nicanor jammed the tractor into low gear and jammed on the brake. The iron giant came to a jerking stop a few feet in front of Mr. Charles.
Both men jumped down from the tractor, yelling wildly in Spanish.
"What is it? What is it?" he yelled at the men, waving the plume of exhaust smoke away from his face.
The smell of diesel smoke was something he never got used to.
Both of them continued to rant in Spanish, waving their arms wildly and frantically. Mr Charles did his best to calm them down. Finally, Estevon stopped yelling and stared down toward the dirt pathway. Nicanor threw his hands in the air, looking around at the endless labyrinth of fruit trees surrounding them.
Boom!
All three of the men ducked and looked toward the sound of the shots.
"That is it... meester Char-ez," Nicanor said, shaking his head as he took off down the path away from the gunfire. Estevon and Mr. Charles were right behind him.
"What *happened?*"
The two men quickly exchanged in Spanish again, both of them shaking their heads as their pace quickened.
Mr. Charles followed the men to their truck parked around the side of the barn. Neither of them seemed to be

unswayed from leaving and never coming back. He had pipe to get in and work lined up for weeks to get the newly acquired orchard up to speed again and producing. The blossoms were nearly fully in bloom and without the proper irrigation, the orchard would be at least another year out before he could even begin to recoup his investment.

"No! NO!" Estevon sniped, "Thees is out of hand! He has gone too far this time!"

"He tried to kill US!"

"Look — just stay. Give me a chance to handle this — I promise you, *that will never happen again.*"

*   *   *

Underneath the rundown remains of his farmhouse, the basement lay dark and wet, like a bunker set under the flooding farmlands of a World War II battlefield. Layers of dingy white paint peeled off the cracking concrete walls and fell to the floor. Chipped paint swirled into a moist menagerie of long black hairs and rodent shit. When it rained, water poured in and advanced across the frigid concrete. Time would dry the floor, but the sour smell crept into every corner and crevice where it lay, as if in repose.

Stagnant and putrid.

But downstairs in his fortress of solitude, she rarely ventured. This was his temple. His only place in a mad world where he could be the master of his own destiny. It was how he wanted it. Everything, it seemed, had to be fought for or manipulated to his liking. For if it were up to the world, his existence would have been far different.

Against the far wall stood an old bench top cabinet. About it were strewn gun parts, small smithing tools, and rusting projects that he would probably never finish. The piles of junk could probably be laid out in a chronological record of his childhood. Radio controlled airplanes, different incantations of small animal traps, and even some old galvanized pipe pieces that he and his young friends had filled with black powder hoping one day to use them to scare up starlings in the fields. His interest in things waned and waxed like the moon, and that day had probably long since passed.

He slipped his frail legs out of his pants, and nearly fell over as he lost his balance. The cold concrete of the basement wall kept him from ending up on his face. He had smacked his head into the walls before. They were every bit as unforgiving as his hateful mother.

The room was entirely too small.

But it was his.

He set his bare foot back down on the tiny rug trying to hide under the metal frame of his twin-sized mattress. The roughly knit rug made his feet itch every time he stood on it.

He stared at his bed.

The wool, military issue blanket was so tightly tucked he could barely pull it open to climb in between the sheets.

There were semen stains. He needed to do laundry.

Everything made him itch, it seemed.

Naked, except for his white briefs, he slid in between the frigid layers of the cotton sheets. Before removing his glasses to set on the nightstand, he carefully scanned over the collection of pistols, rifles, and shotguns littered and standing guard across the shelves next to his bed. These are what made the desolate concrete entrapment a home.

His home.

With a satisfied smile, he confirmed they were all in their rightful place. His glasses hit the nightstand and he lay back into his pillow with a sigh.

He stared at the magazine pictures neatly taped to the ceiling and smiled again. Next to his guns, these were his prized possessions.

They were beautiful, he thought.

His mother, had she known about them, would have demanded their removal and subsequent burning in the barrel behind the barn. But she hadn't navigated the frail stairway down into his dungeon-like tomb in a very long time. He was free to do as he wished here, whether she approved of it or not. He was free to fantasize however he wished. Unencumbered by any parental dose of reality.

And he did so quite often.

For a second he closed his eyes. His hand slipped down under the elastic of his briefs. Quietly, he lightly began stroking himself. He opened his eyes again and joyfully stared at the dozens and dozens of pictures of nude women floating above him. The entire ceiling was covered with Hustler, Penthouse, and Playboy centerfolds. With his free hand, he reached for the lamp on his night stand and tipped the lampshade so the shadows would move. The dim light soaked into the centerfold he wanted to see.

Her arms squeezed her huge breasts upward, making them appear even larger than they probably were. Her lips were puckered toward the camera and her hair was nearly the same color as his.

She was one of his favorites.

Slowly, his rhythm became more accelerated.

She sat with her knees folded to one side. Her thighs were thick, but not fat.

And she was so tan.

He closed his eyes and stroked faster.

He took a deep breath and the springs of his bed quietly squeaked. He opened them again. She was right above him. How could someone be so beautiful?

He arched his back and lifted his hips upward so he could slide his underwear down around his ankles. The sheets were tucked so tightly he could hardly maneuver his hand. With an awkward kick he slid his briefs off of one foot and then the other.

He licked his hand, and imagined slipping himself inside her. In a fluid, choreographed motion, he reached toward the lamp and shifted the aim of the light toward another large-breasted woman directly above him.

She was blonde. And much older.

He loved her, too.

With a shudder, the bed springs screamed and shuddered.

And as quickly as it began, it was over.

He grabbed his underwear from the foot of the inside of the sheets and wiped himself off. He pulled the moisture-laden briefs back on and turned out his lamp; carefully positioning one of his pillows between his arms and legs like he were cuddling intimately with the blonde centerfold.

Soon, he would be—

BAM! BAM! BAM!

He was startled. Upstairs, he heard his mother's recliner squeal and drive forward into its upright position. Her footsteps shook the ceiling above him as he reached for the glasses on his nightstand and flipped on the light.

Who would be here?

Without a sound, he slipped up two thirds of the stairs and heard the front door open. The floor squeaked as someone stepped in. If he remained perfectly still, he would be able to listen in.

"Mr. Charles— do you know what time— what is the matter with you?" His mother, Ruth, asked defiantly.

"Ruth, I gotta tell ya—" Mr. Charles paused; he was so upset it seemed he could barely speak. "That kid of yours has gone too dang far this time!"

"Here, sit down. You know, ever'body gets so upset— what do you *think* he's done this time?" Ruth asked almost dismissively, her voice so quiet and gentle she could calm a winter storm.

He heard one of the dining room chairs screech across the floor as Mr. Charles dropped his heavy frame into it.

"He tried to kill my workers…"

"Why do you think that? Because he was *target shooting?* There's no law against that now, is there?" Ruth interrupted him.

It wasn't as though she were going to the defense of her son. She could not have cared less what he did. She was more interested in upsetting her neighbors.

Especially this one.

"For cryin' out loud, Ruth. Is *that* what you think? Not more than 10 minutes after two o' my men run him off again. *He knew they were back there!*"

"He wouldn't hurt nobody — and he certainly wouldn't do it intentional like..."

"Did you not hear me?" Mr. Charles interrupted, "They was just with him before he did it. They said he was mad that they run him off."

Ruth folded her arms in disgust at the mere suggestion.

"Look, I can't control him. I barely see him, 'lest he comes up from that basement. You just lookin' for a reason to be mad at him. No one has ever liked him. No one. Least of all, all you people who s'posed to be neighbors."

"Ruth, he has problems..."

"Oh, don't I know that. You think you know what his problem is?" Ruth was now becoming very agitated.

She unfolded her arms and took a few steps toward Mr. Charles, "You think I don't know? Goddamit! Why do you think everyone 'round here hates him?" Ruth asked, her face glaring at Mr. Charles.

She continued, " 'Cause he teases the neighbor girl? Is it because he shot his brother's dog? *Why do you think he did that?*"

Mr. Charles stood up to leave. It was obvious he was not going to find a receptive ear in Ruth Perry.

"Where were you all when the boys at the school was laughin' 'cause he don't like his hair cut short?" Ruth began to yell, her quiet and calm devotion to her son quickly vacated.

He Said, She Said: The Spokane River Killer

Mr. Charles turned and hollered over his shoulder as he paced away, "Fine, I'll just let the sheriff handle this then. I mean for cryin' out loud, get him some help or somethin.' With everything that's happened in the last ten years? It's not like he's a boy. He's a grown man. What is he? About 30 or 35 years old now?"

Ruth angrily labored up from the chair, screaming like a banshee.

Mr. Charles continued quickly for the door.

"*I KNOW God damn well what you tryin' to do!*" she yelled, "I know EXACTLY why you're doin' this… you son of a bitch! You and that no good brother-in-law of mine have been schemin' this the whole time!!"

Mr. Charles darted through the doorway. He shook his head without looking back at Ruth and raised his hand to offer as neighborly a wave goodbye as he could muster.

Ruth nearly tumbled as she followed. Her obese frame and wide hips awkwardly bounced after him.

"It won't work!!" she yelled through the doorway.

But Mr. Charles had already gone.

2

The Clock On The Wall

As Okanogan Sheriff's Deputy Mike Johnson maneuvered his patrol car in between a John Deere tractor and a 1930's era Chevrolet truck, Mr. Charles' workers, Niconar and Estevon, stopped loading irrigation pipe onto the flatbed truck parked near the barn and just stared at him. One of them muttered something in Spanish and the other shook his head. The early morning chill of the high desert had long since been chased away by the rising sun. The rocky hillsides and steep faces of the ridgelines above the farm stared down on them.

Deputy Johnson had been with the Sheriff's Department since 1974. He had relocated his family to the small town of Omak after serving as a patrol officer in the Seattle suburb of Puyallup, Washington. He had seen his fair share of neighborly disputes and mopped up the carnage when they went wrong. Cocaine trafficking, methamphetamine production— all of it. The rural lifestyle of Omak was the biggest reason he had packed up his family and moved out of western Washington.

As he opened the car door and stepped out, the workers went right back to loading the flatbed. The police always made the migrant workers a little nervous. His dark olive-colored uniform was perfectly pressed and fitted. Even the leather holster securing his sidearm appeared meticulously conditioned and "form fit" to his hip. His badge glimmered like a diamond on a new bride's finger.

"Hello!" a woman's voice hollered as the screen door screeched and swung open onto the porch.

Deputy Johnson turned as he slammed the door to the patrol car shut to find a smaller-framed woman in her early fifties wearing a full length, blue denim dress and an apron waving at him from the top of the steps.

"You must be the Sheriff!" she continued.

"Morning, ma'am. And, no, I am Deputy Johnson. Is Mr. Charles at home?"

"Oh, sorry, yes, *deputy*. It's all the same. It's all the same you know," she chuckled and beckoned Deputy Johnson toward the front door.

"Can I get you something to drink? Yes, yes, he is inside here. He's been waiting. That business with the Perry boy," she shook her head in disgust and sighed loudly, "It just never seems to end, I tell you."

The deputy followed her inside, removing his hat as he stepped through the front doorway.

"Come in here, into the living room; he's inside there; he's inside waiting, yes. Can I get you something to drink? I have some carrot cake?"

"Of course, that would be wonderful," Deputy Johnson replied as he continued through the foyer and stepped through a mahogany archway into the living room.

The house was full of handcrafted country furniture. Every single decorative item seemed to have a perfect position and orientation. The picture frames all matched and even the cat perch was crafted out of the same blue, plaid material as the sofa, chairs and love seat. Near the large bay window overlooking the orchard which lined the gravel driveway, an organ and bench sat in the corner.

"You must be the Sheriff," a man's voice bellowed out.

Deputy Johnson turned toward the stairway, and a larger man in his fifties wearing tightly fitting navy blue coveralls lumbered down the stairs. It was obvious the coveralls no longer fit the man standing before him. Function clearly outweighed form in this case.

And fashion for that matter.

Mrs. Charles excused herself to go to the kitchen.

The man extended his hand to Deputy Johnson, "L. L. Charles. How do you do?"

"Good sir, good. Uh, yes. And I am Deputy Johnson, Okanogan County Sheriff's Department."

Mr. Charles motioned the deputy toward the sofa. The smell of furniture polish and freshly baked carrot cake swirled about the room. It reminded Deputy Johnson of his own grandmother's home back in Seattle.

"So, I understand you had an incident with one of your neighbors? Douglas Perry?" Deputy Johnson began after Mr. Charles joined him on the sofa.

"That little son of a gun. Yeah. 'Incident' is one way to look at it," Mr. Charles drew a deep breath, and his look became very serious, "You know, I may as well just dive right into it. That Perry boy has been nothing but trouble his whole life. And his mother? She's as cuckoo as he is. One of these days — if you don't do somethin' 'bout it — one of these days somethin' bad is gonna happen. Mark my words. I could tell you stories about that whole dang family. Oh, yeah. *Years.*"

It was very apparent to Deputy Johnson that Mr. Charles was frustrated with the situation. Obviously there was a lot of history between him and the Perry family.

"Well, why don't you tell me about yesterday," Deputy Johnson suggested.

"Well that kid. That, *Doug*. Well, he's not really a kid — he's about 33 or 34 years old now — but *mentally*," Mr. Charles pointed at his head, "But, mentally — he's like a dang teenager. *Or worse.*"

He Said, She Said: The Spokane River Killer

Deputy Johnson began taking notes. Outside, the migrant workers had fired up the John Deere tractor, and the low thundering of the engine nearly washed out the ticking of the antique wall clock hung near the organ.

"So I was out there in the west orchard— with Niconar and Estevon— and we were getting a layout for the new irrigation pipe— I mean that orchard has been dead since we bought it from the county a ways back— you know the Perrys used to own it— but the county took it 'cause they didn't pay the taxes on it," Mr. Charles began, leaning forward and pointing toward the orchard as he spoke.

His voice rumbled across the dark hardwood floors like distant thunder.

"Anyway— *so we own it*— if you talk to Doug, or his nut job mother, they'll probably tell ya we stole it or some crazy notion— but yeah, so we were out there, and Doug was running around like a storm trooper— or like he was spying on us— or who knows what the heck he was doin'— but we had to run him off— you know. I don't need him out there."

Deputy Johnson realized this wasn't going to be quick.

"He does some 'out-of-this-world' stuff sometimes. So, you know—" Mr. Charles began shaking his head in frustration.

"Well, it is your private property. Why you don't want him there does not matter. You have every right," Deputy Johnson interjected, "He is clearly trespassing."

"*Trespassing?*" Mr. Charles grunted in disgust, "Yeah… right."

Mr. Charles shifted his large frame.

"So my laborers, they, uh… they run him off, you see."

Mrs. Charles floated back into the room carrying two plates of carrot cake and set them on the coffee table.

"Tell him about— " his wife interrupted as she produced a pair of fine silver forks and set them near each of the plates.

"I'm getting to that— hold on," he said as he gripped one of the forks and took a bite of carrot cake, "So he sets up his targets— you know the Perry land borders that orchard— and he then he starts shootin'. Well... bullets are zingin' into the trees at us, and so my workers— they run for cover."

His wife leaned forward, "And he's done this before, you know. The Lingle girls used to walk to the bus stop, and he'd be out there shooting away— not at them, but he'd shoot across the road in front of them and kind of laugh. And he'd say, *'I'm not shooting at you — I'm shooting in front of you. It's perfectly legal.'* "

Mrs. Charles sidestepped away from the sofa and sat herself in the matching chair across from her husband.

Deputy Johnson held up his hand to stop Mrs. Charles from speaking any further, "Well, brandishing a weapon where you are intending to frighten or threaten someone *is illegal*. Did you call us?"

Her husband nearly choked on his cake as he blurted out, "Goodness YES! And they would never do anything— he'd go to court, and they would tell him he needed to see a shrink. *They did nothing.*"

"How long ago was this?" Deputy Johnson asked.

Mr. Charles shifted his legs uncomfortably and slid his hips back into his chair. He paused for a moment and his glossy blue eyes stared toward the ceiling.

"Oh... I want to say it was four or five years ago," Mr. Charles said.

Deputy Johnson drew in a deep breath, and as he began to speak, Mr. Charles interrupted him—.

"You see, the problem here is that all the 'powers that be' in this town seem to be the ones who feel sorry for him. For goodness sake— the judge— the judge used to represent him when he'd get into trouble years ago! Now, you're going to tell me that he might not be a little too 'lenient' on little Dougie?"

His wife nodded in agreement.

"Everybody else in this county feels sorry for them. They don't have to live next to him," she added.

He Said, She Said: The Spokane River Killer

A puzzled look came across Deputy Johnson's face.

"Why would everyone feel sorry for them?" he asked innocently.

Mrs. Charles shook her head.

"Oh those two... those two are a piece of work, I tell you. Just a few months ago," she began, "just a few months ago, when it was colder than the Dickens outside, it was... uh...," she looked up at the ceiling, "it was January! And it had gotten down to nearly zero outside every night for about a week— I mean it didn't even get up above the teens during the day— you remember that?"

Mr. Charles nodded toward his wife.

"Well, they had no electricity! I mean, *none*. I heard they couldn't pay the whole bill or something and they tried to call 'em— but they both are just so— but they ended up getting it shut off!" Mrs. Charles continued.

Deputy Johnson stopped writing and leaned back in disbelief.

"Oh, no— it gets better, it gets better. Trust me," she smiled, "So somebody decides they need to be checked on by the police to see if they are ok and what not, and do you think the police wanted to go up there?"

Deputy Johnson interrupted her, "I remember hearing a little about that a few months ago— around the station."

Mrs. Charles continued, "Well the police show up— and Doug won't come to the door, and Ruth won't get out of her bed... I mean... it's pitch black inside that old house! Well, the police don't want this to escalate, because they are so dang— so dang *weird*, so they call one of the lawyers from town, uh— Rod, Rod Reinbold. So he comes up here, and Doug lets him come in and see that they aren't dead in that damn shack— *pardon me* — and they can't do nothin' so they go."

Deputy Johnson sat quiet for a moment, and then asked, "So, how did they end up alone together in that house? Where is the rest of the family?"

Mr. Charles looked at his wife and then over at Deputy Johnson and slowly began shaking his head. He sighed, looked at the clock on the wall and said, "You better settle in."

*   *   *

"DOUGLAS!!... DOUGLAS!!!" her screams nearly vibrated the walls of the run-down house.

"DOUGLAS! I've got DIARRHEA!" she yelled, *"Douglas?! Do you hear me?"*

The upstairs bathroom door slammed shut again. He could hear her muffled groans as though she were giving birth.

Then the door opened up again.

"God damn you! *Get up here!"* she screamed.

He knew her persistence would be unending.

"What?" he hollered from the kitchen, not wanting to go any nearer to the bathroom than he had to. He knew damn well what it smelled like.

"You need to get— *oh God…* " she blurted out and slammed the door shut again.

He waited near the entrance to the hallway and listened to her bowel cry out like a wailing mother who had just lost her three children to cholera. A few minutes later the door opened again.

"I need some antidiahrreal, *now!"*

"But—"

"Now! If I don't get it soon," she muttered as pathetically as she could, "… I'll probably die…"

Doug swallowed hard and looked at his feeble mother. Her muumuu was pulled up above her knees, and her large ass barely fit on the toilet between the bathtub and wall. A black-and-white portrait photograph of his sister loomed above her next to the vanity, the gold paint on the frame cracked and peeling.

"Is that *WHAT YOU WANT!*" she screamed out of nowhere and started sobbing uncontrollably, "and then the Charleses will get *this place too—* AND IT WILL BE YOUR FAULT!!"

Her fat arms bounced as she cried, nearly knocking the toilet paper out of its holder. She looked up at the portrait and then at her son, as he hid just out of view in the doorway.

Doug sighed as deliberately and as loudly as he could, "Ok... okay! I'll go get it."

"Bless you child. *Bless you*," she said as sweetly as she could.

Doug turned down the hallway—

"CLOSE the GOD DAMN DOOR!!" she screamed.

Doug drew his fists upward and shook them at the ceiling as he closed the door. It never ended.

As soon as Doug was out of the house, she blew her nose, and with her obese frame perched on the toilet, she lit up a cigarette and belched.

For the most part, Doug hated going to town. It was an inconvenient necessity, but he recognized that it was requisite to his survival. Thankfully, when his mother needed some sort of over-the-counter medication for whatever crisis she was having at the time, Omak was only a short drive down the hill away.

His car was parked out behind the shop where his mother couldn't see it. He always parked the red Ford Pinto out of sight of the house. He believed that, somehow, if his mother saw it, it would remind her that he had the ability to go fetch whatever it was she felt she needed at the time. He was constantly trying to outwit his mother's incessant control of his life. This time, however, the explosive nature of her digestive malady precluded his ability to circumvent her.

By most standards, Omak was a small town. The endless streams of pioneering orchardists from the early 20th century had all grown old. As the children of the town grew up, most of them tried to find their way *out* of Omak, not *in*. Once out of the grip of the town, they would return only during holiday visits and to tend to elderly parents.

The town was dying.

Sun-bleached plywood signs beckoned summer travelers to the quaint, overpriced campgrounds, burger stands, and antique shops down the main drive. In between the orchards, covered in bird netting and dotted with migrant workers perched atop ladders, the rich, copper-colored Okanogan River flowed gently through town.

For those unfortunate enough to be trapped in this small town with its hot dust, there was at least the reward of gentle breezes and some spectacular sunsets.

But, despite the begging of locals, Omak was just a stopover on the way up Highway 97 from central Washington to Canada. Winding up and around the brushy, dry hills, the highway was a lonely, hot place during the summer. Omak and the adjoining town of Okanogan a few miles to the south, existed mostly unnoticed.

The grocery store was up the hill to the north of town in the 'new' part of Omak, nearer the state highway. The agriculture industry in Washington, and particularly the fruit growers, had experienced a significant economic boom during the 1980s. This influx of money into the area spurred a significant amount of growth and new construction. It turned out to be quite short-lived, but Omak was now clearly divided into "new" and "old" parts of town.

Doug much preferred the newer grocery store as it was big enough and busy enough that he felt he could blend in and not have to interact with anyone. He parked the car as far away from the front entrance as he could to avoid any possibility that he might be forced into a perfunctory (and awkward) conversation with someone parked next to him, and he hesitantly strode inside.

He was very familiar with the pharmacy and knew right where to get his mother her antidiarrheal medication. Quickly, he sneaked to the back of the store, picked it off the shelf, and moved to the checkout line, where there were a few customers in front of him.

This was bad.

Behind him, two boys about 11 or 12 years old whispered to one another and giggled. Without much to do in a place as small as Omak, the boys in the town always seemed to be up to some sort of mischief.

Doug was once one of them.

One of the boys had two candy bars in his hand and was delicately trying to grip two packs of bubble gum in the same hand without losing all of it onto the floor.

Doug turned and looked forward again. He was growing impatient and irritated at the idle chit chat between the grocery clerk and the young woman in line in front of him.

Hurry the fuck up.

Nervously, he looked around.

Without warning, he felt one of the young boys bump into him from behind. As he turned to look, it became obvious the other boy had pushed him into Doug on purpose and was now laughing about it. The boy recovered himself and shoved his friend in retaliation. The two candy bars and the packs of bubble gum flew out of his grasp and towards the end of the condiments aisle.

Both boys stopped and stared at Doug, who was now uncomfortably staring at them. He reached up and pushed his glasses upward on the bridge of his nose.

"Ask him," one of the boys laughed.

"You ask him," he retorted back and began scooping the two chocolate bars and the bubble gum back into his hand.

Doug turned and looked at the clerk. Finally the woman in front of him had received her change and was now moving toward her cart full of bagged groceries.

Again, the boy behind him smashed into his back side. Doug jerked around and the boy jumped back. Doug tried to look mean and irritated.

"AAAAHHHH!!" the boy screamed jokingly as though Doug's appearance had frightened him, "I thought you were a *girl!*"

The boys started laughing.

"What is... what is your problem?" he asked.

The two boys turned away and continued to giggle.

"You better be... better be careful who you... you mess with!" Doug sneered at the boys.

He had heard the comments about his appearance before... at the gas station... in the convenience stores. It was nothing new. People thought he looked weird. So what.

They both stared blankly, and looked at the box of Imodium A-D in his hand.

One of the boys started singing, "Diarrhea, *pphhtt pphhtt*, diarrhea *pphhtt pphhtt*, some people thinks it's funny, but it's really kind of runny, diarrhea *pphhtt pphhtt*, diarrhea *pphhtt pphhtt*."

The boys started laughing hysterically.

"Fuck off... you... off... little fuckers!" Doug yelled at them. The words sounded like they had come from a skipping CD.

The entire store became suddenly quiet. The grocery checker even looked at Doug disapprovingly.

"I mean it. I mean it. You never... you might end up dead... dead in a ditch somewhere," Doug stuttered at them, "You might... might mess with the... the wrong person."

A tall man wearing a John Deere cap and a bright red flannel shirt stepped up behind Doug.

"They're just kids, man. Mellow out, alright?" he commanded Doug.

His voice sounded like wet hickory run through a sluice box.

Doug backed away quickly and slipped his rucksack off of his shoulder. As he did so, he dropped the antidiarrheal medicine on the conveyor. He looked at the clerk and frowned; it was clear to the clerk he no longer wanted it. He just wanted to get out of the store. His hand fished through his bag as he quickly scurried away, and he gripped the pistol he was carrying in the bag without pulling it out. Looking back over his shoulder he could see the man shaking his head and the two boys were now laughing and pointing.

The tall man in the checkout line looked at the clerk.

"What a jerk," he stated.

She picked up the package of Imodium A-D and set it to the side.

"He's just a little weird," she answered, "he lives up on the Flat and he just has some sort of mental condition."

"Mental condition or not, that's no excuse," he answered, "they're just kids."

The clerk stopped and looked at the man, "What are you supposed to do? He's just mentally ill — poor guy. I feel sorry for him."

"Yeah, well, I heard about him — Pogue Flat — they oughta' lock him up. He's trouble."

Even the residents of the town disagreed about what to do with Doug Perry.

Outside the store, Doug fumbled for his keys. He just wanted out of there.

Now.

Obviously, the man in the John Deere hat was going to start some sort of trouble.

That man was coming after him. *He knew it.*

He dropped his backpack into the passenger seat, started his car and jammed on the gas as hard as he could. Jerking the steering wheel to his left he swirled out of the parking lot, off of the asphalt and nearly lost control of the car as he hit the gravel road leading away from it.

He reached in and grabbed his pistol out of his pack.

Thank God he had loaded it.

His mother was going to be so pissed. It didn't matter. She would spend the entire afternoon shitting all over the linoleum and would probably want to kill him by the time he got home. He shook his head.

This was exactly why he hated coming to town.

Always a hassle.

He looked up in the rear view mirror to see if the man in the John Deere hat was in his truck and following him. He was going so fast he could barely keep the little car on the road. The man was probably going to beat his ass — or worse. Through the rooster tail of dust kicked up by the Pinto he couldn't see more than ten feet behind him. His forehead was beginning to sweat a little.

Was he there?

He had to be.

Doug smashed the steering wheel with his clenched fist.

He better not. He didn't want to have to shoot somebody.

He was sure he had seen the man in the John Deere hat before... watching him wherever he went. Images of the people he had seen in the last few months scrolled across his memory as he tried to remember where he had seen him before.

Was he a cop?

Doug jammed on the brakes of the Pinto and the car dove to the left. With a loud thump the Pinto hopped back up onto the pavement as the gravel road turned south and wound down the hill towards the old part of town. The road followed a dry creek bed and Doug knew of an inconspicuous turnout where he might be able to hide and see if the man was following him. He would have to act fast once he pulled into the turnout so he could spin around and face the oncoming road.

Once again he jammed on the brakes, cut the steering wheel to the right, and slid off into the turnout. His heavy glasses nearly fell off of his face. He spun the car around 180 degrees and jammed the transmission into reverse. He backed the car behind the small cutout in the hillside where traffic coming down the hill would likely drive right on past without even seeing a car parked there.

He cut the engine, rolled down his window, and put the pistol into his lap.

And waited.

He was nearly out of breath.

Completely motionless, he sat there hardly able to let a breath out. His thumb slid over the safety of the pistol and he flicked it off and then back on again. He knew that man would be coming past him any second and he prayed he would just drive on by.

To his left, a pair of cowbirds fluttered and danced along an old barbed wire fence running through the dusty sage hill into which the cutout he was hiding was carved. Beyond their occasional chirps and wingbeats, he could only hear the soft breeze flowing across the bare hillside. And it was fucking hot out.

Maybe the man knew he had stopped here.

Maybe he parked his own rig just down the road from where Doug had come and was silently stalking him over the crest of the hill?

Doug swallowed hard.

He didn't know what to do. He could feel the blood in his veins starting to tingle, and his joints began to twitch ever so slightly.

The panic and fear were beginning to overwhelm him. He swallowed again and nearly wanted to cry. His mouth began to dry out, and his bones felt like they were hollow and filled with heated air.

He hated this feeling.

It nearly made him sick.

In his mind he could see the man's car skidding to a stop after coming around the corner. He would jam his car into reverse and whip in next to Doug's Pinto. Screaming and yelling, he would throw the car door open, and with fury and thunder he would lunge toward Doug; his huge hands would grab Doug by the throat or by his hair; and as Doug's glasses flew off his face, he would jerk Doug from the car through the window and pummel him alongside the road.

He could see it clear as day.

Without the safety of being on his farm, there was nowhere to run and nowhere to hide. He was exposed and helpless. At the mercy of the world and the men within it.

He would have to kill him.

And men were such pigs.

Pithy contests of masculinity at every turn. Always trying to prove dominance over the other men of the tribe. Always trying to establish the hierarchy and pecking order.

It sickened him.

They never acted like this toward women. A woman could have told him his John Deere hat made him look like a faggot and he would have shrunk away, embarrassed. But had *he* said so, well, he knew how that would have ended.

Maybe if the man did show up he could just tell him he was sorry. He didn't really mean he would hurt those kids. He was just kidding around. Maybe if he begged for the man's mercy he wouldn't hurt him. Maybe he would just get in his car and leave him alone.

That was all he really wanted.

To be left alone.

For twenty more minutes he just sat there. Frozen, terrified, and nauseated. Different scenes ran through his head.

None of them ended well.

He had to get out of there and hide. *Somewhere.* But where?

And then it hit him.

He knew exactly where he wanted to hide.

As he started the Pinto and pulled out onto the road, a familiar, wry smile crept across his face. Slowly, the tingling in his veins went away, his joints stopped twitching and his breathing returned to normal.

He Said, She Said: The Spokane River Killer

*   *   *

Deputy Johnson set his fork onto the plate and wiped the linen napkin across his face.

"Thank you, that was delicious," he said, "So, you mentioned how everyone feels sorry for them; what do you mean?"

Mrs. Charles scooped up the empty plate and napkin, "Tell him about Kathy."

Mr. Charles looked up at her and drew in a short breath.

"He don't care about *that*," he quipped back at his wife.

She stood motionless, staring at the Deputy, waiting for his approval.

Mr. Charles reached over for the plate nearest him, "Well, ok. So… Kathy, she was his older sister. Horrible tragedy, *just horrible*. She and another girl… Janice? Yeah, Janice was her name. They were both just about to graduate from high school— Kathy and her were headed up toward Winthrop or some place, and she took a corner on the Loup Loup Highway way too fast or somethin' and went off the road. Killed her. One of them walks away with a few cuts and bruises— one of them dies."

"When was this?"

"Back in 1968 if I'm not mistaken. Yeah, it had to be— it was just at the same time Bobby Kennedy was killed, so yeah, 1968," Mr. Charles answered.

Mrs. Charles sat down in the recliner across from her husband.

"That whole family has not been the same," she added, shaking her head.

"How many are there?" Deputy Johnson asked.

Mrs. Charles looked down into her lap, "Well, there was four kids. Katherine, Lawrence, Douglas, and Karen."

Her husband cleared his throat, "After Kathy died, boy they were just… just devastated. Well, the old man, he never seemed to take care of his orchard and grounds the same way. I'd talk to him now and then, you know, neighborly stuff, but he was always tellin' me about Kathy, Kathy, Kathy. But quite honestly, do you blame him?"

"She was beautiful," Mrs. Charles added, "I mean, all the boys loved her; she was smart, popular... I think she was going to go to college in Pullman."

"So where is the father?"

"Bruce? Well, not long after Kathy died, he died also. About a year and a half later. In fact, it was the day after Thanksgiving. Dropped from a heart attack—"

"At least that's what everybody was told," his wife interrupted.

"Now, now. We don't know any different," Mr. Charles corrected his wife.

She did not appear convinced.

"But anyway, he was in the War, too."

"Vietnam?" asked Deputy Johnson.

"No, no. World War II. In fact, he was an officer—and his brother, Robert, died over there at some point, in Germany or France. Bruce was an honorable and well liked man. The whole family was."

Deputy Johnson folded his hands, "I see how that could be difficult, but— lots of families have—"

"Oh, no. It gets worse," Mr. Charles continued.

Deputy Johnson sat back again as Mrs. Charles nodded.

"After Bruce passed, I think Lawrence was 17, Doug was 15, and Karen was maybe 12 or 13. Ruth had no idea how to run a farm. Lawrence tried— but he is— he is just a... *a bastard,*" Mr. Charles said.

"Tell him about Lawrence—" his wife pleaded again.

"I'll get to that. So everyone, it seemed, who knew Ruth— her extended family and stuff— they all wanted to help, but she was just too far gone. Losing her daughter and then losing her husband—"

"She was nutty to begin with," Mrs. Charles added.

He Said, She Said: The Spokane River Killer

"So, Karen, when she grew up, she ran as far from here as she could. I think she ended up in California as a school teacher. I can't hardly remember seeing her around here at all for years now. And Doug, well, Doug is just as goofy as his mother. Those two are just out there."

Deputy Johnson was shocked at what he was hearing.

"One time, Doug, he shot his brother's dog. He shot it *on purpose*," Mrs. Charles began.

"We don't know that it was on purpose," her husband tried to correct her again. But she would not have it.

"Oh yes he did. And the neighbor's dog. That's what he does— he acts out without thinking about what he's doing, and then he lies so that he isn't held responsible for it. Like that time the silver was missing— out of three of our neighbors' houses? Come on. We know who did it."

"Well," Mr. Charles looked at Deputy Johnson, "We could never prove it, but it did seem to point that way. They never have any money. In fact, they lost that orchard on the side, over there; that's how I ended up with it," Mr. Charles pointed toward the Perry farm, "They couldn't pay the taxes on it, so it went up for sale, and, logically, we bought it from the county. Well Ruth doesn't think it was legal and all that. So Doug, in his weird way, thinks that land is still his."

Deputy Johnson looked over at Mrs. Charles, "And Lawrence? You said something about the older brother that might be relevant to all of this?"

Both of the Charleses looked toward the floor and paused.

"Well, we don't know if it's true or not," Mr. Charles began.

An awkward pause followed again.

"But, uh… some of the neighbors and some of the people in town, they say that, uh… Lawrence…"

"*For cryin' out loud, tell him!*" his wife exclaimed.

"The rumor is that Lawrence, he's a real bad dude; I mean— he has ties to Aryan Nations stuff over in Idaho."

"Aryan Nations? Like with Richard Butler out of Hayden Lake? That kind of thing?" Deputy Johnson asked. He knew this could make things a little more serious and complicated.

Mrs. Charles sighed deeply and gave her husband a stern look.

Mr. Charles drew a deep breath.

His wife could no longer take his apprehension, *"He raped Doug... more than once!"*

"What?" Deputy Johnson said.

"All the time apparently. Since Doug was little," she finished.

Mr. Charles nodded in agreement.

"He's been in counseling and stuff. They would probably tell you, since you're a police officer," she added.

"No. No they wouldn't. Not without a warrant or court order; and medical information— I doubt it," Deputy Johnson answered.

What a mess.

Deputy Johnson felt as though he had stepped in wet pile of dog shit on the church lawn.

There was far more going on here than just an unfriendly dispute between neighbors. But one thing was clear: he had to diffuse this whole situation before it got any worse. And it was going to get worse if something didn't happen, soon.

Deputy Johnson stood up and shook Mr. Charles' hand.

"What are you going to do?" he asked the deputy.

"This is much more than I had expected; I'll be honest with you. But I'm going to have go over and interview Mr. Perry and see what he has to say."

3
The Smell Of Gun Oil

Through the window in the corner, buttressed with wrought iron bars and glass old and dingy, the town below looked like it was enveloped in a thick fog. The rest of the shop was in a similar condition. A single glass counter filled with pistols, magazines, and stacks of old ammunition boxes spanned the entire length of the western wall. Behind it stood racks of shotguns, rifles, and archery equipment. On the floor in front of the counter, a few free-standing steel shelving units held reloading accessories and shooting supplies and the like. The office-grade carpet was clean but worn out. Green threads trailed out across the linoleum near the entrance to the store. The smell of gun oil and cleaning solvent felt like traveling back in time to the golden age of hunting and shooting.

Deer camps, empty whiskey bottles, and tall tales of the one that got away.

The shop's owner, Dwight, stood behind the counter sorting through a week's worth of firearm sales receipts. He was not a large man... in his early thirties, he stood only about 5' 6" tall. Dressed in Levi's 501's and a red and gray flannel shirt, his thinning brown hair and thick mustache fit perfectly with the outdoor feel his shop carried.

The afternoon had been mostly quiet; a few customers had come in to purchase some reloading supplies and paper targets. It was a good time to get caught up on some of the paperwork he needed to maintain. He pulled a stack of receipts out from a manila envelope and reached for the paper clip that held them together. Without warning the front door to his shop flew open and Doug whipped through the door with his pistol shaking in his hand. He turned to lock the door behind but couldn't quite figure out how to deadbolt the door.

"Shit!" Doug yelled.

The pistol dropped from his hand and bounced on to the floor.

"What the—" Dwight muttered to himself.

He and Doug had been friends since childhood. Radio-controlled model airplanes, shooting contests, and endless games of hide and seek on Pogue Flat filled his memories of childhood. Nothing Doug did seemed to surprise him.

"What are you doing, Doug?" Dwight asked as he rushed from the counter.

Doug had a flare for the dramatic.

"Leave the door alone. No one is following you," Dwight admonished his friend, "And put that damn pistol away!"

"I just had to teach this... teach this asshole at the store a lesson... a lesson about messing with... with someone *smarter* than him," Doug began nearly out of breath.

Dwight just stared at him.

"Oh yeah?" Dwight smiled.

Dwight remembered how, as kids, whenever they needed a solution to some sort of problem, Doug was always the one who came up a great plan, but that Doug often took it too far.

He Said, She Said: The Spokane River Killer

Doug looked over his shoulder and peeked around the corner of the clothing rack to make sure no one else was in the store. Mounted animal heads and metal placards from Remington, Winchester and Federal hung precariously on the dark, wood-colored paneling. The heads looked like they might fall off the wall at any moment, but most had stood the test of time for over 20 years. It was obvious when Doug walked in that there was no one else in the shop, but his paranoid delusions continuously got worse over the years.

"Yeah— it was a good thing... that I am... that I am always armed," Doug answered back.

He tapped his backpack where had just lodged his pistol and grinned.

"This asshole farmer at the... at the store was watching me... and he probably is working for the Charleses up... up on the Flat," Doug continued, staring toward the front door as though he had heard a noise outside.

Dwight reached behind the gun rack on the wall and removed a thick black binder. He cleared a spot on the glass counter large enough to open the binder and grabbed a pen from his pocket.

"The Charleses?" Dwight asked as he opened the binder and began copying notes into it from his firearm transaction log, "Why in the world would they care?"

Doug snorted and paused awkwardly. He cocked his head slightly to the side, straining to listen toward the front door.

"*You know why,*" Doug retorted.

Dwight continued to write without looking up.

"Well, they'll now know not... not to take me... lightly. He followed me... followed me right out to... to my Pinto. He said he knew who was... who I was, and that I had better... and I, and I..." Doug started laughing and reached into his backpack, "So I jerked this right out... and I shoved it... shoved it right... into his face... and told him to... to go fuck off... himself."

Doug stood there in front of Dwight grinning, his pistol pointed toward the window, trembling in his hand. Dwight stepped back and flipped the pen down onto his binder, somewhat annoyed.

"I just said to— don't pull that stuff out in my store, man. Come on Doug, really?"

Doug chuckled and put the pistol back in his backpack, "Sorry... sorry."

Doug paused and pretended that he needed to catch his breath. But before he could continue his story, something in the gun rack grabbed his attention.

"Let me see that SKS rifle," Doug said to Dwight and pointed to the wall.

Dwight knew Doug was not going to buy it, but it didn't really matter.

"Just got a few of these in," Dwight smiled as he cleared the action and handed Doug the rifle

"Is this... this Chinese?" Doug asked, shouldering the firearm and aiming it one of the mule deer heads near the window.

"No, no. They're Czech," Dwight answered.

Finished with the three-ring binder, he closed it up and placed it behind the rifles on the back wall.

Doug's hands caressed the wood stock. Nothing felt as smooth and secure as oil-soaked, time-hardened wood. When the steel of the receiver graced his cheek, he couldn't help but smile. He flipped it on its side and admired the vents on the forearm.

"How much for... how much three of them?" Doug asked, running the tips of his fingers along the length of the barrel.

Dwight smiled.

"You already have money down on three guns in the back!" Dwight laughed.

Doug shouldered the weapon again and quickly aimed it across the room out the window. His glasses awkwardly shifted to the side. He shoved them back to the center of his nose and swiped his hair away from his face.

"I can make... payments... make payments," he begged.

Dwight smiled and slid open the door to the ammo case. He knelt down on to the linoleum floor and began moving boxes of ammo from the back of the case up to the front.

"What do you want with three of those, anyhow? You always said they were 'Slav' shit!" Dwight said.

Doug lowered the rifle to his hip and slid his hand up and down the underside of the wooden forearm. It was smooth as silk.

"Becau — because I have a situ-aaa-tion. I caught that... I probably shouldn't say," Doug quipped and turned away from Dwight.

Dwight started to laugh, "A situation? *That you shouldn't say?*"

Doug paused. He knew exactly how to make people beg him for his stories.

"I had to run a couple... a couple of wetbacks off my land, yesterday," he nearly whispered.

Dwight just shook his head as he ripped open a cardboard shipping box full of ammo and continued to restock the glass case.

"The Charleses again? When are you going to realize—"

"They were tres... trespassing," Doug interrupted, "So I told them... to get off my land. There was two... two of them. One of them took a... took a swing at me... so I pulled... pulled my pistol out and... told them to start... to start runnin'... or I would... I would kill them both."

"*You?*" Dwight laughed, "You... told them you'd shoot them?"

Doug nodded and jerked the SKS from the counter, cycled the action and aimed the rifle toward the window again pretending he was clearing a room full of would be assailants.

"Bullshit" Dwight laughed, shaking his head.

"They fucking ran," Doug added.

Dwight stood up and reached for the rifle. Doug handed it to him and took a few steps further down the counter.

"And why exactly... did you do this?" Dwight asked.

"They think the north orchard... they think the north orchard is theirs."

Dwight laughed.

"No, they... they don't own it. They stole it. But by the time... by the time I'm done they'll wish they had just... just left us alone," Doug stammered.

After putting all of the ammo into his display case, Dwight stood up and began breaking down the cardboard shipping containers.

Just being surrounded by guns and in a familiar setting was helping to calm Doug down a little. Some people get nervous around guns— not Doug— he relished them. He loved them. He felt safe with them.

"I don't really... really need an SKS... an SKS any way," Doug stated as he continued to stare at the guns hanging on the wall next to Dwight.

"Oh?" Dwight asked.

"I've got a guy in Canada... a guy who is going to... going to hook me up with some full... full auto hardware," Doug started to snort and giggle; he could barely get the words out of his mouth.

He reached up and readjusted his heavy framed glasses and wiped an errant lock of hair out of the corner of his mouth.

Dwight shook his head.

"No, I'm serious. Next month... next month I'll have them. They are bad ass."

"Well, yeah. How did you get hooked up with those?" Dwight asked.

"I can't say. Lawrence... Lawrence said it has to be kept... kept quiet. You know what I mean?" Doug answered.

As soon as Dwight heard mention of Lawrence, he shook his head again. Dwight, of course, knew Lawrence while they were growing up. Doug's older brother always seemed to be lurking around or interfering with everything he and Doug did when they were kids. Dwight saw firsthand how the entire Perry family was devastated at the loss of Kathy and their father, but it manifested itself in different ways with each of the three surviving siblings. Lawrence became very violent, angry, and controlling. He turned to crime and drugs, and his personality, far more dominating than Doug's, allowed him to interact in the criminal world unencumbered.

Their younger sister, Karen, seemed to focus her emotional pain inward and did well in school so that she could get the hell out of Omak as quickly and quietly as she could— which is exactly what she did. But Doug just never seemed to move on. He seemed to stay right there as a 14-year-old boy who could stretch the truth, tell stories, and just hide in the background. As Dwight and their other friends continued to mature and grow older, Doug seemed to have been left behind.

"Well, I would just be careful, man. If you get caught with those, they'll take your collectors' firearms license away; know what I mean?" Dwight cautioned him.

Doug had applied for and received a Federal Firearms License a few years earlier. He used it mostly so he could buy and sell guns at wholesale prices. Other than that, he didn't even really need it. But he liked to be able to tell people that he was a gun dealer.

Doug giggled again, "Yeah, I know. They would never... would never find them anyways. I've taken steps to… to ensure that if they ever come… ever come looking… it will not go well for… well for whoever comes looking."

*   *   *

Rising upward toward the sky, the clock tower of the Okanogan County Courthouse, built in 1914, resembled an 18th-century Spanish Mission. An addition to the building had been built in 1950, and most recently a movement had formed to register the building as a National Historical place. The hand-cut stones and meticulous landscaping created a prominent landmark above the gently flowing Okanogan River in the valley below. Set against the rocky sagebrush scablands of the surrounding hills, the courthouse and grounds felt like an oasis in the desert.

Deputy Johnson stepped through the giant archway trimmed in red ceramic tiles and into the sheriff's station.

"I hear you got to finally meet our friend, Doug Perry?" a deputy joked as he moved toward the water cooler in the station house.

Inside, the tile floors glimmered with fresh wax and the montage of desks, telephones, and file folders cluttered the enormous hall.

"Not officially," Johnson replied, "I need to get some background and then run back up to the Flat to interview him."

"Johnson!" a voice yelled from one of the glass encased cubicles toward the end of the station.

Both deputies looked toward the end of the room where the Sheriff was standing.

"Good luck," the other deputy chuckled as Deputy Johnson navigated his way through the matrix of justice into the Sheriff's office.

Deputy Johnson stepped into the Sheriff's office and moved one of the steel office chairs away from the desk so he could sit down. Across from him, the Sheriff leaned back in his chair and took a deep breath. His office was small but not cramped. File folders, law books, and pictures, of what Deputy Johnson assumed to be the man's family, adorned the desk and the few empty spaces on the shelves. Through the window to the left of the desk, the sunlight cascaded down onto the shrub-infested hillside. The deep blue skyline beyond the hills was filled with fluffy, white clouds.

"How did the Perry thing go?" the Sheriff asked, once Johnson was settled into his chair.

Johnson was surprised that a simple disturbance call, even one involving a firearm, would garner so much attention.

"I, uh, I took the complaint from L.L. Charles this morning; it seems the neighbor, Douglas R. Perry, threatened and discharged a firearm in the direction of two of Mr. Charles' workers," Johnson began.

"They didn't want to talk to you did they?" the Sheriff laughed.

"No... no, they didn't," Johnson answered.

"Probably undocumented, but even if they were, they don't seem to like police much. Given the fact of where they come from, I can't say as I blame 'em."

Johnson nodded his head.

"Based on what Mr. Charles subscribed to, I think I'll pay a visit to Mr. Perry and see what he has to say," Johnson continued.

"Yeah, you're going to have to. Without a statement from the two workers, you are not going to have much. And let me tell ya', you are stepping into a hornet's nest up there on the Flat with this one. Doug and his mother are quite a pair," the Sheriff said.

"I am getting that impression. I am going to run a report of his priors—"

"Don't waste your time... here," the Sheriff dropped a file folder on his desk and slid it over to Deputy Johnson, "He's been quite an 'active' member of the community. Most of what is in here is just officer's notes — prosecutor seems to have a tough time gettin' much on ol' Dougie. He's quite a handful. He does have one conviction in here from '79 for concealment of an unlawful weapon. But he just got a slap on the wrist. Claims he didn't do it, and if he did do it, then it's because he's 'mentally ill' every time he gets in trouble."

Johnson opened the file folder and quickly skimmed through the notes.

"Harassment, burglary, theft, reckless endangerment, disturbing the peace... and we couldn't get him on any of these?" Johnson asked, looking up at the Sheriff.

"Lawyers and mental health counselors. That's really all I can say 'bout this guy. And that's only the calls that were worth putting notes on. We've gone up there dozens of times on welfare checks because the power will be off, or no one has seen lights on or movement in that old house for days at a time."

Johnson continued to look through the notes in disbelief.

"The only thing we can do with this guy is be proactive. But I just wanted you to keep your expectations reasonable. He really knows how to play the system. He shot one of his neighbor's dogs once; for all intents and purposes we thought we had him. It seemed very clear that he lured the dog onto his property so he could shoot it. When it came to brass tacks — couldn't prove a thing. And just the fact that every one of his neighbors has had similar run-ins doesn't count for much in court," the Sheriff added.

"Says here that he and his mother were caught stealing silver dinnerware from a neighbor's home? And that they recovered the silver in a pawn shop — and that the pawn shop owner provided records that Doug and his mother had pawned it? How does that not get a conviction?" Johnson insisted.

"Simple. The neighbors refused to cooperate and testify in court. They are terrified of Doug, and they have no faith

He Said, She Said: The Spokane River Killer

that the system is going to do anything but give him more counseling," the Sheriff answered.

"With all due respect, sir, I don't accept that. This guy has been terrorizing these people for years it seems, and we are the one entity that is supposed to stand in front of him and say 'no more.' If this pattern continues, it is going to blow up on us— he *will do something drastic.* Without a doubt— he is a ticking time bomb," Johnson answered as he stood from his chair.

"Is that all, sir? I'm headed up to the Perry house to interview him. If he corroborates any of what I heard from Mr. Charles— I'll bring him in. I am sure I can get a statement from the two men that work for Mr. Charles."

The Sheriff stood up and opened his door for Deputy Johnson, "Do what the law demands, but I just wanted you to have some background. And take somebody up there with you— just to be safe."

*   *   *

As Doug turned the Pinto out of the parking lot at the gun store and onto the road up to Pogue Flat, he felt uncharacteristically secure. Nothing lowered his stress and tension level like being surrounded by dozens and dozens of rifles, pistols, and shotguns.

He loved them. He loved everything about them. How they smelled. How they felt in his hands. The comfort of a perfectly balanced stock, action, and barrel. He loved the way that magazines full of cartridges thumped and clanked when they hit the counter. The metal on metal scraping as a magazine slid gently into a receiver. The perfect little click when it sank home.

His familiar wry smile was back.

The drive to Pogue Flat was only a few minutes up the hill, take a right and then a left a few more minutes away. The sun had dropped down behind the hills, and he had a special evening planned in his basement. He loved to plan his evening as he drove. It was almost as fun as actually doing it. He and Dwight used to set up their tents in the old orchard and spend the dark hours planning the next day's events. Doug always seemed to have the best ideas, but no one ever wanted to follow them through.

It was disheartening sometimes.

But tonight he was going to go through the old stack of Playboy magazines he had discovered a few days earlier in the shop. His father had been very good at keeping them hidden from his mother and his siblings. After his dad died, Doug continued to find little stashes of three or four magazines at a time. Most recently he had discovered four issues from 1966 underneath a stack of newspapers his father kept next to the old wood stove to help start fires. When he discovered them earlier in the day, he couldn't take his eyes off one particular playmate: Karla Conway. Her beautiful face and body were encapsulated in what looked like a series of film strips across the cover of the April, 1966, issue.

She was mesmerizing.

Her white dress.

The way the strap was falling off her shoulder. Her blonde hair, so light and breezy.

Doug could hardly wait.

As he came to a stop at the top of the hill, he reached over into his backpack and gripped the pistol. It was still there. He looked left, and then turned his car onto the road leading up to the Flat. He knew he was going to be in for it from his mother. He had been gone for hours, and his failure to return with her anti-diarrheal would only compound matters. If he was quiet enough, he could slip the car through the gate and off of the gravel driveway onto the grass alongside it. She might not even hear him come home. Slipping through the front door and downstairs would be another matter entirely.

"SHIT!" Doug screamed and jerked the wheel quickly to the left as he jammed on the brakes.

BAM!

The headlights shattered as chunks of plastic from the grill of the small car scattered across the road. His tires screeched to a stop as the car lurched toward the ditch on the opposite side of the road.

A fucking deer.

For a moment he sat there... dazed. The little car just sat quietly idling as he gathered himself.

Off to the side of the road he could see the deer lying in the ditch on its side. Its legs were outstretched and stiff. Every few seconds it would lift its head trying to stand up. But the legs just kept jerking randomly. Doug shook his head as a truck pulled up behind him, slowed down, pulled out around him, and continued down the road.

He reached for the door handle and slowly opened the door. He could feel the door was jammed against the fender and had to push much harder than normal to get it open. Once it was nearly fully open, the door jerked and the fender crumpled with a loud crack.

He didn't even want to look at the front end of his car.

The stammering legs of the deer near the ditch caught his attention.

"Serves you right... stupid fucking thing!" he yelled toward the deer.

It just continued to struggle.

Doug took a deep breath and reached in to the car across the seat for his back pack.

"I should let you... let you suffer," he muttered.

His hand fished around the bottom of the pack until he felt the grip of the pistol. With an exaggerated jerk he pulled it from the bottom of the bag.

He flipped the safety off and pointed the gun in the direction of the dying animal in the ditch.

Then he stopped and put the safety back on.

Curiously, he stared at the beast struggling and suffering in the throes of death. As it lifted its head and tried to look in his direction, its tongue furling about its mouth, he just stared. Underneath the white fur of its belly he could see a small amount of blood puddling. As its chest raised and lowered, the deer coughed, more blood gurgling from its mouth.

He took a couple of steps closer.

The animal, writhing in pain, tried to stand once again, her eyes fully opened and nearly popping out of her head. Doug cocked his head to the side.

She blinked.

Begging for mercy.

He circled a few steps to the right of the animal, approaching it from its rear. With a swift motion he kicked it where its tail met its pelvis.

"Stupid! Stupid!" he mumbled.

The deer let out a painful, high pitched bleat, Doug could see its tongue fully extending from its mouth. Its ears pinned back and then relaxed. Doug let out a long breath, the tightening wrench in his abdomen subsided ever so briefly. For a minute or two, he just stood on the gravel shoulder, relieved, and watched the poor animal suffer. Eventually, the entire scene became a bore to him, so he placed the pistol back in his backpack and drove off toward his house.

The deer suffered for hours, struggling near the ditch, before finally succumbing to its injuries.

The last thing Doug needed was to have to get his car fixed. The entire front end looked damaged, but at least he knew how to do a lot of the work himself. There would be no way he would be able to pay off the guns he had on layaway now. Just as it was beginning to get fully dark, he pulled up to the road near his house. Across the field near the gate to his driveway, he could see headlights. A car was parked just outside of his gate. He leaned forward against the steering wheel and reached for his back pack.

He Said, She Said: The Spokane River Killer

Okanogan Sheriff?

Doug turned into his driveway and rolled down his window as he came to a stop in front of the patrol car. A tall sheriff's deputy stepped out of the car and approached his window.

"Do you mind stepping out of the car for a minute, sir?" the deputy asked.

Doug had to think quick.

"Let me park, out of the way," he hollered as he let the car roll through the gate and clearly inside his property line.

He shut the car off, grabbed his backpack and hopped out of the car.

"What's the trou... what's the trouble?" Doug asked as he swung the metal gate shut, separating him from the two officers.

"Are you Douglas Perry?" Deputy Johnson asked as he stepped up to the gate.

"What if I... what if I was?" Doug retorted.

"I want to ask you some questions about a disturbance yesterday," Johnson responded.

Doug looked at the ground and behind him toward the house. The porch light was still on, but the curtains all looked to be drawn shut. Nothing quelled his mother's activities quite like the recalcitrance of her bowels.

"I didn't hear any... any shooting," Doug stated quietly without looking at either of the two officers.

"Who said anything about shooting?" Johnson asked.

Doug swallowed really hard and stepped back from the gate.

"You guys are always comin'... always comin' up about my... my shooting. It's not illegal... illegal, you know!"

"Were you shooting yesterday?"

Doug stood motionless and looked back toward his house, "Yeah, actually, yeah... I was doing some... some target practice, I think?"

"You *think?*"

Doug wiped the hair from his face.

"Why don't you come out here so we can talk about this?" Johnson asked as he motioned for Doug to open the gate and join them on the road.

Doug licked his lips and wiped his arm across his face from left to right.

"I don't have to," he stated boldly.

"Doug, you might have hurt somebody. Where were you shooting?" Johnson asked.

"They were on... on my land! Those two stupid... stupid spicks are lying!"

"Doug, how did you know that two men made a complaint? Sounds like you might know more than you're telling us. Look, why don't you come out here and tell us your side, and I am sure we can get this all straightened out, ok?" Johnson implored.

Doug dropped his backpack onto the dirt and looked at it. The other deputy stepped away from the gate a few yards to the side.

"No! No!" Doug yelled and lowered his chin to his chest, "I won't say anything. Am I... am I under arrest?"

"No, Doug, we're just trying to sort this out."

"Then, no! No! Just leave me... leave me alone. I don't... they took... I just... *Go AWAY!*" Doug yelled, barely able to breathe.

"Doug, I want you to know that we are investigating this. Not talking to us will only make it worse. We can get an arrest warrant if we have to. But why don't you just come with us down to the station, and we can get your side of what happened?"

Doug grabbed his pack and backed a few more steps away from his gate.

"You pigs can do... can do whatever! Just leave... me alone."

"Doug, this has to stop. Running away from it isn't going to help the situation-"

He Said, She Said: The Spokane River Killer

"Fine! You want to... want to go to war... war with me? Fine! I'm not scared... scared of the... the police. Fuck you. *Fuck you!* I know my... I know my rights. Go eat a... a donut or something. Charge me then. Charge me... I always win. Fuck you!"

Doug turned and walked straight in toward his house. As he walked away he threw up his middle finger right behind his head.

Fuck you, pigs.

Jon Keehner

4
In Small Town America

"Look, Mike, it's not about whether he could have killed them or not—"

"Then WHAT is IT?!" Deputy Johnson yelled back at the prosecuting attorney handling Doug's case.

His medium-sized frame jerked to a stop in the county office building hallway where Mike had tracked him down. The black marble floors of the structure were so polished the reflection of the ceiling made the entire interior of the building seem larger than it really was.

Perhaps that was the point.

Prosecuting Attorney Ron Herrick was in his early forties. His hairstyle and mustache were woefully out of style, and his ill-fitting suit was indicative of a recent divorce—handled poorly. The tan line on his ring finger where he had probably worn a wedding band for 10+ years gripped the handle of a worn, brown leather briefcase.

He smelled like Aqua Velva.

"Do not raise your voice to me, Deputy," Ron tersely replied.

Ron was no stranger to Doug Perry. He had prosecuted him on many occasions and knew full well the extent of

He Said, She Said: The Spokane River Killer

Doug's mental challenges. Mike, on the other hand, had not yet been exposed to the plight of Douglas Perry. It had been three days since Doug had more or less told Deputy Johnson to go fuck himself at the gate to his family's property on Pogue Flat.

"He could have killed them. Next time he might! He has done this before— I mean— you know!'

"You see there— that is the problem. You think it matters if he could of— *you* deal in reality. *I* deal in what I can prove in a court of law. And if these two guys, whatever their names are—"

"Niconar and Estovan," Mike interjected.

Ron reached up and slid his hand down his mustache, his thumb and index finger tracing the sides.

"Right. Whatever. You see that? We don't even know if these guys will testify— you saw how nervous they were with the police. We don't have the budgets to go after cases like this with unreliable witnesses—"

Ron started striding down the hallway again as Mike trailed behind pleading his case.

"They're not unreliable— they are migrant workers— and they—"

Ron halted in front of an old pane window looking out toward the foothills of the North Cascade mountains. The old window framed the scene perfectly. For a second Ron stared longingly out the window oblivious to the ambitions of the sophomore deputy chasing him down the hall.

Ron snapped back to attention and said, "Call 'em whatever you want. I call 'em unreliable, because that's what they are. If we try and go to trial on this as reckless endangerment, I'll get laughed at. A jury here will never—"

Mike interrupted him again, "Yes they will. Everyone knows that he is going to eventually kill someone. This whole town is ready to lynch him if he keeps it up."

Ron started to shake his head in disbelief.

"Lynch him? Are you out of your mind? No one is going to lynch him. The system is full of checks and balances. You respond and investigate, I prosecute, judges make sure they get a fair trial, and juries determine their fate. It works, Mike. *Let the system work.*"

"*The* SYSTEM?" Mike laughed. "The system that lets him kill his brother's dog? The system that lets him steal silver from his neighbors and take it to the pawn shop? The system that lets him terrorize teenage girls by pointing his guns at them simply because they have to walk past his and his deranged mother's property to get to the school bus??"

Ron tried to open his mouth to speak but Mike continued.

"This guy has a history of gun violence—"

"He has never killed anyone—" Ron pointed out.

"NOT YET!" Mike railed. "Can't you at least charge him with a felony? We have to keep the guns from him or he is going to kill someone. Mark my words, counselor, he will kill someone."

"Mike, look, Doug Perry has been very good about walking a fine line. His attorney and him have made sure— hell, we stipulated once that his guns be stored at his attorney's house while actions were proceeding— the judge gave 'em back to him at the end of it all. Ordered him to get mental health counseling—"

"Isn't that enough? Can't you remove his guns for--"

"Of course not. You know that. Congress has not given government the authority to remove firearms solely based on a mental health issue. There are ways, but it is VERY VERY difficult. As soon as the government starts taking away constitutional rights from the 'mentally ill,' how long is it gonna be before people stop seeking treatment for depression or other conditions— stop seeking help, because they are in fear that if they do— they will have to give up their guns?"

Mike pursed his lip and shook his head in disbelief.

Ron continued, "Let me explain something to you about Doug Perry. We will send him a citation for felony reckless endangerment. It's a Class C felony—"

"That's all I'm asking—"

"Hold on, let me finish. We will *charge him* with a felony, and he will go see his attorney, and his attorney will come and see me. Doug will have cried and screamed how he won't give up his guns and he never meant to hurt anyone and how Larry used to ass rape him in his dungeon of a basement. And the judge will listen. And we will plea this down to a misdemeanor, and Doug will be forced to continue his counseling at the mental health center."

"Can you at least demand he surrender his firearms?"

Ron began to laugh.

"Look around you. Do you see where we are? No, he isn't going to have to give up his guns. Sure, the judge might make him store them at his lawyer's house for a few months, but Doug will take a few over there-- just enough so it looks like he is complying, and he will keep the rest. Last time he did this his attorney nearly had to rent a truck, because Doug had so many Goddamn guns.

"Do you not see a problem with that?" Mike begged.

"Of course I do. But this is what we get here in small town America. This isn't Seattle, and this isn't Spokane. We don't have teams of lawyers and support staff and cubicles stuffed with probation officers, or "community supervision officers," as they like to call them now. There is me, my secretary, a couple of clerks, and two judges. That is what we get. That is what we work with. If Doug Perry were in Seattle or Spokane— he would probably get the justice he deserves— but not here. It ain't gonna happen."

"Exactly! That is why it is so important to get him on a felony charge so that when he gets caught with his guns, maybe we can get the Feds involved. With all the gun traffic moving across the state lines into north Idaho— he has to be involved somehow."

"Doug?" Ron laughed out loud, "Doug Perry is too scared to travel away from his basement for more than 2 or 3 hours at a time— he is not involved in 'arms trafficking.'"

Ron looked at his watch.

"Look, I have a meeting in three minutes. Keep your chin up, deputy. It'll all work out, I'm sure."

Ron shuffled his way down the hall and through a narrow doorway out of sight. The old walnut door slammed shut leaving Deputy Johnson alone in the hallway. He stared out the old pane window at the gray clouds backing up in the distance over the mountains. It was going to be shitty weather for the next couple of days. Deputy Johnson let out a deep sigh and turned for the staircase at the other end of the hallway.

Nearly six weeks later Doug begged and pleaded for the courts to give him another chance. He realized that discharging a firearm over someone's head could have disastrous and unintended consequences— consequences that couldn't be taken back. Firearms were serious business, and he should exercise safety and caution when handling them. He completely agreed. He promised he would abide by the terms of his community supervision and that he would be a model citizen. He understood the ramifications of his actions and had finally learned a valuable lesson. This, according to him, was going to be a turning point in his life.

Finally he would behave appropriately.

Finally he believed the counseling would work.

This was going to be the time.

On June 22, 1987, Doug plead guilty to a misdemeanor and was ordered to continue to see his mental health counselors.

Deputy Johnson knew they were making a huge mistake.

5
Will Run With Blood

"DOUGLAS!" Ruth screamed down the stairs.

Shit.

He jerked his hand out of his pants and turned toward the stairs. He reached for the glasses on his nightstand and he wrestled them awkwardly onto his face.

"WHAT?!" he yelled back at his mother. He hated it when she screamed like this.

For a second he thought she hadn't heard him so he yelled up the stairs again.

"WHA—"

"DOUGLAS!" she yelled again just he spoke. It seemed they spent more time yelling over each other than anything else.

He dropped the old Penthouse magazine on his bench and stood up. He glanced away as his head bounced off the hanging light bulb and nearly burned his hair. The shadows cast from the swaying bulb looked like marching ghosts across the concrete walls.

What the fuck?

Now he was irritated.

From the doorway at the base of the stairs he could see his mother's ominous physique at the top. She did not look happy.

She rarely did.

"You have to be at the doctor's office at two o'clock!" she yelled.

Doug waved his arm dismissively at her and turned back toward his bedroom.

My counselor is not a doctor.

"DOUGLAS!" she yelled again.

"I KNOW!" he hollered back.

"It's important, Goddamn you. DOUGLAS! If you don't go they will take this place from us. Do you understand ME?! *THEY WILL TAKE OUR HOUSE!!*"

Guilting him into compliance seemed to be the only way she felt he would do anything she asked. When he would leave the water faucet on just a little bit, it was his "fault" that the water company was going to come and shut off the water. When he left his basement light on during his trips to Dwight's gun shop, it was, according to her, going to be his fault the power company turned off the electricity. Part of him knew that she was full of shit — but he worried that it might be so. He worried just enough that every time she said it, the knot in his stomach twisted just a little tighter.

A knot that rarely seemed to loosen.

Douglas flipped his daypack up onto his bed and unzipped the top pocket. Stretching across his bed he grabbed a Makarov pistol and a couple of extra magazines for it. With his other hand he pulled open one of the drawers of his bureau and gripped a small box of ammo for the pistol. He took a deep sigh and slid all of it into the pocket and zipped it shut.

His lawyer had warned him not to take any guns with him when he left the farm. But there was no way he was going to leave the house without at least some form of protection. No one really cared if he had it — it was just what everyone was "supposed" to say. Like when his pitiful excuse of a mother told him he would cause them to lose the house or get the power shut off. He knew it wouldn't *really* happen. Hell, he had the gun in his pack the day he went to court.

They knew he had it.

And yet no one said a word.

One vile task after another. That was all these people who were trying to run his life did. One vile task... after another.

"DOUGLAS!!" she screamed again.

"Fuck! I'm coming!"

He flipped his daypack onto his shoulder and pulled his pony tail out from under the strap. He fished his glasses off the nightstand, kissed his finger tips and slid them across the new centerfold he had laid out on his pillow as though he were blowing his lover a kiss.

"Until tonight..." he smiled.

*   *   *

His counseling offices were just north of the old part of town up the hill a ways. Omak was growing, and it seemed everywhere he looked something new was under construction.

Inside the office, he checked in with the receptionist and sat in the waiting area clutching his daypack. Across the room a young girl no more than 13 or 14 years old sat staring blankly off into space. Her mother kept patting her knee as though somehow this was going to make things better. Clearly she was not happy. Next to the fish tank near the receptionist's window an older man sat with the same blank stare. The misery and disappointment of these people dripped from their souls right onto the floor and pooled like blood.

"Douglas?" a woman's voice called through a door at the end of the room.

He jumped up and threw his bag over one arm. She led him down a short hallway to the end of the building and around the corner. The fresh paint and new carpet smelled sweet to Doug. Everything about this place seemed alarmingly "pleasant" to be around.

Unlike the girl or the man in the waiting area, he knew better.

The fix was in.

This was where they take you to break your spirit. This was where truth went to be put on meds.

"Right in here; Ms. Greeley will be with you shortly," the woman politely informed him.

She sounded like she were rehearsing for a television commercial selling convalescent care to old folks.

It nearly made him sick.

He reached down and felt his pistol through the pocket of the daypack. He knew he wasn't supposed to bring it with him to appointments. When he first started going he told Ms. Greeley that he wouldn't leave his house without it. Of course she had a cow. Even after he told her that he had a Federal Firearms License she still demanded he leave it at home.

That's when he knew.

He knew they were in on it, too. Just like his pathetic mother had claimed. Just like he had read in the old books and diaries Larry had left in the corner when mother kicked him out of the house years earlier.

He read them. He knew about how the government was trying to take away all the rights of its citizens. Hell, they elected a damn actor as president, and it turned out *even he* might be corrupt. Something big was going down that went even further than the president. He read about "New World Order" and other things. Jim Jones in Guyana and even the Moon cult were probably onto something.

Stupid nips.

But he wasn't scared of them. He had told them before, and he would tell them again— as long as they knew he was not to be messed with. Earlier in the summer he had even told Ms. Greeley that he had a MAC-10 machine gun buried in his yard. She asked if he was still worried about the government trying to come and take away his rights.

So he told her.

He knew she couldn't say anything unless he said he was "going to go kill someone." He didn't even know if she believed him.

"It's fully automatic," he said to her at the time.

She just scribbled and reminded him that he couldn't bring any firearms to his appointments.

"Hi Doug, how are you?" Ms. Greeley asked as she gallantly strode through the door into the office.

"I am... I am good... I guess?" Doug answered.

"Well that doesn't sound like a good start; what's going on?" she asked as she slid into the chair across from the couch and pulled out her note pad. As she crossed her legs in the chair he caught a quick glimpse of her panties between her knee high boots.

He smiled.

"I don't know," Doug began.

He looked toward the floor and remained silent. He knew she wouldn't say a word. He could stay silent and the whole half of an hour would go by.

"I'm just tired of coming here, I guess," he looked up at her hoping she wouldn't be mad.

He hated it when they got mad at him.

"Yeah, I wanted to talk a little bit about that," she began, "You have missed quite a few appointments—"

"Six."

She stopped and looked at him disapproving of his interruption.

"Seven. Actually."

He looked back down toward the floor

"Part of the reason that talking these things out helps is because it is consistent. We need to try and have a few consistent weeks. Do you think we can do that?" she asked.

Doug paused.

For almost a minute she stared at him disapprovingly.

"I just don't like... I don't like coming... coming here. It's a waste... a waste of time."

"Well, Doug, the court doesn't seem to think so—"

"The COURTS can go to HELL!" Doug shouted.

He was becoming very irritated and annoyed. This whole counseling thing was just a way for them to get his guns and get his land any way they could. Every time he came here it was the same song and dance. She would pepper him with suggestions and ask how he felt and he would just block it all out and get angry.

Every Goddamn time.

"How do you feel right now, Doug. What *emotion* are you feeling? Let's try and identify that, right now..."

"What?" Doug looked at her again.

He reached down toward his bag.

Don't do it.

"Right now— this is good— what emotion are you feeling?"

"I'm pissed off!"

"Pissed off at what? Or who?"

Doug leaned backwards away from her and tucked his chin toward his chest.

Was this bitch nuts?

He didn't answer her. He drifted away from the room, away from town, and into another place. For a few minutes he bit his lip and started to pitch forward and backward.

No.

He punched his thigh trying not to give in. He raked his fingernails across the skin on his forearms to make the thoughts go away. He hated this.

She just stared at him, intently.

" I don't want to talk about it!"

She said nothing.

He looked at the ceiling and started to slap his knees together and rub his hands across his thighs. He looked at her again and she had not moved a muscle.

This wasn't supposed to happen.

He shook his head.

NO!

He didn't want to remember. But he couldn't stop it.

He closed his eyes and they started to tear up.

"What is it, Doug. What do you see? *Who do you see!?*" Ms. Greeley shouted toward him.

* * *

"Deputy Johnson?" the man's voice quickly got Mike's attention.

"Just Mike, sir. I'm off duty today," Mike replied.

Mr. Charles stood before him with a handful of pipe fittings and some teflon tape. With only one hardware store in town it was not uncommon to run into someone you knew at least once a year there.

The two men sidestepped their way around the corner out of the main traffic path of the aisles.

"So, uh… how is that Doug Perry thing going?" Mr. Charles began, "We still see him out in the yard when we are up at that end of the field. He must not have gone to trial yet, I suppose? How many years do you think he will get for damn near killin' two of my workers?"

Mike drew in a huge breath and let it go.

"That bad, huh?" Mr. Charles chuckled.

Mike didn't like giving his word and going back on it. With almost 15 years on the job he was not naive to the ways of the court system in rural America. But he had rarely seen a case where the victims were literally being terrorized at the hands of someone else, and that person was getting little more than community service and counseling.

"Mr. Charles—"

"L.L.— that's what everyone calls me," he awkwardly joked, hoping to ease the burden of what he knew must be difficult for the deputy.

"You see, it's like this: without knowing that Estevon and uhhh... uhhh... shit, I can't believe *I forgot* their names—"

"Nicanor."

"Yeah— Nicanor. Anyway— without knowing if they would even testify— the prosecutor was—"

"Worried?"

"Yes, he was very worried."

"I understand that, deputy—"

"Mike, please—"

"I understand that, Mike. But Nico and Estevon are here legally. In fact, Nico is taking his citizenship test next month. They would have come to court," Mr. Charles shook his head in disappointment.

"It's more than that, sir. For some reason, the judge and the prosecutor and Doug's lawyer— they have this little "system" worked out that they believe is the best thing for Doug—"

"What about the best thing for us? Livin' up on the Flat?" Mr. Charles exclaimed.

He was irritated.

"I understand—"

Mr. Charles slipped to the side away from a man trying to get into the basket of plumbing sealants.

"Well, even if he only gets a little jail or prison time— and taking away his guns will make things a little better—"

Mike couldn't hide the shame on his face.

Mr. Charles looked at him and then nearly gasped.

"He's not even going to get any time is he? They are just going to take away his guns?" he stated assumingly.

Mike let out another drawn out sigh. He shifted his feet and looked around as though he were about to tell a dirty joke in church.

"The prosecutor and his lawyer already had him plea to a misdemeanor. They aren't going to take away his guns. In fact, this case was resolved a few months ago."

"Are you KIDDING ME?" Mr. Charles grumbled.

He shifted back and forth in his tight blue overalls.

"He damn near shoots two of my workers— and we don't honestly know if he meant to kill them, or maybe he did and just *missed*. And my wife and I report it, and with all of the other looseness going on around that Perry farm— you tell me that no one even bothered to let us know? *What if he had decided to retaliate against us?*"

"I am quite sure he was not going to do so— his counselors—"

"*HIS COUNSELORS? Jeezus man, listen to yourself!*"

In 15 years of being on the job, Mike empathized with many a crime victim. But this case really gnawed at him.

"So counseling it is then, eh? More 'mental health?' Mark my words, deputy, that boy— man— is trouble. He is a time bomb waiting to go off. What the hell am I doing here at the hardware store anyway? You ain't gonna stop him. The judge ain't gonna stop him. Sounds like no one gonna stop him? Sounds like I ought to be over at the gun counter. Good day, deputy."

Mr. Charles stormed off.

God I hope he is not serious.

*   *   *

"Who makes you angry, Doug? Who? *Tell me!*"

For a second he could see his brother coming down the stairs into his basement. As he stood in front of the workbench in his basement, Larry's shadow would creep across the wall and his stomach would turn to knots.

No.

"Let it go Douglas, let it go," she begged him.

He would come up behind him and put his arm around his torso. Doug could feel his brothers erect penis through his sweatpants against his lower back.

No.

"Time," he would say, and Doug would turn off his mind and turn off his eyes and turn off his ears. He would drift away to the field and he would see Dwight and they would be chasing radio-controlled airplanes around the field behind the house.

Doug would hold his breath.

If he let in the sounds he could hear Larry whispering girls' names and he would suck on Doug's ears. He would lick his neck and then he would start pumping slowly on his thighs while he pulled Doug's pants and underwear down. He would put his hands on Doug's shoulder blades and push his upper body forward. When Larry's arms let Doug's body go he knew it was only a few seconds— Larry would be taking his own pants down. He had to relax or it was going to hurt. The final warning was when he would hear Larry spit and lick on his hand before stroking his penis to lube it up — and then he would feel it—

"Please, Doug, " Ms. Greeley asked again.

Doug opened his eyes and gave her an evil stare. He looked toward his daypack and muttered something unintelligible under his breath.

No.

He would never tell.

"It's this *fucking place!*" Doug yelled at her, "You all just want to take me away from the farm. Take the land away from. Keep under your thumb because we don't look like you and act like—"

Doug was breathing heavy and beads of sweat appeared on his brow.

"I know what you all are up to. I won't be fooled. My mother is right— she knows how you all operate together. That's how the Charleses got our land from us. That's how I keep ending up here— how much do you get paid for this!?"

Doug stood up and began to pace around the room. Ms. Greeley started to realize that this was one more of Doug's common outbursts.

Doug knew he couldn't trust her. How would she ever understand? She would just tell Larry what he had said, and then— *oh, God no.*

He needed out of here; he need this whole counseling thing to end. This was enough. He could just go back to the basement and finish his projects. If he could just get out of here, he promised himself he would finish putting the Mauser trigger group together that he had promised Dwight months ago. If he could just get out and back to the Flat, he would not bother the Charleses or their stupid workers. He would leave the neighbor girls alone and maybe even quit shooting at the feet of the neighbors' dogs.

If he could just get out.

"How many more sessions do I have to do? How much longer do I have to keep coming here?" Doug yelled and sat back on the couch burying his face into his hands.

Ms. Greeley realized that Doug was deflecting again.

"The court order says until such time as I can assure the court you will no longer pose a danger to others," she answered politely.

He hated it how she would always answer so formally. Everyone around this place from the receptionist to the damn janitors always acted like he was a fragile cupcake or something.

Why couldn't they just be real?

"Well obviously that will... that will never happen, right? Because I will always... I will always be a danger to anyone who... who threatens me or tries to... tries to fuck with me!"

"Then we have a lot of work to do, Douglas."

He hated that even more. Her condescending sarcasm was enough to make him want to kill her.

"No! No more!" Doug screamed and stood up.

Ms. Greeley looked worried.

"I am telling you right now… if you do not… if you do not tell the courts that I am fine and that… that I am fine… we are done here— then I guarantee you— I absolutely GUARANTEE you— this place will… will see blood. Oh yes, it… yes it will… will run WITH BLOOD!!"

Doug shouldered his backpack and strutted down the hall and out the door.

Ms. Greeley continued to write notes in her book and then sighed.

Doug's court-mandated counseling was over.

6
A Rotting Carcass

April 25, 1988.

Where are the fucking keys?

Doug began scattering the tools and miscellaneous gun parts across his bench. He had last used the car the day before when he had gone to see Dwight. It had been weeks, maybe even months, since he had actually gone to town to visit his friend. Even in as frail a mental condition as he was, he occasionally felt the joy of simply meeting up with an old friend. He had stopped taking his meds a week earlier, and the positive effects of the medication lingered on well enough that he felt somewhat normal. The side effects of the medication had subsided a day or two after he stopped taking them, and it was a rare time that he ever felt this good.

But his car keys were nowhere to be found.

Then he heard the footsteps across the kitchen floor above him.

He froze.

Please. Not tonight.

"DOUGLAS!" she screamed.

Doug closed his eyes and sadly shook his head. There was no point in looking for his car keys now.

"DOUGLLLLAAAS!!" she screamed again as the hinges on the door squealed his demise again.

"What?!" he yelled up the stairs.

Nothing.

It was dead quiet.

He turned and slowly stepped up the stairs. At the top he could see the door was halfway open and the lamp next to her recliner in the living room was on.

She would pace across the floor for a while and soon, the drawers and cupboard doors in the kitchen would be opening and slamming shut. The squeaking and creaking on the floor above him would quickly become stomping and soon she would be screaming at the top of her lungs in a fit of rage. If he was lucky, she would wear herself out and disappear into her bedroom for the night and fall asleep to reruns of The Maury Povich Show.

Otherwise, he'd be in for a long night while she screamed and yelled and belittled him for hours and hours. She would rant about how he was nothing like his sisters; they were young and beautiful. But for some reason, he and Lawrence, (she always had to bring Lawrence into everything), were pathetic, sick little faggots. She even blamed him for *letting* his older brother sodomize him. She figured little Doug probably liked it, or he wouldn't have allowed it. Maybe it would turn him into a man.

As the minutes passed, he realized she was probably going to take herself to bed. Just as he started to look over his gun projects to decide on what to do next, the hinges on the door to the basement squealed open and the door slammed into the wall upstairs.

"God DAMN you, Douglas!" she screamed down the stairs. Her voice was so strained she could curdle milk.

He knew what he was in for.

"Douglas! God Damn you! Douglas! Get your little ass up here! NOW!! Aaaaaahhhhhh!!" she screamed even louder.

"DOUGLAS!!!!"

He Said, She Said: The Spokane River Killer

There was no way she would ever make the trek down into his basement. He could simply refuse to take part in her tirade. But he also knew she would scream and yell down that flight of stairs for *hours* if he didn't respond.

She knew he was down there.

He slipped a pair of worn out jeans onto his legs. He nearly fell over when one of his feet got caught up in the gaping hole in the knee. He fumbled his glasses onto his face and begrudgingly slipped up the stairs.

She was nowhere to be seen. The only light came from the kitchen.

"You've really done it this time!" his mother screamed at him and threw something made of glass shattering into the sink.

She wouldn't even look at him. He just stood in the doorway above the stairs to use the door frame as a shield if she really decided to go off this time.

She had thrown glass jars at him before. Once it nearly blinded him, leaving a 3-inch cut above his eye. It bled on and off for almost a week.

Blood fascinated him.

There was no point in responding. It was better to just take as much of it as he could.

"That man and your Uncle Dick— they know exactly what they're doing. *And you're helping them!*" she continued to yell.

She had a knife in her hand, and for some reason she had decided to cut up an onion. With every strike of the cutting board as she sliced away, he jumped.

"You better figure out a way out of this one," she said in her normal voice, "or they are going to finally get this place. The whole goddamn thing!"

"But... they can't—" he meekly offered.

She immediately turned and stared at Doug, the knife extended straight out of her hand towards him.

"You shut up!!" she screamed, "You shut up— right now. This is all your fault. They will take everything, because *you* got yourself thrown in prison! That's what they'll do to you. You know that?"

A horrified look came across Doug's face. He waited for her to continue, but she just kept dicing the onion. And not saying anything. For nearly a minute it seemed. He knew she was just waiting for him to start talking so she could cut him off and continue berating him.

He said not a word.

"And what do you think will happen to a *scrawny*, little, long-haired, baby-faced *runt* like you? Huh?" she finally broke her silence.

Her voice sounded low and gravely like some sort of demon were channeling itself through her.

He just sat there.

"Little... boys... like you," she continued, her words slow and methodical, "they get to be... they get... taken down-- and the *things those evil men do!!*"

Her voice kept shifting from low and demon-like to a blood curdling scream. And then low again.

He didn't want to believe her. He knew she was lying, but somehow he wondered if maybe it were true.

"You... you will end up licking some man's— *you'd probably like it!*" she screamed again, "*You little homo!*"

Suddenly she stopped.

For a few seconds she went completely silent and stared at the picture of Kathy on the wall. Her face and features went soft like she were going to cry.

Kathy... her beloved Kathy.

There were pictures of her all over the house.

Ruth let the gas building up inside her intestines free. It smelled like a rotting carcass along the highway. But worse.

The pendulum on the wall clock just ticked- back and forth as though time had stood still.

And then her nostrils flared and the fat below her chin curled under as she bit her bottom lip and began to shift in front of the kitchen sink.

"FAGGOT!!" she screamed at the top of her lungs again.

She turned, almost dropping the knife, and extended her arms outward towards him as if she were going to strangle him. The kitchen chair kicked out from behind her and screeched across the floor, tumbling into the cabinet beneath the sink.

"You rotten little beast!" she screamed and nearly plunged the knife into his wrist.

Doug turned and headed toward the dining room; he was much faster than she was, and if he could just stay away from her for a minute or two, she would calm down and probably go pass out in her recliner.

She always did.

But something was stirring in her this time. This time she had it in for him, and she would not be denied. Instead of chasing after him toward the dining room, she went back toward the kitchen and circled around through the pantry and met him in the dining room, heading him off from the opposite direction. He ran directly into her.

"You little *BASTARD!!*" she screamed at the top of her lungs.

All Doug could imagine was that she was going to plunge the knife right into his throat and kill him. He reached out and pulled her hand toward him to spin her around. She was not very nimble. He grabbed her by the hair on the back of her head and slammed her onto the hardwood floors on her back.

She flailed like a wounded turtle.

In a flash he saw the knife, and without thinking, he punched her and punched her and punched her in the face until she dropped it. She screamed like the feral cats he had seen scream while they were fucking.

But louder.

Blood gushed from her mouth and her nose, and she wailed and stopped moving. The knife slid across the floor and bounced off the doorway and back into the kitchen.

She moaned and bellowed like a dying beast.

He had shoved her before, and once he had even hit her. But he was just a kid then. As she lay on the hardwood floor nearly choking on her own blood, he wanted to laugh.

He wanted to go get the knife from the kitchen and shove it right through her heart.

As the clock in the hallway ticked back and forth, Doug could hardly catch his breath.

For minutes he just stared at his pathetic mother.

"Douglas?" she finally whimpered.

Doug shook his head and gathered himself.

"What?" he asked.

"Can you get me a wet towel from the sink and help me up?" she cried.

Douglas went into the kitchen and grabbed one of the hand towels draped across the oven door.

He unzipped his pants and pulled out his penis. Out of sight of his mother around the corner he pissed all over the towel and into the sink. Without a word he zipped up his jeans and took the towel to his mother. She grabbed it from him without even noticing. She dabbed the piss-soaked rag all over her face and continued to groan.

"Help me up, boy," she moaned and tried to roll over.

"F... F... Fuck you."

He turned and went back down the stairs.

"Don't you walk away from me! DOUGLAS! You little son of a bitch!! Come back here! Come back here at once or I will make you pay!!!"

When he got downstairs he dug through one of the boxes of Playboys until he found the perfect one. He laughed thinking about his blubbering mother upstairs wiping the blood off of her face with his piss-soaked towel.

He Said, She Said: The Spokane River Killer

He slipped his pants down and flipped open the magazine.

He wanted so desperately to make love to a woman.

Upstairs, his mother dialed 911.

*   *   *

"DOUG! . . . This is Deputy Johnson . . . I want to talk to you. Will you come upstairs?" the deputy hollered down into the darkness.

She had called the fucking police?

Doug could not believe what he was hearing. There was a cop — *inside his house?*

Deputy Johnson stood braced against the side of the doorway, out of the line of sight from the concrete stairwell leading to the basement. The mortar-lined walls leading down were cracked and a dingy off-white. Through the doorway behind him he could hear Ruth arguing with the other deputy.

This was not the first time he had been called to the Perry house. He had been on the force in Okanogan County for more than fourteen years.

Deputy Johnson peeked around the doorway for just a second and jerked his head back and yelled down again, "Doug? . . . I just want to talk; we need to get this sorted out. Will you just come up here so we can talk?"

With his head turned slightly to the side the deputy listened intently for any sound which might give an indication as to what Doug was up to.

Nothing.

He waited silently at the top of the stairs. The smell of cat urine and feces was nearly overwhelming. If the cats even had litter boxes, they probably had not been emptied in weeks. Maybe if he waited Doug out, he would hear something or perhaps Doug would get sick of waiting and just come upstairs. Cautiously, the officer stepped away from the doorway and leaned in to the living room where Ruth was trying to describe to the other deputy what had happened.

Johnson interrupted, "Maybe we can have dispatch try and get Rod on the phone? At least give it a try."

Local attorney Rod Reinbold was well liked in Omak. He had represented Doug a few times before and on more than one occasion he had successfully helped defuse some pretty tenuous situations involving Doug and the police.

Leaning back toward the downstairs doorway, Johnson heard a door squeaking open and the otherwise dusky basement became bathed in light as the door opened just a touch.

"Doug? . . . Doug I need you to come up here please."

Patiently, the deputy waited and listened for nearly a minute.

"Listen Doug, we aren't going anywhere; this is only going to get worse for you the longer this goes on. Is this really how you want this to go down?"

Once again the basement faded to darkness as the door to Doug's bedroom slammed shut.

Deputy Johnson shook his head and sighed.

Downstairs, Doug paced back and forth along the end of his bed. As quickly as he sat on the worn-out spring mattress, he jumped up again and mumbled to himself. He looked around the smattering of gun parts, firearms magazines, and military surplus gear he had amassed since he was a child. He sat on the bed again and buried his face into his hands as his elbows rested on his knees.

He didn't mean to hit her. But she just kept nagging and nagging. Why wouldn't she just shut up about it?

Doug could hear footsteps creaking the hardwood floors up the stairs. He had no idea how many cops were up there or how many more were going to show up. But he wasn't leaving.

No way.

He Said, She Said: The Spokane River Killer

"Doug," Johnson's voice boomed down the stairs again just as the motor to the deep freeze in the corner kicked on, completely startling him. His heart raced.

"Doug! Just come upstairs and we'll talk this out; we tried to get a hold of Rod, but he's out of town right now."

Doug shook his head.

Rod? Why were they trying to get Rod?

Standing up, Doug clutched his fists together and brought them jerkily up to his chest. His thumbs nervously twirled in a circular motion around each curled index finger.

He sat back onto the wool blanket covering his bed and then shot up again to pace from wall to wall. As the freezer motor continued to whir, the crackling of the police radio upstairs made him even more nervous.

Why couldn't they just stay out of it? Why couldn't they just leave?

The freezer abruptly shut off.

Silence.

"I am going to come downstairs, Doug. I just want to talk. I just want to hear your side of things, OK?"

Now Doug was horrified.

Downstairs?

No.

He paced even faster around the tiny concrete clad room.

No... no... NO!

He ripped his glasses from his night stand and threw them onto his face. His hands massaged the hair out of his face, and he grabbed his Makarov pistol. With a single fluid motion, he hit the magazine release and dropped the magazine out of the pistol to confirm it had ammo in it.

He could barely swallow the lump in his throat.

Desperately he wanted a glass of water.

Carefully he cracked his bedroom door open again to peer out into the cluttered basement.

"Whoever comes... down," Doug paused and licked his lips, "down those... down those stairs... I'll SHOOT THEM!" Doug's voice cracked nervously as he half-heartedly yelled toward Deputy Johnson.

Doug stood in the doorway to his bedroom with the Makarov shaking in his hand near his thigh and waited.

Johnson shook his head in disbelief again. This was spinning out of control.

But so be it.

He knew to be cautious. Two summers earlier a tribal policeman named Louis Millard was shot and killed in the nearby town of Nespelem on the Colville Indian Reservation. These things could get out of hand quickly. And Johnson knew it.

"Look, Doug, let's not let this get out of hand any further. OK?" he shouted.

"I've got this place... this place wired! It will all blow... blow up — I mean it — this whole damn... whole damn... this whole damn house will blow up!"

A fucking bomb? Johnson wouldn't put anything past Doug.

Every few minutes Doug heard the front door open, and more and more people were showing up. It was obvious the whole police force was probably upstairs listening to his mother cry about how he had pummeled the shit out of her.

And he was getting thirsty.

He knew he should have grabbed his chocolate milk before he came downstairs, but striking his mother made him curiously aroused.

He found it exhilarating.

Maybe he should just go up and talk to them. They probably just want to see if he's OK, and his mother will tell them she doesn't want to press charges, and he can have a glass of chocolate milk and make love to another centerfold.

Yes.

He just needed to go talk.

"Fine!" Doug yelled upstairs.

"Douglas?" Deputy Johnson yelled back down, "Fine what? Are you coming up? We just want to talk to you."

Doug didn't want all those cops there. He would talk to Johnson, because he knew he had to talk to one of them. But the rest of them? They had to go.

"I'll come up if... up if it's just you!" Doug yelled up again.

"Sure, Doug. No problem. I am just going to tell my partner to head back down to the station house. It will be just you and me and your mother, OK?"

Johnson motioned for his partner to walk out the front door and the other officers to remain motionless.

"I heard more than just your... more than just your partner come in!"

"No, Doug, that was just some paramedics we called to help your mom. She is okay; turns out she just has a little bruise. That's all. She'll be fine. If we can just see that you're OK, we can talk and then maybe we can just let this all go, huh?"

Doug tossed the underpants he had used to wipe his semen from his hand into the corner. He pulled open his drawer and slipped on a new pair. He found the jeans he had been wearing and pulled them up around his waist.

"I'll be up in just a second," he called up the stairs.

"No problem, Doug. It's just me and your mom. I'll have her get some dessert out? How about some ice cream, huh?"

Doug was somewhat surprised that cops could be so reasonable. Maybe he had been wrong all this time not to trust them. It seemed as though he had beaten the shit out of his mother — but it turned out maybe not? Maybe Doug was just letting his mind get the better of him?

He grabbed an old white t-shirt as he sprinted up the stairs for a bowl of ice cream. His elbow smacked into the doorway at the top of the stairs as he pulled the shirt over his face blinding him for just a second.

WHAM!!

As he hit the top step he was tackled to the ground with such force he thought he had broken his orbital bone.

"*WHAT THE HELL!!!*" he screamed as his shirt slid around his neck and he could now see nearly half a dozen uniformed police officers in his living room. His face was pressed against the floor, and in the corner of the living room he could see his mother struggling to breathe. Her face was swollen to nearly twice its normal size.

"Douglas Perry you are under arrest!!"

Before he even realized the extent to which he had been duped and the serious nature of the trouble he was in, Deputy Johnson jerked his arms behind him and placed him in handcuffs.

"You lying pigs!" he yelled, "You can't do that!! That's... that's entrapment. I'll fucking... I'll fucking kill you... I'll kill all of you pigs. You better believe it... I'LL BLOW UP THE... THE GODDAMN POLICE STATION!!!"

An hour later Doug was sitting in solitary confinement in the Okanogan County Jail.

He was furious.

But he knew he would be home before any of those dumb cops finished their shifts.

He knew.

7
Bits of Broken Glass

Sunrise over the Okanogan Highlands of northeastern Washington never seemed to get the credit for the scenic beauty that it deserved. By late April, daybreak was still cool and crisp, but the morning frost rose quickly into warm mist. Officer Johnson thoroughly loved his morning coffee and the warmth of the day to come.

Especially today.

Today, Doug Perry had finally slipped up. Threatening law enforcement officers with rigged explosives and then following up that threat by further threatening to blow up the Omak and Okanogan police stations was going to be more than enough to get him a search warrant for the Perry basement. If everything the folks living on Pogue Flat were saying was true, he should finally be able to convince the prosecuting attorney to charge Doug with a significant crime— a crime for which the judge could not sentence him to "time served" and "mental health counseling." If Doug had the number of firearms he suspected he did, then the threats Doug made would seem even more plausible to a jury. Even Deputy Johnson doubted that Doug had actually "wired the door with explosives" or that he even possessed the knowledge and means to do so. But the search warrant would finally allow Deputy Johnson to see what the hell was going on inside that basement.

But he had to act fast.

Essentially, Johnson had 72 hours from the time of Doug's arrest to make a case for something more severe than simple assault on his mother. That 72-hour time clock would expire on Thursday night, so he had today and Wednesday. Prosecuting Attorney Herrick had agreed not to charge Doug until the very last minute; therefore, there was no way Doug's lawyer could bail Doug out of jail.

By 11:15 in the morning, Deputy Johnson had secured a warrant to search Doug's basement for guns, ammunition, or explosives. The warrant was based upon statements Ruth had made to the officers while on the scene attempting to arrest Doug for assaulting his mother and on information relayed from the mental health center in Omak to the investigating officers that Doug's prior counselors believed he may be in possession of automatic weapons, and, thereby, was a danger to himself or others.

When Johnson arrived at the Perry farm, he was surprised to see Ruth sitting outside the front door in a chair and staring off into the fields to the south of Smith Road.

"Ms. Perry?" Johnson asked as he slammed the door to his patrol car shut.

She continued to stare and say nothing.

It was nearly noon, and the radiant heat from the morning sun had already warmed up the Flat. So much so that tiny beads of sweat had formed on her brow as she sat.

A moment later Deputy Thompson, who was going to assist in the execution of the search warrant, pulled his patrol car into the driveway and parked.

The smell of burning applewood floated in from somewhere up the valley. In the distance a chainsaw faintly roared and bogged its way through the late spring task of getting the orchards on Pogue Flat ready for the season.

He Said, She Said: The Spokane River Killer

"Ms. Perry?" Johnson continued, "We have a search warrant for the part of the house where Doug lives— down in the basement. So we are going to need for you to stay out of there while we do our work... ma'am?"

In her hands she clutched a framed photo of a young girl. The glass from the frame was jagged and broken and it looked like Ruth's hands were covered in dried blood.

Out of nowhere she turned to look at Deputy Johnson, and an evil scowl came across her face.

"Do... what you want AND GO!" she screamed at Deputy Johnson.

He was caught off guard by her odd behavior, but at this point he was far from surprised by it.

Inside the house, the living room was still in disarray from the night before. The sofa was knocked out of the way, and the recliner and end tables were still lying on their sides where Doug had been wrestled to the floor and handcuffed.

Small bits of broken glass lay scattered across the rug. The house smelled like someone had pissed (or worse) in the corner. The officers each pulled latex gloves onto their hands.

The door to the basement was off of its frame, and fragments of wood and plaster littered the doorway from the night before where the explosives detail had made sure the door was not wired with explosives as Doug had claimed.

"Do you really think we will find anything down here?" Thompson inquired as they shined their flashlights down the stairway.

"I don't know for sure, but I know this guy is way worse than the lawyers and courts think he is," Johnson responded and stepped carefully down onto the first stair.

"What makes you think that?" Thompson asked.

The wooden stairs creaked and groaned as the two large men descended into the abyss of Doug Perry's childhood.

"Just a gut feeling. I have seen these kind before. Yeah— they are mostly talk, and they hardly ever follow through with anything they plan or set out to do. But they always end up escalating, and then some random, unrelated event will go down, and something really bad happens. Not that they intended— but because they just don't have the capacity to see that playing bad ass with guns or threatening people and police— no one ever puts a stop to it, so they keep pushing more and more— and it will never stop escalating until someone puts a stop to it."

Through another doorway the officers could see Doug's bed and nightstand. The benches and tables in the basement were covered in old tools, boxes, and dozens and dozens of antique military firearms in various states of disassembly.

"You think Perry's that bad?" Thompson joked as they headed toward the bed.

Through the doorway Johnson shone his flashlight on the walls and ceiling of Doug's bedroom. The walls and ceiling were entirely covered with magazine centerfolds pulled from porn magazines and glued to the concrete walls like wallpaper.

Tits, asses, and perfect smiles.

Everywhere.

"Yeah," Johnson looked back at Deputy Thompson, "I think Doug Perry is really that bad."

For nearly three and a half hours the two deputies continued the demented journey through Doug's childhood. Stacks of Penthouse, Hustler, and Playboy magazines littered the floor and bench areas. Cardboard boxes full of empty ammunition casings and rusting gun tools— many of which the two deputies failed to recognize— were strewn about like torn-out pages of a disturbed teenager's diary. Old drawers from what looked like the remnants of a machinist's bench had been stacked along the wall nearest the entryway to Doug's bedroom. Oil soaked and rotting, they seemed like they had not been moved in years, maybe even decades.

Gun parts.

Shop manuals.

Rat shit.

It seemed like they were finding nothing of any use.

"Holy shit," Johnson hollered from the far corner of the basement.

Deputy Thompson strode over to the corner and stared down into a wire basket that had been covered by another stack of Penthouse magazines.

"Are those what I think they are?" Thompson asked.

They were covered in cobwebs and sawdust.

Johnson pulled the other officer back. He was genuinely shocked.

"We better get the team back down here — don't disturb another thing."

* * *

Doug paced back and forth in his block staring at the other inmates. The green jumpsuit they made him wear every time they put him in here made his thighs itch. He hated them. Like a small child visiting the zoo for the first time, he would stare at the other inmates wondering what they might have done to land themselves here. They were different than he was. They were real criminals. Hardened and brutal.

The jail was a relatively quiet place. The block consisted of 12 cells. Two inmates shared a cell, and in each cell was a bunk bed, a sink and a toilet. In the corner of the block there were 4 showers in complete view of the lounging area. Other than the dialog emanating from the television hung outside the cell out of reach of the inmates, hardly a sound could be heard. When the buzzing from one of the electronic locks snapped Doug from his daydream, he would scurry to the Plexiglas window in hopes they were coming to call his name.

So far they hadn't.

And Doug was getting irritated.

He had been in jail a couple of times before—once for shooting at a neighbor's dog and once for getting a little too friendly with the same neighbor's daughter. Although he liked to act as though he were an "old hand" at incarceration, he really wasn't. He was, however, familiar enough with the ins and outs of the justice system in Okanogan County that he already knew how this was going to play out. The fact that it took days or even weeks for the inevitable outcome to surface seemed to cement his fear and loathing of the general public even more.

All this shit was perfunctory at best.

By the time the bailiff finally did come to fetch him for his meeting with the public defender, he more or less had already played the scenes out in his head. He knew his mother would refuse to make a statement or (God forbid) go to a court and testify that Doug had assaulted her. He knew that there was no way the county was going to pay to put him in jail and have to feed him and provide any type of medical care. They all knew that he would end up causing more problems in the jail by simply being there than it was worth. The system would be better off if Doug just stayed away and went to counseling. This way, other inmates wouldn't get in fights with him— fights that would lead to more charges being filed and more court time wasted by people who couldn't afford to pay the court costs anyway.

Doug simply needed more counseling.

The bailiff steered Doug around the corner and into a small meeting room near the booking station of the jail. He could hear a young lady berating one of the officers in Spanish while her child screamed in the background.

Stupid bitch.

Inside the bleak space sat a small conference table and four chairs. The bailiff uncuffed Doug and motioned for him to wait quietly. Doug rubbed his wrists and pulled his hair back behind his ears as he sat down in the furthest chair, facing back toward the door.

He Said, She Said: The Spokane River Killer

A few minutes later a short, awkward-looking man with a graying crew cut, wire-rimmed glasses, and a horribly tailored corduroy sport jacket slithered into the room. A few moments later they were joined by the Prosecuting Attorney, Ron Herrick.

The short man sat next to Doug and handed him a business card, "I am here from the defenders office to represent you."

Clumsily, he outstretched his other arm to shake Doug's hand.

"I am sure you remember, me— don't you Doug? Ron Herrick," the other man stated as he sat across from Doug and his lawyer.

"Well, I think we all know where this is headed, Doug," Ron continued.

"I didn't do anything... do anything, wrong," Doug began.

His lawyer interrupted him and raised his arm, motioning Doug to remain quiet.

"I have already negotiated this with the prosecutor, Doug. We all know you didn't mean to threaten the police or to threaten anyone with explosives. Mr. Herrick has already agreed that he is willing to let that go— and to simply plea this out to a gross misdemeanor of assault."

Doug started to speak and was again rebuffed by his attorney.

"Say nothing, Douglas. These could have turned into very serious charges. Explosives, *death threats* against law enforcement. Battery against your *mother?*"

Doug felt as though he were being scolded by his own lawyer.

"I think you should plea this out, and Mr. Herrick has agreed to simply recommend that you stay on community supervision for another two years and attend counseling appointments as regularly as the mental health unit thinks you should. And I can see no reason why we shouldn't accept the offer."

Inside his head, Doug was laughing hysterically. These two idiots were scared of him. They obviously knew that Doug was smarter and more clever than they were, and they simply did not want to put him to the test.

He had gamed the system again.

And he could hardly wait to laugh in Deputy Johnson's face the next time he saw him.

"Do I have to... have to say I am sorry... am sorry to my mother?" Doug whimpered as pathetically as he could. He started to make his knee shake as he stared down at it for effect.

"No, Doug. Just go to your appointments, and for crying out loud, *PLEASE,* quit getting yourself into trouble!" Mr. Herrick implored.

"So when can I go?" Doug asked.

"We will draw up the paperwork; your attorney here will look at it, make sure it's right, and we will put you on the calendar for tomorrow. If the judge accepts the deal, which I am quite sure he will, then you should be able to go home right after the hearing tomorrow."

Once back in his cell, Doug could hardly keep the smile off of his face. He wondered if Deputy Johnson would be at the hearing and if he would object somehow.

He wanted him to.

He wanted to see the look on that stupid cop's face as, once again, Doug Perry was smarter than everyone else.

He even got down on his knees and mockingly prayed to God that Officer Johnson and all of the police from Omak and Okanogan County would be at his hearing and watch as he strode out of the courthouse victorious.

It was going to be epic.

"PERRY!" one of the bailiffs yelled as he approached the cell block.

Doug was surprised to be called to the entrance of the cell block again. He had just returned to his cell.

What could they possibly want now?

"We need to take you down to the rooms again," the bailiff informed Doug as he stepped into the doorway and waited for the electronic lock to close behind him so they could open the next door.

"Why?" he asked, surprised.

"It's for questioning by a couple of Okanogan deputies," the bailiff answered as he cuffed Doug for transport through the facility.

Doug couldn't believe that the deputies had already heard about his plea agreement. And now they were here to do *what?*

This was going to be his chance to rub it in to these two dickheads. Just like he told them outside of his gate the first time they tried to fuck with him.

This time the bailiffs took him down to the basement floor instead of the tiny conference room he had been in before. However, unlike before, they cuffed him to the desk and left him alone in the room— although this room had two-way mirror in it, so Doug knew someone was probably watching him right now.

But why?

Nearly 30 minutes later, Deputies Johnson and Thompson joined Doug in the interrogation room.

"Hi Doug. Sorry to keep you waiting so long. These things are sometimes frustrating like that. We would like to talk to you to try and clear some of this up," Johnson began as he sat across from Doug and opened up a small notebook.

Thompson sat kitty corner from Doug and opened a large three-ring binder in front of him without so much as looking up at Doug at all. The room was small and brightly lit. It was obviously designed so whoever was stuck in this rat hole would want to get out as soon as they could, and therefore, would start talking.

Clear some of this up?

Doug knew he had these idiots beat already. But like a cat that's killed too many mice, he wanted to toss the half-dead carcass around just a bit.

These stupid cops didn't even know I've already cut a deal.

This will be fun.

"If you aren't going to charge... going to charge me, then you need to let me go," he pleaded as he reached up with his cuffed-together hands and pushed his glasses back up the bridge of his nose.

"Well, we would love to get you right out that door, Doug," Johnson began, "but we have to wait for your attorney to get here."

"I haven't done nothin'. So if it will... so if it will speed this up, then we don't have to wait," Doug suggested.

A familiar smile crept under his thick glasses and matted hair once again.

"So you'll talk to us? Without your attorney present? Is that what you're saying?" Thompson asked.

Doug couldn't believe his good fortune. He was going to get to string these morons along— *without his attorney always cutting him off.*

"Of course I will," Doug replied, "I have nothing to hide."

Johnson produced a document for Doug to sign that showed Doug freely and willingly agreed to talk with them without his attorney present.

"So, as you know, Doug, we served a search warrant on your mother's house, and we searched your basement," Johnson began.

Doug was not expecting to hear that. He had not heard from his mother since he had been arrested and could not see any reason why they would want to go inside his basement.

"We are a little concerned that some of the items we discovered might be stolen property—" Thompson began as he rose from his chair.

Doug immediately cut him off, "What! No. No way! I am not... I am not a th... th... thief!"

Doug was really caught off guard by the fact they thought he was a petty thief.

How dare they.

"Everything in that basement is *mine!*" Doug yelled at them, "Mine! And no one else's! I inherited most of it from my father— I am no thief."

Fact was, Doug was a thief. On numerous occasions he and his mother had stolen silver and other small items of value from neighboring homes. But Doug knew that none of those items was in the basement. He and his mother had always sold them off in the Little Nickel want ads or driven to Wenatchee to pawn them off there. None of it was in the basement.

"Ok, Ok, no need to get excited. We just wanted to clear that up— I mean it looked like you might have some stolen stuff down there, so we just need you to sign a statement saying that *everything* in the basement is yours and not your mother's, or not stolen, or whatever. Are you willing to do that, Doug?"

Doug thought for a second that maybe he should change his mind and ask for his attorney. But really? For this? These guys didn't even know he already had a deal in place.

"Yeah— whatever. I'll sign a statement... that says... a statement that says... that says it's all my stuff, sure."

Deputy Thompson produced a blank sheet of paper and pen for Doug to write his statement with. By now Doug was getting bored with his little game and wanted to just go back to his cell. He finished writing his statement, signed it, and slid it and the pen over to Deputy Johnson.

"If we are done... we are done here, I'd like to... like to go back to—"

"NO WE AIN'T DONE HERE!!!" Johnson yelled as loud as he could, jumping up from his chair toward Doug.

Doug screamed in horror and fell backwards away from Johnson.

"You think you can threaten to blow up a police station and law enforcement officers and just walk away?" Johnson continued to yell.

Doug looked toward Thompson hoping he would come to his aid but Thompson merely put his hand to his mouth without even looking and filled his cheek with a handful of sunflower seeds. He didn't even glance up from his three-ringed binder.

That's what this was about?

Doug recovered himself in his chair and yelled back at Johnson, "All of you in this town... in this town know! You know who... who I am and... and what I can do! None of you dumb... of you dumb cops... is as smart... as smart as me. So just let me go back... go back to my cell."

Johnson stared right into the back of Doug's skull as he towered over Doug, leaning forward across the table.

Thompson spit one of his seeds into the trashcan next to him.

For nearly a minute they all remained frozen in time. Each wondering what the next move was going to be. Finally, Johnson broke the stalemate.

"Well, Doug, you want to know what we found? But you already know what was in that basement, Don't you? And there is no getting out of it— you just signed a statement making it very clear that everything in that basement was yours!"

Doug seemed caught a little off guard.

Fucking bastards.

He knew he should never have trusted these cops. They tricked him.

"We found your pipe bombs, *all of them,*" Johnson continued.

Doug nearly stopped breathing.

Pipe bombs?

Doug wanted to start laughing hysterically at the deputy, but he knew he might send him into a rage if he did that. Doug vaguely remembered as a kid when he and one of his friends put some black powder into some threaded cast iron pipes and put cannon fuses in them. They tried one of them but it didn't explode so they gave up trying. He must have dumped the other five somewhere into the basement and forgotten about them.

"Those are from when... from when I was a kid. They don't... don't even work," Doug retorted.

"Well I've got some good news for you, Douglas. The Washington State Patrol is going to examine them and even detonate one of them. And when they explode — and when the prosecutor hears about the threats to blow up the police stations and everybody in it — then we will see where you stand then, eh?"

Doug had been waiting for the right moment to drop the dime on his plea deal — the moment that he could rub all of this in Johnson's face and go home. And it was finally here.

"Well, guess what... you stupid... guess what you stupid pig?" Doug started to yell back, his voice screeching and broken.

"I already made a deal... made a deal with Mr. Herrick!" Doug screamed.

Johnson looked unfazed.

"There is no bomb charges. Or no... or no threats charges!"

Doug smiled wryly as he stared at Johnson. Thompson, for the first time, looked up from his three-ring binder and was *smiling?*

Doug continued, albeit a little bothered that Thompson was smiling at him, "And the plea deal is... plea deal is tomorrow! And you... you can't do a thing... a thing about it! Once again... once again... I win. I win, you fucking... I win, you fucking pigs! Tomorrow afternoon I'll be back up on... back up on the Flat cleaning up whatever... whatever mess you left in my... in my basement. Then I'll go to town and see... and see my friend Dwight — and maybe I'll see you in... see you in town somewhere too?"

Doug had bested them again. He sat back in his chair and turned away like a teenaged girl who had won her phone privileges back from her evil stepfather by threatening to tell mom what really went on last summer in the bathhouse.

Or so he thought.

The smile on Johnson's face got even wider. Thompson simply continued to spit seeds into the trash can.

"Do you want to tell him?" Johnson asked Thompson.

Thompson sat silent for a moment.

"This has been your case. You tell him, " Thompson stated mildly.

As a staleness hung in the air like the stench of a rotting roadkill, Doug's nose and upper lip twitched for just a second.

"You see, Doug," Johnson began, pausing to savor the moment, "it kind of works like this. I already know you have a plea deal worked out on the assault charge. I already know that the county doesn't have the resources to deal with a deranged lunatic *like you*."

Was he bluffing? Doug wasn't sure. And it made him uncomfortable.

"I know that you have the system here in Omak figured out. I know that you think you are smarter than everyone else around you. You can outwit the counselors. Outsmart the lawyers and judges. You have been threatening and terrorizing the people up on the Flat for more than 10 years now. Stealing their silver when they go to town. Shooting their pets when they wander helplessly and innocently into your yard. You have done it and got away with it--"

"Bailiff! I want to go back to my cell!" Doug yelled, straining to look past Deputy Johnson.

"But your reign of sick and twisted terror is over, Doug! You know why?"

"Bailiff! Get me out of here. I want to go back to my cell!"

"You want to know why?? DOUG!!"

Doug could hardly swallow the lump in his throat.

Thompson spit more seeds into the trash.

"Look at me Douglas!! You will never manipulate this system again, because this time I called the Bureau of Alcohol, Tobacco, and Firearms in on this one. I am guessing you don't have a license to possess an explosive device like the ones we found—"

The Feds?

"And when the ATF gets done with you— not up here in Okanogan County, no sir— for this little prize, you have won a trip to Spokane to go to Federal Court!"

He called the ATF?

"And I am guessing, *Doug*, that after speaking at length with ATF Agent Hearst and the Federal Prosecutor— you are going to be convicted of a felony. Do you know what that means? *Doug?*"

Doug wanted to scream, but he would never give these two pigs the satisfaction.

"That means you will lose your right to have firearms, *FOREVER!* No more guns, no more bullets, no more nothing!! You are done."

"Fuck you!! Fuck you!! I'll never give up my guns! You will never take them away from me!"

"And that is exactly what I am counting on Dougie boy! Because *every time* you screw up and get caught with a gun or even looking at a gun in a gun magazine— you will be back in front of a FEDERAL judge— not Okanogan County. Not even Spokane County— as I have no doubts you will be manipulating them before too long. Get used to it. Your love of guns will be your downfall, Douglas Perry. *Your love of guns is going to make sure you die in a prison cell some day. Some way, somehow. I fucking guarantee it.* Bailiff! Take this piece of pond scum out of my sight. Take care, Dougie. Enjoy Spokane."

Spokane?

8
Other Parts of the Town

On May 2, 1988, Doug was transported from Okanogan County to Spokane, Washington. The trip from Omak to Spokane wound south along a two-lane highway through the rocky scablands of central Washington. For miles, dust-laden hills and irrigated crops reminded Doug of Omak. Eventually the highway intersected with U.S. Highway 2 and turned to the southeast. As the black SUV drew nearer to Spokane, Doug became more and more uneasy. Within a few hours he noticed the roads were getting busier, homes were becoming less and less scarce and it seemed everywhere there were cars and trucks and people making their way through the thinly forested hills.

He had no idea where they were taking him. He had overheard one of the agents say that he was going to be detained at the Spokane County Jail but there seemed to be some dispute as to his ultimate destination.

And for how long.

He Said, She Said: The Spokane River Killer

He simply wanted to go in front of the Federal Judge and explain how Deputy Johnson "had it out for him," and then get back to Omak as quickly as possible.

Spokane was not a "big city" as far as urban centers in the USA go. It was large enough to have its fair share of city problems like violent crime, homelessness, drugs, and prostitution. But it wasn't big enough to have any of the attractive benefits of being a large city, like professional sports teams or some sort of telltale landmark. Spokane was a geographical oddity in some ways. Parts of the city literally butted up to agricultural land, mostly wheat and barley. The heart of the downtown district was dissected by the Spokane River which flowed out of Lake Coeur d'Alene just across the state border in Idaho to the east. The river meandered its way from Idaho through Spokane Valley and through a series of scenic falls before exiting Spokane to the west. Beyond the city it eventually made its way through rocky canyons lined with Ponderosa trees to the Columbia River about 60 miles to the northwest.

Directly west of Spokane, Fairchild Air Force base was home to squadrons of the Air Force's Strategic Air Command. Established in 1942, Fairchild housed over 5,200 Air Force personnel and contributed greatly to Spokane's economy and growth.

The small communities and suburbs surrounding Spokane were filled with people whose interests were more aligned with outdoor pursuits like fishing, hunting, and camping— away from the city— than theater, concerts, and civic events.

But times were changing.

Spokane was determined to become "more sophisticated."

Fourteen years earlier, Spokane had hosted the 1974 World's Fair. Just north of the financial centers and high-rise apartment dwellings, a park had been constructed spanning the Spokane River. Carnival rides, event centers, and a gondola that took passengers out across the Spokane Falls entertained thousands of people who attended the events.

The World's Fair marked a coming of age for the city. Prior to this, it had often been viewed as the dirty, younger sibling of Seattle, 275 miles to the west. Most of the tall buildings in Spokane were under thirty stories. It certainly was not a "burgeoning metropolis," but the city had a "new" feel to it.

During the early seventies, in preparation for the World's Fair, political leaders and event planners made great efforts to clean up the downtown district before the judging eyes of the world fell on the Lilac City. Prior to this, the downtown streets were full of prostitution, drug dealing, panhandling, and other unsightly crimes. At first, the efforts by police were met with stiff resistance. It seemed the people engaging in the lifestyle had nowhere else to promote their activities. A few months into the campaign, city leaders realized that if they wanted the "undesirables" out of the downtown district so that the world would not remember "Expo '74" for its ready availability of heroin, cocaine, and pussy, it had to "look the other way" when the activities sprang up in other parts of the town.

Which they eventually did.

And the other part of town it sprang up in was — Sprague Avenue.

When the SUV that Doug was riding in finally exited the Interstate, it swung left around a huge off-ramp and struggled its way through the downtown traffic a few blocks north until it came to rest underneath a giant railway overpass. The road seemed an afterthought as it dove under the railway. Much of Spokane seemed like it hadn't been planned out very well at all.

Above him on the tracks a freight train thundered and shook the ground. Empty fast-food bags, beer cans, and cigarette butts littered the tracks and empty side streets. As he sat in the SUV, stuck in the traffic monotony, he could see a couple of whores through the chain-link fence separating the sidewalk from some sort of mindless construction going on in the alleyway.

One particular whore, a lovely brunette in white "boy toy" shorts and a bikini top caught his attention. As the freight train rumbled through, she sat on the hot rocks, a few feet from the passing cars and chewed a piece of dried out grass, staring at the graffiti on the boxcars. She wondered where each of the trains had been and where they were going. Sometimes she thought of stepping right in front of one.

A means to an end.

A way out.

Engineers and brakemen would yell at her as they rode by, laughing and flipping their middle fingers at the whore near the tracks.

To these men she was a worthless piece of shit.

To these men — men who after having only a couple of beers would probably fuck her in an instant if given the chance at any one of the nearby taverns — to these men — she was living trash.

Within minutes, the thunderous clapping of the endless stream of boxcars and iron rails would subside back into the dreary wailing of heavy traffic. Sirens, horns, and squealing brakes.

Assholes yelling obscenities.

This festering pustule was Sprague Avenue.

This was how the city of Spokane maintained its precious reputation.

As the SUV finally proceeded through the intersection and turned left toward the detention center, Doug almost thought he had made eye contact with her.

He smiled for the first time in nearly a week.

The following day, Doug learned that he was being charged with "Knowingly and willfully possessing a firearm (destructive device) which is not registered to him in the National Firearms Registration and Transfer Record."

The agent investigating his case was Layne Hearst.

Agent Hearst had spoken at length with Deputy Johnson and a number of interested parties in Okanogan County about Douglas Perry. Hearst was under no illusions about why Okanogan and the Omak community in general were so interested in the prosecution of this case. After a thorough review of ATF records he determined that no record existed which registered a destructive device to Douglas R. Perry, and, therefore, he was in violation of United States law for possessing the pipe bombs Deputy Johnson had discovered in Doug's basement.

On May 4, 1988, Doug went before the U.S. Magistrate for the Eastern District of Washington and was ordered to be temporarily detained pending a hearing in two days in which Doug would be appointed counsel. In order to show that Doug qualified, financially, for legal assistance he disclosed that he had not worked since 1978. He was legally disabled and collecting $704 per month from Social Security psychological disability benefits. Clearly he qualified for legal help, but he was convinced this entire episode was a joke. There was no way Doug should be in prison or locked up for a few pipe bombs left over from when he was a kid.

He wanted out of jail, now.

He wanted to get back to Pogue Flat.

Prior to his detention hearing on May 6, 1988, defense attorney Philip Wetzel was appointed to represent Doug.

Known as "Dutch" by his peers, Philip Wetzel first obtained his license to practice in Washington in 1979. A very skilled criminal defense attorney, Mr. Wetzel was respected and liked by his peers. This was exactly what Doug needed if he were going to have any hope of returning to the Flat.

Immediately, Doug's defense questioned whether there was even probable cause to move forward with such a case. It became clear, rather quickly, that this case was "payback" against a member of the community whom the local police, and specifically Deputy Johnson, simply did not like.

Doug was different.

Doug was weird.

He was a long-haired, grown man still living in his mother's basement. He masturbated to the porn wallpapered on his ceiling and he was obsessed with firearms. This was a case of a mentally ill person saying something he clearly did not mean, and a deputy who took it upon himself to be the arbiter of justice.

Or so claimed Doug's defense.

As quickly as his attorney and his staff of investigators could do so, they began gathering information that would speak to their client's suffering mental health.

They only had two days.

Doug just wanted to go home.

Inside the downtown Spokane Federal Building, Agent Hearst was actively pursuing the opposite outcome for Doug Perry. He and Deputy Johnson had spoken at great length about the situation between Doug and the local residents of Pogue Flat. It wasn't often that the ATF took it upon themselves to become the arbiters of local justice, but in this case it was astoundingly clear. Doug Perry needed to remain out of Omak, and he needed to be locked up; whether in a mental facility or a jail did not matter much at the time.

A hearing on May 6 to determine whether probable cause existed to move forward with the case would begin to establish Doug's fate.

Doug's defense had contacted his counselors back in Omak hoping that they would remain neutral, testify truthfully and help Doug get back to the safety of Omak. A number of the counselors had already been contacted by U.S. investigators and many were genuinely scared for their safety.

This was not going to be easy for Doug's defense.

It was impossible for his counselors to discuss private and privileged medical information unless they felt that Doug was an immediate danger to himself or others. This put many of them in ethical dilemmas. They could choose not to discuss anything and thereby risk Doug's imminent release and probable return to Omak where most of the counselors felt he they did not have the resources to deal with his conditions. Or they could choose to discuss their interactions with Doug under the pretense that he might be a danger, but if the court released Doug— then they were hanging out in the wind with a mentally ill client, who has a demonstrated propensity for violence, living among them in their small community again.

Neither option was very appealing for the employees of the small town mental health clinic.

Rob White had been a therapist in the clinic since 1980 and was the most senior of the staff. He agreed to review Doug's records all the way back through 1975 and agreed to summarize his findings and opinions for the court. He explained the apprehension on the part of his colleagues to involve themselves one way or the other because of Doug's continuous disregard for social norms and clinic rules.

In 1986, White explained, Doug had slapped another client while at the clinic and that he had telephoned the clinic on another occasion upset about how the court proceedings were going and told the clinic that the court would "see blood" if the court and the clinic did not work together to resolve his legal complications. A year prior, in 1985, Doug had brought a firearm with him to the clinic and was told very clearly that he was not allowed to do so. However, in 1987, almost a year after making the threat that the courts would "see blood"-- he brought a gun with him again.

Neither the courts or the clinic did anything about it.

As far as Doug was concerned, there were no consequences.

White also testified that, in his professional opinion, Doug suffered from a paranoid personality disorder, and, therefore, Doug expected people to either exploit him or harm him.

He Said, She Said: The Spokane River Killer

With only two days to prepare, a half-hearted summarization from his therapist was all his defense could muster.

Agent Hearst, however, followed up and testified that he had received information from an Okanogan Sheriff's deputy who had responded to a domestic violence call a little more than a week earlier. The domestic violence case, although already resolved in Okanogan County, resulted in a search and seizure of a number of galvanized steel pipe bombs, one of which was nearly a foot long and two inches in diameter. The search came about when the defendant threatened to "blow up the police station and anyone who came through the door" to the defendant's basement, Hearst testified.

The Judge did not appear convinced.

Hearst wasn't done.

He also informed the Court that they were investigating Doug Perry for possession of other illegal firearms, including a number of fully automatic weapons hidden on the property near his mother's house. In a written statement to the Court, a childhood friend of Doug's explained that on the day before his arrest, Doug had told his friend that he had arranged to buy some machine guns from an Aryan Nations' group operating in northeastern Washington and northern Idaho. Doug also bragged to this friend about how the Aryan Nations were trying to recruit Doug into their group. The informant who made the statement had known Doug since childhood and did not believe that Doug's statements were credible; therefore, he felt there was no need to report them. In his words, Doug had always stretched the truth and made up stories in order to garner attention and feel like he belonged to something. His friend wanted to make the statement in order to show that Doug was not in the right frame of mind to be left to his own devices.

Hearst also noted for the Court that Doug had been convicted of reckless endangerment in June of 1987 and that he had also been convicted of concealment of an unlawful weapon in 1979. This was important, Hearst explained, because the Deputy from Okanogan County had spoken with local residents and many of them were very concerned for their personal safety should Doug return to Omak. His history of verbally harassing neighbors and his wanton discharge of firearms in the community had them all on edge.

Something bad was going to happen in Pogue Flat if they didn't do something.

And do it now.

Doug could not believe what he was hearing. He wasn't a danger to anybody unless they bothered him first. The neighbors?

They got what they deserved anyhow.

This was a farce. He almost wanted to just plead guilty to everything so he could go back home to his basement.

And make love to one of his girls on the ceiling.

His lawyer quickly advised him against pleading guilty so he could "just go home."

It seemed pretty clear that this obviously was a case of a deputy with a chip on his shoulder. He clearly was trying to railroad Doug so he could make himself look good. The judge would obviously see this and dismiss all charges and Doug would be home before nightfall.

He wondered if he should call Dwight to come and pick him up.

Doug snapped out of his daydream when his lawyer nudged him in the ribs.

Without a doubt, the Judge ruled, there was Probable Cause to move forward with the case.

What!?

"That's bull, that's bullshit!" Doug muttered, half under his breath.

His lawyer looked over at him with a deadly serious expression on his face.

"I can't go back, go back to *jail*," Doug continued, louder.

"Your Honor, if I may," his attorney motioned toward the Judge, "Clearly, Mr. Perry has ongoing mental issues that cannot be addressed properly in the Spokane County Jail. May we continue the detention portion of this hearing until Wednesday... *the 11th* ... so that we might explore the option of having Mr. Perry evaluated at Sacred Heart Hospital? In fact, I am meeting with them here after lunch; perhaps we could continue even this afternoon?"

"Are you asking for a mental evaluation order? Because you can have your psychologist or doctor evaluate Mr. Perry in Spokane County. We do it all the time," the Judge responded, somewhat sarcastically.

Doug shifted nervously in his chair. He hated the fucking jail.

"I think with the depth and potential severity of Mr. Perry's condition we would be better served with the ability to observe Mr. Perry in a mental health facility for a period of days. If the hearing is in five days— on the 11th — then we can get a better understanding of Mr. Perry's mental condition and will be more able to offer ... uh, offer more effective solutions if ... I think based on the testimony of Mr. White, my client deserves a comprehensive analysis that can only be provided through an inpatient and observation type of setting — such a setting as can be ... can be found at Sacred Heart."

Doug's heart was pounding nearly out of his chest.

"As you wish counselor. Put together an order for observation at Sacred Heart, and I'll sign it this afternoon. Include the continuance for May 11th."

Doug nearly fell out of his chair.

He had won the first battle.

9
Suffer the Beautiful Girl

Sacred Heart Hospital was a short distance to the south of downtown, nestled in between the South Hill and Interstate 90 where it cut through the southern edge of Spokane. Its prominent position at the base of the hill broadcast its importance to the community. Opened in 1887, Sacred Heart Hospital preceded the opening of Spokane's other major hospital, Deaconess, by nearly nine years.

From the parking garage, Doug and the bailiff transporting him entered a cramped elevator and rode up a couple of stories. The doors opened into a glossy, bleached-white hallway bustling with doctors and nurses. A pair of orderlies jumped out of their chairs behind a curved desk and informed the bailiff that the handcuffs were no longer necessary. The bailiff chuckled and handed one of the orderlies a clipboard asking him to sign.

Doug was Sacred Heart's problem.

For now.

He had spent most of his life, so far, convincing people that the outbursts of aggressive threats and behaviors were a reactionary microcosm of a life filled with tragedy and emotional and physical abuse directed toward him.

He was a victim.

It was his role to respond as he did, and as long as he was fulfilling the roles laid out before him, everyone was happy: his counselors, the courts — even his mother.

If he wasn't acting weird, then somehow he was condoning the abuse and bullying he had suffered.

And he would *never* condone it.

An orderly in a bright white uniform gently asked if Doug would follow him down the hallway, and he would show him his room. He explained to Doug the rules as they meandered down the hall, but Doug knew how it worked with the "mental people" (as he liked to call them.)

Follow the schedule, show up on time, take your meds, don't get in hassles with the other residents, and talk during group.

The next morning after breakfast, an orderly informed Doug that he needed to see Dr. Keller for his evaluation. He handed Doug a map of the hospital and gave him directions about how to get there. For nearly two hours Doug sat on Dr. Keller's couch in his office and spewed forth his tale of woe.

Afterward, Doug was not exactly sure how he thought the evaluation may have gone. He explained to Dr. Keller that he did not like the side effects of his medications — especially the anti-depressants. What did Dr. Keller want from him? He even admitted that he knew things would probably get worse if he went off of them.

They made him feel like he was un-alive.

Begrudgingly, he agreed to maintain his medications throughout his stay at Sacred Heart. It was better than going to jail.

And besides, he wasn't going to be there that long anyway. He knew that the judge would eventually order him to continue counseling, store his guns at a friend's house for a month or two until things cooled off, and leave his neighbors on the Flat alone for a while.

All he had to do was convince the doctors at Sacred Heart that he was mentally ill enough to not be responsible for what he had done, but healthy enough to be granted his freedom, with reasonable community restrictions of course.

He had been playing this game his whole life.

And winning.

Later in the afternoon, Doug was moved out of isolation and allowed to join the general population ward.

Obviously the evaluation must have gone well.

Another orderly, whom he had seen the night before when he arrived, helped him bundle up his paperwork and showed him down to the common areas of the general population.

Like most of the doctor offices and therapist lairs he had been to before, the melancholy artwork permanently bonded to the wood paneling on the walls failed to comfort the mentally infirm as much as those who had politely donated the outdated garbage believed it might. The cheap, sub-office-quality carpet always managed to entrap the vile smell of piss, puke, and blood from resident "episodes" of prior days. Its pattern of black and red fleur-de-lis reminded him of playing hopscotch on the playground at his elementary school back in Omak.

Tattered and sun-bleached boxes of board games, decades-old couches and chairs, and buzzing fluorescent light fixtures.

Worse, it smelled like stale popcorn.

The subdued moaning of the chamber's occupants completed the virulent feel and taste of a poorly maintained 1975 movie theater.

He even wondered if there were semen stains on the sofas.

Mounted high on the wall, out of the reach of any of the occupants who may want to launch the appliance toward one of the unsuspecting tenants, a 19" color television outshouted the moaning and groaning of the drooling residents perched and propped in the corner, their heads held upright with a tepid mix of pillows and pharmaceuticals.

He had no intentions of being roped into a checkers game with an older gentleman wearing lavender-striped, button-up pajamas, mucus dripping from his nose. And listening to the old *non compos mentis* cotton ball on the couch nearest to him regale him with tales of grandchildren that exist, unbeknownst to her, only in her mind, seemed less than optimal.

And, like a gazelle in the Savannah of Africa whose gaze first meets the pride of female lions stalking through the tall grass toward him and cannot decide whether to run or hide— there she was.

He was entranced.

Across the room full of damaged sickness and sorrow, sat the most beautiful princess he had ever seen.

Her eyes sparkled like tiny crystal jewels. The corners of her mouth turned slightly upward making her appear as though she were perpetually happy. Her teeth were a beautiful white, and one of her fronts was just a little crooked. It made her look like a little girl grinning at Santa Clause. The way her sandy brown curls dropped in front of her eyes as they nearly kissed her cheekbones. The way she blinked her eyes. Her thick black lashes.

He knew he must be in love.

He had to remind himself to breathe.

She was every bit as gorgeous as the women plastered to his ceiling in the basement back on Pogue Flat.

Even more so.

He didn't even notice that the white-clad orderly who had escorted him through the hospital had left his side and abandoned him to his peers.

And his fate.

Somehow he had to meet her. But how?

As he watched her, he could see she was not involved in much of the goings on in this den of sickness. She was in her very own place.

Severely medicated, no doubt.

In his fantasy, he imagined her a sophisticated woman... a woman too good for a shithole like this. He imagined she was probably a model for Zebra Club or Generra or something en vogue. She probably worked for some high profile corporation, or maybe she was even an actress.

A wry smile crept across his face.

Whoever she was, she was perfect.

He slipped across the room toward an old green sofa positioned just a few feet away from the card table she was sitting at. He had no idea how he would be able to talk to her. He didn't even know if he wanted to just yet. It would be so much easier if she saw him and gave him some kind of sign.

He was not good at girls.

The old woman badgering on about her fake grandkids had removed herself to the craft table and left an opening where he could sit on the couch directly across from her. A teenage girl sat with her knees tucked under her, and just as he was about to sit, she attempted to unfurl her legs and lie completely stretched out on the couch. Awkwardly, he sat down on her legs and both of them jumped back.

The young girl was not pleased that Doug wanted to sit there.

With a scowl, she tucked her legs back up underneath her and sighed loudly.

Doug looked over at the woman to see if she had noticed.

Thankfully, she did not seem to have any reaction at all.

"You stink you fucking dirtbag. Why don't you bathe or something? Jesus fucking Christ."

Doug tried not pay the young girl any attention.

"Are you not listening you hippie fuck? You too cool for me— with your long hair and your geeky glasses? What are you supposed to be— Nikki Sixx? With glasses?" she yelled as she stood up and placed herself right in front of Doug.

He continued to sit on the couch and try and pretend that she wasn't really there.

"Oh yeah, you just sit there and pretend you cannot hear me."

She looked around the room to see who was paying attention to her. It seemed the entire group of residents were staring at her or Doug in silence. Save for the same reruns on TV or the occasional fight against one of the staff members, she was perhaps the most entertainment any of these people were going to get.

Doug, for his part, wanted to stand up and smash the bitch right across her face. She only looked like she might have weighed 90 pounds or so. One of those girls who is so little and scrawny that she could always play the sympathy card if someone ever did rightfully bust her across the mouth when she needed it.

If she knew exactly who she was tangling with, he knew she would be trembling in her little tight jeans and athletic shoes while piss ran down her leg from her festering little snatch.

He knew.

Before she could continue on her rant, Doug stood up and pushed her gently aside so he could move toward the entrance door of the common area. Without looking back he continued down the hall and went back into his room, closing the door behind him.

What a little bitch.

Doug spent most of the ensuing weekend trying everything he could to get near the target of his affections. On more than one occasion he was sure she had made eye contact with him and smiled, however brief it may have been. Every time he thought he might be able to go sit next to her or across from her, something would get in the way, or he would lose his nerve.

Everything had to be perfect when he first talked to her. Perfect.

He was becoming so obsessed with her every move that when his attorney reminded him of his probable cause hearing on Monday afternoon, he even asked if he was required to be there. When his attorney told him that he could probably do it without him being there, Doug dropped the phone and wandered off looking for his new-found love.

Doug's attorney phoned him later in the afternoon to explain that the court had found probable cause to continue with the proceedings and that Doug willfully and knowingly possessed the explosive devices that Deputy Johnson had discovered during the search in April. Doug's only concern was the effect the outcome of the hearing might have on his ability to remain in Sacred Heart.

By Tuesday night, Doug's obsession began to reach the boiling point. He had to talk to her no matter what. After dinner he could usually find her sitting in the corner of the common room at the card table playing solitaire. The previous few nights had found the chair across from her occupied by the old man in the lavender pajamas who would just sit and stare at her.

She paid him no mind.

It were as though she ordained the man to be there. A placeholder of sorts against the maneuvers of horny and virile men.

For her, this place was a vacation. A respite from the continuous hustle of life on the streets of Spokane. She knew it would be coming to an end soon. As soon as the doctors forced her back onto her med regimen, she would be kicked out back to the curb and left to the fate of the city.

A city far from home.

But tonight, the dreary old man who had guarded her virtue the previous three nights was spending the evening in his room, thoughtfully on display for a family who cared less for him than they did their own guilt at failing to help him.

This was Doug's chance.

With uncharacteristic boldness he strode over to the card table and sat down across from her. Without so much as acknowledging him, she continued to count out three cards in her hand and flip them on to the table as she played her solitaire game.

He felt flushed with embarrassment.

"You play cards?" she asked, her voice soft and sweet.

She did not even bother to look up at him.

Was she being shy?

"I play… I play gin rummy," he replied, trying to sound as masculine and mature as he could.

He had never been this close to her before. He couldn't say the wrong thing.

"Gin rummy's a kids' game," she replied quietly as she flipped over a red king and moved it into an empty spot in her game.

He swallowed hard and stared.

Dumbfounded.

He was actually talking to her.

She looked up from her game and smiled.

A wave of relief washed over him. Her eyes were stunningly beautiful.

She stopped counting out the cards and stared back at him. For a few seconds an awkwardness hung in the air like two lovers waiting to kiss.

"Cat got your tongue?" she asked and bit her lower lip, giggling to herself.

"No… I just… I just…" he began.

She cut him off quickly.

"Just what?" she asked.

He could hardly keep up with her, she was so pretty he just wanted to stare into her eyes.

"Well, maybe we should just start with your name? Maybe?" she asked, turning her head slightly to the right and giggling again.

"Uh… name?" he fumbled, "uh… yeah, Doug."

He didn't know if he should extend his hand — she was not another man — but doing nothing seemed somewhat awkward. Girls were simply too confusing. All of the women in his life were either yelling at him, counseling him, or glued to the ceiling of his basement back on Pogue Flat. He had never really met a real one before.

"Clairann," she proudly offered back, "Clairann, from Sequim, Washington. On the Peninsula. Ever heard of it?"

He swallowed again and continued to stare at her.

"Hello? Anyone in there?" she joked and continued to silently count out groups of three playing cards while simultaneously scanning for where they might be laid down.

"Sequim? Yeah… I have… I have heard of it," he answered her. His heart was beating so fast he thought he might hyperventilate.

"I grew up in Omak. We have a fruit orchard there. Well we.. we used to." Doug continued.

He noticed that his speech was deliberate and clear. His nervous staccato was almost entirely gone.

"Oh, yeah? I grew up on a dairy farm. It's one of the oldest over there," she smiled, she waved her hands in the air like she were introducing a famous movie title, "The Eberle Farm!"

As she said it her face went sarcastically from happy and joyous to demure and twisted. He could tell it was not a happy place for her.

"Yeah… I am not too keen on my home in Omak, either," he responded in kind.

For a minute she focused on her card game, and Doug began to feel as though his opportunity was being wasted.

"Yeah, well what do you know?" she said in a dark and evil voice.

Doug was not sure what to make of it.

Quickly, she looked up and smiled, "Well, let's go to the rec hall. What do you say?"

Her voice had returned to the cheery and upbeat timbre that she had when he first sat down.

She wanted to do something? And she invited him to do it with her? He was flabbergasted.

He knew at that moment that she was the woman who would complete him. She was perfect in every way.

She was going to be his.

He just had to make sure.

By Wednesday morning, Doug was overtly infatuated with his newfound friend. He tried to get Mr. Wetzel to handle this hearing without him as well, but there would be major complications if Doug failed to appear this time.

Reluctantly, Doug acquiesced.

All of the testimony had been made on Friday, the continuance granted was for the sole purpose of exploring the ability for Sacred Heart Medical Center to admit him into their mental health program pending the disposition of his case. Although the Magistrate found that Doug was clearly a danger to himself, others, and to the community, the Magistrate, upon receiving confirmation that Doug would be admitted to Sacred Heart, also found that the "Government has not by clear and convincing evidence shown that there are not conditions that this Court can fathom that would permit the release of the defendant from custody."

The Court determined that Sacred Heart was a reasonable alternative to detention lockup in the county jail.

Upon arriving back at Sacred Heart after the hearing, Doug could hardly contain his excitement. He was going to be able to stay with her after all. He felt like a kid who had just received permission from his parents to spend the night at a friend's house, and he wanted to dart upstairs to surprise them.

"Do you have his Order of Release? I need to see it."

Mr. Wetzel handed him a copy of the signed order.

His conditions for release were clearly laid out in the Order of Release signed by U.S. Magistrate James Hovis:

On May 6, 1988, this court held a probable cause and detention hearing. Stephanie J. Johnson appeared for the government. Defendant was present with appointed counsel Phillip Wetzel. ATF Agent Layne Hearst, Deputy Sheriff Mike Johnson, and mental health professional Rob White, testified and were cross-examined. Both sides argued. The court found probable cause to believe defendant is guilty of the charged offense. Upon the motion of the defendant and with the consent of the United States and upon the court finding that good cause existed for such continuance, the detention hearing was continued until May 11, 1988. In a later order, this court allowed defendant's release for care to the Sacred Heart Medical Center.

On May 11, 1988 at the hour of 1:30 p.m., the detention hearing continued. Stephanie J. Johnson appeared for the government. Defendant was present with appointed counsel Phillip Wetzel.

The government in seeking defendant's detention, contended defendant, if released, would present a danger to the safety of the community. Consistent with 18 U.S.C. 3153 (c), the court considered the pretrial services report. The pretrial services report, testimony of Layne Hearst, Mike Johnson and the proffer of the defendant show and the court finds: Defendant is a lifelong resident of Okanogan County. He resides at Route 1, Box 242, Omak, Washington. Defendant's resources are limited. Defendant receives $700.00 per month in Social Security Disability payments. Defendant's mental health is very bad. His physical health is fair to poor. Defendant has a history of endangering the safety of others. Based on the testimony of the mental health professional and others, the court finds there is clear and convincing evidence that the defendant, because of his mental condition, will be a danger to his safety, the safety of others, and the safety of the community.

The government has not by clear and convincing evidence shown that there are not conditions that this court can fathom that would permit the release of the defendant from custody.

IT IS ORDERED,

That the defendant be released from custody on the following conditions that will be strictly complied with:

1. Defendant shall remain at all times in the locked Acute Care Unit (Step 1) of the Sacred Heart Medical Center. While Sacred Heart does not have the responsibility to detain defendant they are requested to notify the United States Marshal's Office, or any other authorized officer, of any attempt the defendant may make to leave.

2. If the United States Marshal's Office determines, notification by Sacred Heart or any other means that the defendant has attempted to leave, they or any other authorized officer is directed by the court to take the defendant into custody and to report that fact to this court on the next court day for further determination by this court.

3. Defendant shall comply with all the rules and regulations of Sacred Heart during his stay there and shall not be disruptive.

4. Defendant shall be responsible for the costs of his care at Sacred Heart. If necessary, the United States is authorized to advance said funds but in any event the final responsibility hall be the defendant's.

5. Defendant shall surrender as soon as possible his dealer's license to the ATF pending disposition of the charges herein.

6. The government has reserved the right to move this court for such psychiatric evaluation at such place and times as they may petition this court.

7. If his conditions improve, the defendant may move this court for relaxation of the conditions herein. However, such motion must be accompanied by the written evaluation of a mental health professional supporting such relief.

DATED this 11th day of May, 1988.

James B. Hovis
United States Magistrate

"Whoa whoa whoa—" the clerk decried as he stood up and handed the document back toward Mr. Wetzel, "He can't stay here under those conditions. There is no way we will take responsibility for notifying the U.S. Marshal's Office — or anyone else for that matter."

Doug looked at his lawyer desperately.

"What do you... what does this... this mean?" Doug asked.

Mr. Wetzel looked back at the administrator and took the order from his hand, "Look, this is an order from a United States Magistrate, you—"

"I don't— we don't have to do anything" he cut off Mr. Wetzel, "I am just letting you know we will release him tomorrow around this same time. Our administrators will be in touch in the morning. But we have a very clear policy. We are not a lockdown facility."

Doug couldn't believe his ears.

"But I have to... have to stay here!" he cried.

He looked around the hallway as though the crowd of indigents living in this shit box might suddenly and miraculously come to their senses and assist.

"Look, Doug, don't worry. I'll call the U.S. Attorney and we will get this worked out in the morning."

"Are you sure?" Doug quivered.

He was finally getting to know her. If he left now, he may never see her again.

10
A Violent and Frequently Labile Woman

Patients were generally expected to remain in their rooms until 6 a.m. barring some sort of emergency. Doug was unable to sleep at all. He even tried masturbating himself, but with all of the uncertainty surrounding his immediate future, it was no use.

The moment the minute hand on the industrial clock near the door to his room struck 6 a.m., he was up. He had no need to get dressed as he usually slept in his jeans and shirt in case a situation arose which he would need to escape with no time to dress himself.

It just made sense.

For more than 30 minutes he tried calling his lawyer, but no one was answering. They probably wouldn't arrive at the office for at least another hour. The idle time was killing him.

The cafeteria didn't open for breakfast until 7 a.m. What the fuck was he supposed to do for the next half hour?

"Hey, I'm just headed out for a smoke. Wanna join me?"

He jerked his head around behind him.

It was her.

She stood a few feet away wearing pink slippers and a long, blue night robe that nearly dragged the floor as she walked. In one hand she held a little red lighter and a long white cigarette rested between the fingers of her other hand.

He wondered what, if anything, she was wearing beneath the robe. His imaginative powers nearly resulted in an erection.

"Well?" she asked again and started toward the hall which led to the outside smoking area.

"Uh… yeah," he finally answered, "I don't… I don't smoke, though."

She giggled.

"Of course you don't."

Like a newborn puppy, he followed a few steps behind her down the hallway.

She pressed her arm into a swinging glass door and opened it up into a small courtyard near the back corner of the hospital campus. A small concrete patio had been poured recently, but most of the courtyard was covered in beauty bark. Someone had spent some time planting native grasses and some bushes around the pair of pine trees near the picnic table in the corner. The entire area was surrounded by a solid wood eight foot fence. A sand filled concrete ash tray stood near the glass door, and another next to the picnic table. The grounds were remarkably free of the expected cigarette butts. These people couldn't manage their mental faculties, but could manage to keep the smoking area clean? It was these kinds of inconsistencies in life that gave him the most pause.

She spun herself around and parked her ass on the top of the picnic table. She lit her smoke and tapped the palm of her hand on the table right next to where she sat, motioning him to sit right next to her, which he quickly did.

"So you're up early today," she said as she let out the first drag of her smoke.

"Oh… I … uh, I just had to call my… call my lawyer," his nervous staccato was back.

She was a master at determining when men were lying. Which, in her reality, was not that difficult since they seemed to lie to her all of the time.

"You're lying. Why are you lying?" she laughed.

At first he was caught somewhat off-guard by her honesty, but he quickly realized she was simply being playful.

"Well, no... I mean...," he mumbled almost incoherently.

"What's going on?" she asked sincerely.

"Oh, it's nothing. The judge screwed up when he... when he did some stuff yesterday. But, my lawyer, he will fix it. I pay a lot of money for him, so... a lot of money."

She laughed out loud and a huge bellow of smoke drifted right in front of Doug.

"*You pay a lot of money?*" she laughed again, "Yeah. Right!"

Doug just smiled at her. He felt completely at ease whenever he was talking to her. He just had to make sure he didn't screw it up.

"So, you never really told me why you were here, exactly," she said in a more serious tone as she put her cigarette out into the ashtray and grabbed another smoke out of her pack.

The sun was finally starting to shine through the trees surrounding the hospital grounds, and it was becoming a hot summer day. In the distance he could hear the morning traffic on Interstate 90 start to build up. People were going to work and leading their lives. Here he was sitting with the prettiest woman he had ever seen— and he was in the nut house.

"It's bullshit really. Some cop back in Omak doesn't like that I see through the government bullshit," he began, his voice relaxed and clear again.

"A cop?" she asked curiously.

"Well, yeah. I deal guns. A friend of mine and I supply the Nation up there and in parts of north Idaho..."

She stared at him disbelievingly, but intrigued nonetheless.

"Guns?" she asked, delightedly, and slid a little closer to him.

She knew how men wanted to feel.

"I own a 20-acre orchard; I let my mom live there, and we... we don't really have to do fruit any more as I... I make enough with my gun deals. Well, my mother, if she doesn't get what she... what she wants then she starts to make stuff up. So she called the cops and said... said I had hit her."

She knew right away she had him. Whenever a man starts to open up — and lie to her, he was hers.

To do with as she pleased.

"So, they showed up at my house. I told them... told them they had no right to come to my house without a... without a warrant and stuff. But they have been after me for... me for years. But I knew they had nothing, so I told them I would go with them. I warned them... warned them that if they didn't treat me fairly, I'd blow up their police station — which is a fact — I could if I needed to. Well, they got so... got so scared up there in Omak — they had to bring in the ATF and stuff."

Clairann looked at him with wide open eyes and a huge smile.

"Sounds like you're kind of a big deal?"

Doug smiled.

"Still haven't answered my question though. Why you *in here?*"

As quickly as the breeze quit gliding through the woods, his smile turned blank once again.

"It's easier to be here... rather than jail. The judges and the lawyers and stuff — they like to think they are 'helping' — I don't know... don't know why more people haven't... people haven't figured that out yet. Why go to jail? When you can go here?" he laughed.

Maybe he wasn't so crazy after all, Clairann thought to herself.

Outside of the fence around the smoking area, they could hear the morning shift arriving in the parking lot. Doors slammed, employees greeted each other with disingenuous pleasantries and moribund greetings they didn't really mean.

"So why are you here?" he asked her in as genuinely considerate a way as he possibly could.

"Wouldn't you like to know?" she giggled at him.

Suddenly he saw her as vulnerable. She turned away from his gaze and clutched her hands between her knees as she continued to look away. He did not want to press her too boldly.

"It doesn't matter, I just—"

"No. It's okay. I asked you..." she replied and looked at him directly. Her face had changed shape and her voice even sounded a little different.

Had he gone too far?

Without a word, she leaned backwards placing her elbows on the table. Her entire posture seemed different and he was not sure what to make of it. She even slid herself a few inches away from him. As though suddenly she were no longer interested.

He felt a wave of apprehension roiling over him.

And then, without any warning she leaned back upright and moved herself back toward him, touching the side of his legs. She fished another smoke from her robe and smiled, biting her bottom lip like an excited schoolgirl who just discovered she had made the cheerleading team.

"Doug?" one of the orderlies hollered through the glass door as he stood half in the building and half in the courtyard.

Doug looked over at him, *not now.*

"Doug, you have an important phone call," he continued to holler.

"You go on," she motioned pleasantly, "Why don't you come to my group session this afternoon? If you really want to see why I am here. Come at 2 p.m. in room 415. It's open to anyone who I put on the list. I'll put you on."

"They're waiting for you on the phone, Doug," the orderly advised, motioning for Doug to come along.

Doug hopped up from the table and strode toward the door. He looked back at Clairann, "I'll be there. I promise. 2 p.m. Room 415."

*   *   *

For almost half an hour Doug sat in the little donated dining room chair next to the phone in the common area and argued with his lawyer. It was unfathomable to Doug that the court could order him to stay at Sacred Heart and then change their minds. His lawyer kept telling him that they were not changing their minds — Sacred Heart was unwilling to be required to monitor Doug's presence or absence in the facility in order to report to law enforcement should the latter scenario ensue. Mr. Wetzel had placed a call to Miss Johnson of the U.S. Attorney's Office and despite his pleadings, she was adamant about motioning the court to revoke the previous Order of Release and lock Doug up in the county jail.

Mr. Wetzel was able to convince Dr. Keller to provide a written affidavit supporting the notion that the best place for Doug was to remain at Sacred Heart — just not with the stipulation that Sacred Heart had to take responsibility for his whereabouts. They simply were not set up for such conditions. If that were, in fact, what the Court required, then he suggested Eastern State Hospital may be the best venue.

At 11:00 a.m. the Court convened to hear the motion from the U.S. Attorney's Office. Mr. Wetzel picked up Doug from Sacred Heart and brought him to the hearing. Doug's only concern was that he be able to return to Sacred Heart in time so that he could join Clairann in her group session. To be invited to such a session was an honor that was not the slightest bit lost on him. He knew exactly what it meant to be invited.

He was not going to let her down.

The U.S. Attorney's Office jumped on the chance to revoke his conditional release, arguing vehemently that Doug was a danger to more than just himself. He was a danger to others as well:

AFFIDAVIT OF STEPHANIE J. JOHNSON

I am an Assistant United States Attorney assigned to the prosecution of this case.

I received information from defendant's attorney, Dutch Wetzel, on the afternoon of May 11, 1988, that Mr. Wetzel returned defendant Perry to Sacred Heart Hospital. Mr. Wetzel also advised me at that time that Sacred Heart is unable to comply with the Court's order of release dated May, 11, 1988 and will only keep the defendant Perry for 24 hours from the time of his readmission May 11, 1988.

I believe based on Mr. Wetzel's representations, that the Court's conditions of release cannot be complied with by Sacred Heart.

I have received information on May 12, 1988, from Layne Hearst, Special Agent of Alcohol, Tobacco and Firearms, that he is presently investigating the alleged possession of additional firearms and machine guns by the defendant Perry. Special Agent Hearst conferred with the prosecutor of Okanogan County on May 12, 1988. The prosecutor advised him that authorities in Okanogan County have recently received information that the defendant Perry may have firearms, including machine guns, hidden on the premises of his mother's home.

This Court's order on May 11, 1988, stated that "Based on the testimony of the mental health professional and others, the Court finds there is clear and convincing evidence that the defendant, because of his mental condition, will be a danger to his safety, the safety of others, and the safety of the community."

This Court has heard testimony at the detention hearing on May 6, 1988, of the defendant's prior criminal record of endangering the safety of the community, his mental health history of making threats of violence, testimony of Deputy Mike Johnson of the Okanogan County Sheriff's Department that the neighbors of defendant Perry are concerned for their personal safety, testimony of Robert White of the Okanogan Mental Health Clinic that, based on his review of defendant Perry's medical records from 1975 to 1988, it is his opinion that defendant Perry is a danger to himself and the community.

This Court on May 9, 1988, held that there was probable cause to believe defendant Perry knowingly and willfully possessed 5 pipebombs which were not registered to him with the National Firearms Registration and Transfer Record, in violation of 26 U.S.C. 5861(d). At that time the court also heard testimony from Deputy Mike Johnson of the Okanogan County Sheriff's Department that defendant Perry threatened to blow up the Okanogan County Sheriff's Department and possessed the ability to do so.

I submit that, based on the evidence to this Court, defendant Perry should be placed in a custodial situation and that release of defendant Perry would pose a danger to himself and the community.

I further submit that, based on the evidence in this case and the pending investigation of Special Agent Hearst, modification of the Court's order of release allowing defendant Perry to remain unconfined at Sacred heart Hospital would pose a danger to himself, the patients at Sacred Heart, and the community.

Stephanie J. Johnson.

However, Dr. Timothy Keller maintained that Sacred Heart was the best place for him, but the conditions of his release simply needed to be modified. In his report to the Court from May 12, 1988, Dr. Keller stated:

He Said, She Said: The Spokane River Killer

This 36 year old was referred by Federal District Court for psychiatric evaluation after an arrest in which he was charged, among other things, with possessing illegal weapons. History was obtained from the patient, from his lawyer, Phillip Wetzel, from Mr. Rob White in the Okanogan Community Mental Health Center and from Mr. Lang of the Federal Alcohol, Firearm and Drug Administration.

PROBLEM: Mr. Perry has a long history of somewhat isolated, recently antisocial activity. He is the youngest of three of an Okanogan orchardist. His mother reportedly is a violent and frequently labile woman who suffers from manic-depressive disease. Doug was repeatedly raped and abused by an older, now homosexual and drug-dependent, brother. Doug has had long-standing interpersonal difficulties. He has been living in the country outside of Okanogan on land inherited from his father. He has collected a rather extensive series of firearms, mostly World War II issue which he has restored and hopes ultimately to sell at a profit. However, during this time, there have also been several incidents of threats, shooting of a neighbor dog, and most recently, his arrest following the discovery of a group of pipe bombs among his other weapons.

Mr. Perry has been in consistent counseling at the Okanogan Community Health. He has generally refused to take medications, stating that he develops atypical reactions, in particular to antidepressants.

Since hospitalization at Sacred Heart, Perry was initially hospitalized in the Acute Care Unit. He is a small, wiry man with long black hair. He has a rather abrupt staccato way of speaking. His speech has a rather belligerent, aggressive quality, although he has at no time during his hospitalization made any threats. He moved from the Acute Care system up to a Level II which permitted him to go off unit with staff, to participate in activities and group programs. He has handled all of these levels of responsibility reasonably well. There was one minor verbal altercation with an adolescent female patient who criticized Doug for his long hair and "hippy" appearance. Doug became angry and there was an exchange of words. Doug subsequently asked to have some time alone in order to cool his temper off. Doug tends to minimize the *threatening aspects of his behavior in Okanogan. He expresses fairly strong paranoid thinking, believing that he will be persecuted and rejected for his desire to isolate himself in his individualistic beliefs in ways. He seems to have little capacity of empathic insight into the feelings of others. He does comment, 'I am not dumb. I am not going to go threatening or hurting others. I just want to be left alone.' He did state that he was having trouble settling down, that he has used a combination of Vistaril and Librium at night to help him relax and sleep. Indeed, this combination of minor tranquilizers was prescribed here and he appeared to respond reasonably well to it.*

Mr. Perry is on Social Security disability for the past year with a diagnosis of a paranoid personality disorder. I would certainly agree with this diagnosis. I find no evidence of a schizophrenic or otherwise psychotic thought disorder. There are also elements of adjustment reaction given the acute nature. I believe many of his threats to the ADF officers occurred in this context.

With regard to further disposition, Sacred Heart is willing to continue to evaluate and treat this man, although personality orders tend to be notoriously difficult to treat in the short-term and are generally not responsive to medications. In order to evaluate and treat him, we will require that he be able to participate in the full range of the Psychiatric Unit activities including participation in the Level System with the levels of individual responsibility permitted within that system. His inability to participate will compromise both his own treatment program and the treatment program of other patients. If a secure facility is required, he might more appropriately be transferred to Eastern State Hospital.

I would expect Mr. Perry to do poorly in jail because of his small stature and experience of homosexual rape. He has an intense and somewhat realistic fear of incarceration. He has not appeared at any time during his Sacred Heart hospitalization to be a significant danger to himself or others. However, this is a reasonably structured environment with a wide tolerance for deviant behavior and speech. In a situation in a community in which he feels more cornered, Mr. Perry's behavior might be more unpredictable.

In summary, if Sacred heart does continue to evaluate and treat Mr. Perry, we would ask for a release from the restrictions on Mr. Perry's personal responsibility within the hospital setting and authorization for him to participate fully in the hospital program.

Timothy Keller, M.D.
Sacred Heart Medical Center

As the judge read over each of the affidavits and listened to the pleadings of the litigants before him, Doug stared blankly at the clock on the wall. He knew, based on his extensive courtroom experience, that if the hearing did not conclude by noon, they would have to reconvene after lunch, probably near 1:15 p.m. If that were the case, he would need them to finish by 1:30 at the latest so that he could make it back to the hospital for Clairann's group at 2 p.m. By 11:45 a.m. he knew there was no way this was going to get resolved before lunch.

"I think I have heard everything I need to on this, counselors?" the judge suddenly spoke.

Doug snapped his attention back to the bench.

He was going to make her group session after all.

"I've made my decision."

11
State of Unkemptness

"It is not this court's position to get into the business of forcing mental health facilities to become the arbiters of incarceration. As much as I think Mr. Perry deserves and needs some type of mental health care at this time, our legislators have simply failed to provide us the tools we need to do so. Our criminal justice system is a poor substitute for an effective mental health system. Given the circumstances, I have to weigh Mr. Perry's rights against the rights of the community's safety. Having done so, I must revoke yesterday's Order of Detention and remand Mr. Perry into custody at the Spokane County jail pending trial."

Doug looked at his lawyer.

He was going back to jail?

He wanted to stand up and scream at the judge, or his lawyer, or somebody. How could they do this? At least he would be able to go back and see her before they took him into custody.

Or so he thought.

He Said, She Said: The Spokane River Killer

Within a few seconds of the judge's order, the bailiffs came over to escort him through the side door and transport him across the river to the jail.

Somehow he had to get word to Clairann.

By 2:15 p.m. she knew he wasn't coming.

Like most men, he probably just wanted to fuck her and had no interest in even knowing anything about her life.

It reminded her of her ex-husband.

Life was never easy.

She grew up in the small coastal town of Sequim, Washington. Nestled in between the shores of the Strait of Juan De Fuca and the Olympic Mountains, Sequim was situated a mere 30 miles to the southeast of Victoria, British Columbia. In 1950, her father had traveled to his ancestral homeland of Switzerland and returned with a wife, a registered pediatric nurse by trade. Together, the Eberles began working on her grandfather's 220-acre dairy farm. Her older sister, Viola, was born in 1952, and a brother, Edwin, was born in 1954; however, he died as an infant. Clairann was born in February of 1956 and loved living on the farm. She enjoyed all aspects of living on the dairy farm and loved school activities.

As she grew older, something was simply not quite right.

The family had difficulty discerning and accepting her outbursts and strange behavior. Diagnosing and treating mental illness was still one step away from the frontal lobotomy and electroshock therapies of the butchers from earlier times. The little community of Sequim, not unlike Omak, had few if any resources available for diagnosis and treatment.

Eventually, with limited options, Clairann began self-medicating and spiraled downward into a shit-spooned trough of poor decisions, drugs, and alcohol. She married, had a daughter, and just a year earlier had given up a son for adoption to her parents, who would raise him as their own.

Prostitution, drugs, pain, suffering.

All of them the cost of untreated and undiagnosed mental illness during the 1980s.

But like most men in her life, Doug had failed her also.

He failed to keep a simple promise.

And for that, he would pay.

And pay dearly.

So would many others.

*   *   *

The victory for the U.S. Attorney's Office was short-lived. Within a day they received a motion requesting a de novo Review of the entire detention hearing process. A de novo review was similar to an appeal; however, the appeal court would simply review the case as though they were looking at it for the first time rather than remanding it back to a lower court if they disagreed. The reviewing court could simply order Doug to a mental health facility without further involvement from the lower court. They simply were not going to let the mental health issues rest.

For Doug, this was all he knew. It was all he had ever known.

He had known no personal responsibility for anything he ever did. Whether he knew it was right or wrong made no difference. According to the system that he had been dealing with, if he knew it was wrong and did it anyway, then he must be mentally ill. And if he didn't know it was wrong and did it anyway — then he was obviously mentally ill.

The system itself was the very definition of insanity.

It made it easy to keep him from jail, but it rendered any treatment for his mental health worthless by design.

The ATF, with the assistance of the Okanogan Sheriff's Department, continued to dig and dig. On May 13, 1988, one of Doug's counselors in Omak agreed to make a statement in support of Deputy Johnson's request for another search warrant of the Perry property up on Pogue Flat. Numerous grammatical errors, spelling errors, and odd phrasing suggest it may have been rushed.

Statement of Corrine Greenley taken on 5/13/88 at 1645 hrs.

I have been a counselor with Doug Perry for about 3 years. During the Fall of 1987 I was told he told me that he had a Mac-10 machine gun. But previous to this about 1 1/2 years ago he told me that he had machine guns. But when he told me about the Mac-10 he said that he had it buried. I believe that he has more than one machine gun just by the way he talked to me about them. At one time he stated to me that he could lose his license if his machine guns were found. He did not say how he got the machine guns but he has his ways. I also got the feeling that he has silencer for his weapons because of the way he talked about them. At one time he also referred to a Army surplus machine gun that he had, I don't remember when that was.

Corrine Greenley

Based on Mrs. Greeley's statement, on May 16, 1988, Judge Dave Edwards signed another search warrant. It became clear to Mr. Wetzel that his client was probably not exaggerating his claims that Okanogan County was out to rid themselves of Doug Perry any way that they could.

As Doug languished in jail he became more and more depressed. He rarely left his cell for fear of being attacked or abused by other inmates. He was well aware how others perceived his unique mannerisms. He had dealt with it his whole life.

Somehow he just wanted to get a message out to Clairann. He was sure she must have heard what happened to him. His mother had been confined to Eastern State Hospital on a number of occasions in the past. He knew they had a lock-down facility. His attorney and family friend in Omak had spoken of it on numerous occasions.

He jumped upward from his cot and smiled.
Rod!
He will help. He always did.

Rod Reinbold had been practicing law in Omak since the mid-seventies. A reputable and honest man, Rod displayed great compassion toward all of his clients. They were human beings deserving of fair treatment under the law. Doug and his attorney spoke with Rod a number of times seeking his input and advice. Mr. Reinbold did not represent Doug in his current dilemma but was willing to act as a friend if it would help Doug. His involvement and advocacy for Doug was, and is, highly commendable.

On June 1, 1988, he provided the following affidavit to the court:

Rodney M. Reinbold, being first duly sworn upon Oath, deposes and says:

I am an attorney practicing in Okanogan County since 1974. I represented Doug Perry in one of my first cases. Since that time I have had frequent contact with the Perry family. In the past I have been brought into the Perry family problems as an intermediary. I have represented Doug Perry in several minor criminal problems and I represented Doug in the Social Security appeal process. Doug lives with his mother, Ruth Perry, up on Pogue Flat out of Omak, Washington. They live in a small house which does not enjoy the benefit of hot running water. Doug's portion of the house is in the basement and consists of a small room. It is primarily there where Doug kept his gun collection. On several occasions I have been asked to take possession of Doug's gun collection. These were times when I was not representing Doug but acting as a friend. On one occasion, I had the entire gun collection in the basement of my house. On another occasion, I had the gun collection in the basement of my office.

Doug Perry has never lived away from home. For most of his life he has lived in his mother's basement up on Pogue Flat. The Perry's have had frequent difficulties with neighbors. Doug's mother, Ruth Perry, has a long history of mental illness which has required frequent hospitalization at Eastern State Hospital. She is presently at the mental institution at Eastern.

Doug was diagnosed as having a paranoid personality by his psychologist in connection with the Social Security hearings and was granted a disability on that basis. Doug experiences great fear when exposed to new situations, strangers and stress. It is unlikely that Doug will directly provoke a confrontation with another human being because of his extreme fear. Doug Perry's natural tendency toward self-defense however is easily triggered by his fears. He reacts poorly to confrontation with law enforcement officers and tends to be suspicious of those who invade his turf. To alleviate that situation I have asked Doug to call me when he has difficulties in this area. It is not uncommon for me to receive a call from Doug indicating that the police have been to his house or that a stranger has been to his house for one reason or another. He usually allows me to call the Sheriff, find out what it's about and then he allows them to come to the house. This rather sensible procedure was not followed on the night when Doug was last arrested. If that procedure had been followed, I'm sure that the situation would never have progresses to the point where Doug threatened to use force against the law enforcement officers as alleged.

Based upon my fourteen years of knowing Mr. Perry it is my opinion that he is not aggressive. Rather the opposite is true. He tends to be fearful. Doug has called me on several occasions from the county jail and I have spoken with him. He tells me that he is presently being held in solitary confinement. He is not receiving the medication that he should be receiving. He has a long-standing order for a lithium-based medication. Apparently the jail physician feels that he would be better benefited by Xanex. This tends to aggravate Mr. Perry's paranoia and he is now living in solitary confinement without the benefit of any medication. The present situation can only ultimately aggravate Doug Perry's case in the long term.

As an observer of Mr. Perry, I would recommend the following:

1. Doug should stay in the Spokane area. The neighbors have become extremely suspicious of Doug Perry. Doug and Ruth have had a number of confrontations with the Charles family. This confrontation includes a family dispute between the Charles and the Perry's involving property that the Charles bought from the Federal Land Bank. This property was pledged by Dick Perry as collateral for a loan. Ruth has had a long-standing dispute with Dick Perry contending that she was the rightful owner of this orchard. I have examined the case and there is a legitimate dispute concerning the ownership of the orchard. The dispute has caused extremely poor relations between Ruth Perry and the Charles family. These bad feelings have aggravated Doug Perry's fears of the Charles family. Doug Perry's fear of the Charles family has in turn increased their suspicion and fears of Doug. It would be best for both of them if Doug lived in some other location, out of harm's way. For that reason it would be better if he lived in Spokane during the pendency of this suit.

2. Day treatment for the chronically ill. Doug needs to be involved in a day treatment program for the chronically mentally ill. This program could provide daily supervision so that the court could be assured Doug is not using guns. The program could also help Doug to make arrangements for housing in the Spokane area, coordinate his Social Security benefits, and ease his fears of the new environment.

A release from prison into the hands of a day treatment program would be consistent with the philosophy of the Legislature in terminating institutional treatment in favor of out-patient treatment for the mentally ill. In my opinion, the community's interests are best served by deploying as soon as possible a day treatment program consistent with the safety of the community and the welfare of the patient.

I have spoken to the Okanogan County Sheriff about a long-term solution along these lines. The program presently has his tentative approval, however, Jim Weed wanted to check with the members of the Pogue Flat community before endorsing such a plan and I believe he is in the process of doing that.

Rodney M. Reinbold

He Said, She Said: The Spokane River Killer

On June 2, 1988, the U.S. Attorney's Office filed their response to the defendant's request for de novo review of detention hearing. In it, the United States Attorney lays out a fairly damning summation of Doug's history in Omak. The town was scared of him.

And probably should be.

"1. A second Search Warrant was executed on the Perry property on May 16, 1988. Okanogan County deputies discovered a 30-caliber Browning machine gun and spring and a box of pills.

2. Corrine Greeley, Okanogan Mental Health Coordinator, provided information to the Okanogan Sheriff's Department that defendant had buried a machine gun at his residence. A buried machine gun has never been found.

3. Dwight Caryl, co-owner of Timberline Gunsmithing, a licensed federal firearms dealer in Omak, Washington, has advised Agent Hearst that on approximately April 24, 1988, defendant Perry told Caryl that defendant Perry had machine guns and five pounds of plastic explosives at an Idaho residence. Defendant Perry also told Caryl that he had been contacted and recruited by people from the Aryan Nations.

4. Mike Johnson, Okanogan County Sheriff's Deputy has advised Agent Hearst that he has received information from a confidential informant that defendant Perry purchased a Mac 10 machine gun approximately two years ago. A Mac 10 has never been found at the Perry residence.

5. Additionally, Officer Johnson has advised Agent Hearst that Rod Reinbold, an attorney in Omak who has previously represented defendant Perry, has been asked by Omak police to talk to defendant Perry when defendant was agitated. Reinbold has refused to speak with defendant. Reinbold also refused to come to police department when requested to speak with defendant Perry. It is Officer Johnson's opinion that Reinbold is afraid of defendant Perry.

6. Based on Deputy Johnson's past experience with defendant Perry and defendant Perry's criminal record, Deputy Johnson believes defendant is a substantial risk to the community of Omak because defendant is mentally unstable and uses firearms to intimidate and harass. It is also Deputy Johnson's opinion that if defendant is released, he will return to Omak to retaliate against police officers and neighbors, since they have provided testimony against the defendant.

7. Agent Hearst inspected pills taken from defendant Perry's residence. Hearst will testify that bottles of pills were stuffed in a heater duct at the residence. Hearst will also testify that there were approximately 10 full bottles of pills prescribed to Perry from Omak Mental Health Clinic."

Upon receipt of Mr. Reinbold's affidavit, the U.S. Attorney desired to determine if there might be more to what Mr. Reinbold knew of Doug Perry. On June 8, 1988, investigator Sandra Brewer interviewed attorney Rod Reinbold. Rod had known the Perry family for quite some time. In a lot of ways he was the "relief valve" for the Perry family whenever they got into trouble.

Wednesday afternoons were slow in Mr. Reinbold's office. Rod cordially welcomed Sandra into his office and after some informal chatting, she began the interview.

"Mr. Reinbold, do you know Doug Perry?" Sandra began the interview.

Rod leaned back in his chair.

"Yeah, I have known Doug for about," he paused and looked toward the off-white ceiling, "Since about 1975. In my first case."

Sandra continued to write without looking up.

"What sort of cases did you see Doug for?" she asked.

"Oh, Doug has…, uh, had a couple conflicts with the neighbors and I represented him, uh, in those cases," Rod smiled back, nodding as he answered.

"Did they involve firearms?" Sandra continued.

"Yes, the first one involved when Doug, uh, Doug allegedly shot a gun over the neighbor's head."

Rod immediately began shaking his head and leaned forward as he continued, "There was never a suggestion, uh, that he, uh, intended to shoot the man."

Sandra looked up unamused.

"He was, uh, shooting the gun in the air to scare him away," Rod said and paused. He drew his elbow up to the table and leaned his chin onto his hand. His index finger rode along the side of his nose. For a second, he stroked his beard.

Sandra just stared.

"On another occasion, Doug was accused of shooting a neighbor's dog," Rod stated matter-of-fact like.

She stopped writing and sighed, "So how did those cases turn out?"

"The first case, we took it to a jury trial and we had a hung jury. Then I was relieved of my duties on the case because," Rod chuckled, "his mother fired me. Another lawyer took over the case and I understand that they were working out some sort of plea bargain where Doug pleaded guilty to a misdemeanor."

"Do you feel that Doug is a threat to other people?" she asked.

"Doug is not a threat in this sense. He's not aggressive. There would be in my opinion," Rod paused, "now I don't think Doug would be the first person to pick up a gun and do something aggressive with the gun. I do have a feel though, that if Doug is cornered, he'd be a problem."

Sandra nodded her headed in agreement and continued to listen.

"What Doug is, I represented Doug in a hearing—"

"For?" Sandra interrupted.

"His social security hearing—"

Sandra nodded again.

"Particularly enough that I became involved in the psychology— and Doug is a paranoid person, extremely so. An example of his paranoia was when we went down to the hearing, he put his gun in his backpack, and Doug carries a gun all the time."

"Why does he carry a gun all the time?" she asked.

"The reason he carries a gun is because he's afraid of other people. He also took in his backpack a two-to-three-day supply of food in case he had to walk home. That's the way he thinks, always is prepared for the worst, and he expects the worst," Rod paused, "The psychologist that interviewed Doug recognized that he was extremely paranoid."

"Is he mentally retarded?" she continued.

"He has a high I.Q. in terms of verbal ability. He has a high I.Q. in terms of math. When I say 'high,' I mean *the genius level*."

Sandra sat back and a confused look crossed her face.

"He does have a high I.Q. in terms of verbal ability, but he's also afraid to leave his house."

"Does he have any type of a social life?" she asked.

"He has no social life whatsoever—"

"Women? Dating? Anything?" Sandra interrupted, shaking her head.

"He's had maybe two girlfriends in his whole life. Both relationships were very short term. He never goes to bars. He never leaves his home at night and is never out of his mother's basement."

"So what does he do?" she asked.

"Usually, a typical day for Doug Perry is to get up at 10:00 a.m. and stay close to home. He likes to eat at home but does have a social security disability."

It was clear from this interview that Doug was a troubled young man.

Sandra tapped her pen on her writing pad and asked, "Do you feel that if he was in another town, he might be better off, especially if he got treatment in another area?"

Rod immediately began nodding in agreement.

"Yes. He needs to... my ultimate recommendation for Doug is that he get away from his mother," Rod began.

"Why is that?" Sandra quizzed.

"His mother is certifiably schizophrenic. She has been all her life. The combination of Doug Perry with his mother is a poor combination."

"What do you mean?" she asked.

"They tend to create and generate fantasies. She will say that the Charles' are going to do something and Doug doesn't have the ability to distinguish the fact from fiction. He, too, will make up terrifically complicated stories. When they are both having an episode, the worry is that something is really going to happen. They need to be separated."

"Couldn't he just move somewhere else in Omak?" she asked.

"At least," Rod pleaded, "Doug needs to get away from the area. He's become an issue with the neighbors."

"Which ones?" she asked.

"The Charles', I think, have no compunction in exaggerating the stories to get rid of Doug Perry."

"Why?" Sandra interrupted.

"They feel it's a question of self-defense."

"What— can you give me an example?" she asked.

A good example of this is last year when Doug got into his latest episode with the law. He was target shooting in his yard. The Charles' turned that into 'we thought he was shooting over some pickers' heads and aggravating our help.' Well, I don't think, myself, that he was doing anything like that."

"So why, do you think, they would say that?"

"I don't know what the Charles' problem was, but after they had an argument with the Perry family and heard Perry out there shooting his guns, it isn't too much for these people to imagine that the people might exaggerate the story a little bit to solve the problem."

"That doesn't really explain why. I mean... why go to…"

"It's either that or become involved in violence yourself."

"Are they the only ones?" Sandra asked.

"Those neighbors aren't good for Doug because they don't give him any slack at all and the Lingo's on the other side, he shot their dog. They have similar feelings of Doug Perry. It's not good for him to be in that environment because, unfortunately, his paranoia is turned into a little more reality. The best thing for Doug is he needs to get away from his mother; he needs to find a place to live in another community. Then he needs to be plugged into a day-treatment program for chronically mentally ill people," Rod answered.

Both of them sat in silence for just a moment.

Rod leaned back in his chair again and continued, "Maybe he needs to go to a mental institution for a short time. At least in a mental institution, he would be plugged into a treatment program, and day treatment is not designed to make people better. Day treatment programs will accept a chronically mentally ill person for what he is."

Sandra asked, "Are you afraid of Doug Perry at all? One of the deputies stated you refused to respond to Doug Perry's residence when asked."

Rod chuckled, "The deputy, Mike Johnson, claims that I was once called by the Omak City Police. Number one, Doug Perry, to the best of my knowledge, hasn't been involved with the Omak City Police. The reason for that is that Doug Perry would have to get up his nerve to come to town. I don't recall being called by the Omak City Police or by any police when I didn't come. The police have called me, the Sheriff has called me, that Doug Perry would not answer the door. 'Would you come?' I have done that and Doug has answered the door and (I) have said that here's what they want.'"

One of the psychologists' reports indicated that Doug had been sexually abused, experiencing 'homosexual rape' at the command of his older brother, Lawrence. Sandra was interested in confirming what Mr. Reinbold may have known about it.

"Do you know Doug's brother, Lawrence?" she asked.

"Yes, he has a very erratic personality. He always carries a firearm," Rod began.

"Have you seen this yourself?" she asked.

"Once when he (Lawrence) was loading apples on his mother's truck, Lawrence displayed a firearm."

"Does he have as many firearms as Doug?"

Rod shook his head.

"He doesn't have as many firearms as Doug does," he answered.

"Speaking of the guns," Sandra began, "did you know of Doug's firearms?"

"Yes. I've had them myself."

Sandra looked puzzled and asked, "Why?"

"I've been asked a couple of times to take possession of his firearms. Usually, when he gets into trouble, the first thing the judge wants to do is see that he doesn't have his firearms. I've allowed Doug to… one time he put all his firearms in my basement, and the next time I had them put in the basement of our law office."

"What did he have the firearms in? Were they in a container?" she asked.

"No. They were by themselves," he answered.

"So how did you get them?"

"One time I went out to his house; I was assisted by the deputies; they put them in my truck and I think they confined their search to Doug Perry's room. They took all the firearms out and put them into my truck and I took them to my law office."

"And the time after that?"

"That was the last time. The time before that, I went out myself to Doug Perry's house and, with his mother, got his firearms."

"Did he ever mention to you about the pipe bombs and blasting caps he had?"

"No."

Sandra paused, hoping he would elaborate. After a few awkward moments, she continued.

"Was Lawrence Perry out there a lot? Was it very frequently?"

Rod shook his head, "No, not a lot. Lawrence had some conflict with his mother. She lived in the other area of the house. Doug Perry did not consider the whole house his. He lived in his room, which was his. He always lived in the basement of the house."

"Have you heard from Doug?" she asked.

Rod leaned forward, "Yes. I'm very disturbed about the conditions he's being held in there. He's called me, said he's in solitary confinement, he hurts, he was crying, he's losing hope."

"Is Doug very open with you?"

"You might say I was his best friend, but I don't feel that way with him. He talks a lot."

"Do you think he would have told you about the machine guns and blasting caps?"

"No," Rod shook his head, "I've always thought he shouldn't have the guns."

"Do you feel Doug sometimes fantasizes and does not tell the truth?"

"Yes. He tends to exaggerate his life. He'd like you to believe that he has other friends and shares with his friends. I heard a story that the Aryan Nations were contacting him. He might like to believe he's a part of an organization not just part of himself. He'd like you to believe… he tells me all the time… he's told me before that he hates himself but takes care of his physical needs, that life is punishing him. The truth is he's basically afraid. He imagines that sort of life that the Aryan Nations would want him but the chances of that is very slim. He tries to convince himself that his life is richer than it is. It's hard to admit that his life is as bad as it is."

"Is it true that he has a federal firearms license?"

"Yes. He brags a lot. He always had a federal firearms license. He was still able to get a concealed weapons permit. It was just this year he hasn't gotten a license for his concealed weapons license."

"What about his gun collection?"

"It is not as exotic in terms of — I've heard that he's got some sniper guns. But his guns are fairly normal. One of the guns that I've heard is a snipe gun is a 22. It's just a 22 that the stock folds down," Rod began waving his hands around above his head and smiled, "It's exotic and erotic but it's nothing but the same as a 22. These guns are no secret."

"What about the machine gun?"

Rod stopped smiling and leaned forward.

"*Lawrence Perry* may have had the connections at one time to get the parts but Doug Perry himself does not have the connections. Doug doesn't *have the nerve.*"

"But his brother may?"

"Yes. His brother may have had the contacts. I think you'll find they're very old and something his brother did and brought the parts home and piled them up in the junk. *You gotta appreciate this:* The house doesn't have running water right now. It isn't clean. It isn't kept. The blankets are old. The house is in the state of unkemptness. There are things in that house *that these people don't even know they have.* It's that kind of a house. There are boxes on the floor, things could lay around there a long time. *I know.* And it's dark. When I went by Doug Perry's house that night, we had to walk down the stairs with his mother in a state of hysteria because her son was in jail and I had to walk down in the basement with her that night and I don't know where she's taking me. I haven't been down there before. There's no lights. I have to walk down a steep set of stairs in the dark and open the door to Doug Perry's room and there wasn't a light on. That's the way the house is. It's a dark, unlit house that has areas with many rodents."

"Has the house always been like this?"

"It's been this way since his dad died. She was functional until her daughter was killed and then she lost contact with reality. Doug said Lawrence molested him when he was a child. Whether that's true or not, I have no way of knowing."

Later that afternoon, Sandra Brewer and Jill Thomas also interviewed Judge David Edwards, District Court Judge in Okanogan County. They summarized their interview as follows:

Judge Edwards stated to us that he had known Doug Perry approximately thirteen years. He stated he met Doug when he was his court-appointed counsel. He represented him at least a couple of times. He also remembers Doug in District Court as Doug has had cases in front of him. Judge Edwards also stated that he had talked countless times to Doug in person and on the phone.

Judge Edwards stated that Doug Perry has always had guns all his life and has had a love for guns and his collection.

Judge Edwards stated that he personally had never been afraid of Doug Perry. He did feel that Doug is paranoid and that his environment and his mother does affect his reaction. Judge Edwards stated that Doug Perry did need support and relief from his mother. He stated that Doug Perry had been saying that if he couldn't get away from his mother, he'd go crazy. Judge Edwards also stated that Doug had tried through several social agencies to get some help. Judge Edwards also felt that if it were not for his mother, Doug would not be in this situation. He feels that Doug Perry does need treatment and locking him up would make him worse. Judge Edwards feels that his environment affects how Doug Perry reacts and acts. This is a quote from Judge Edwards: 'If you take time to deal with him, it usually works out. Personally I'm not afraid of him but if you are a person who doesn't know how to deal with him, then there is potential for violence.'

He Said, She Said: The Spokane River Killer

Judge Edwards also stated that he felt Doug Perry needed a structured support system. Another quote from Judge Edwards: 'If you hope to have a behavior that is not a threat, you cannot just lock him up, it would create a worse problem. My guess would be that he would do very well at Sacred Heart Hospital. I'm not a professional but I think treatment is the best hope for community safety. My big hope was that the federal system would provide a meaningful alternative; a lock up situation may not be the best. Doug has mental illness, it needs to be addressed. Treating him like a criminal will never accomplish anything at all, but make it worse for society.'

Judge Edwards also felt that if Doug did not have access to his guns he would be unable to obtain guns through any strong arm measures because of his physical stature and personality. Judge Edwards also stated that he felt the Sheriff's office made more of the incident than they needed to, especially the way it appeared in the press.

Judge Edwards also stated that Doug Perry does not socialize well with people and that he thought Doug would be responsive to treatment if it was adequate. Judge Edwards felt that there probably wasn't adequate treatment in Omak but that if Doug did get adequate treatment he would be very amenable to the treatment and Judge Edwards stated that he was very familiar with Sacred Heart Hospital's psychiatric treatment. He feels that Doug would probably thrive well there and that he did trust Sacred Heart's judgment as to a treatment program for Doug. Again, Judge Edwards did want to emphasize that Doug Perry does have a mental illness. He is not a criminal and the problem does need to be addressed as a mental illness to keep any further occurrences of this nature from happening.

Before they left Omak, Sandra also stopped by Dwight Caryl's gun shop. An employee explained that Dwight was not in but that he could be reached by telephone if she wanted to use the phone near the front counter.

June 8, 1988

Phone Interview of Dwight Caryl
Interview by Sandra Brewer

I spoke to Dwight Caryl over the phone on the above date. Dwight Caryl stated that he had been a friend of Doug Perry's for several years. Dwight Caryl is a gunsmith in the town of Omak.

Dwight Caryl stated that Doug Perry had always had an interest with guns and had a gun collection.

Dwight Caryl also stated that he felt Doug Perry had "lost contact with reality in the last few years." He did not know why or what caused this. Mr. Caryl also said that Doug was a loner and did not talk much about his family. Mr. Caryl did state that Doug and his family had quite a dispute going with the neighbors over land and boundaries.

Dwight Caryl also stated that Doug Perry was very hard to believe anymore and seemed to talk in fantasies rather than realities. Mr. Caryl felt that Doug Perry made up stories quite often and didn't seem to be able to distinguish the truth from the stories.

End of Interview.

With so much evidence mounting up against him, it was clear the only hope Doug had of getting out of jail and communicating with Clairann was if he were admitted to Eastern State Hospital. On the same day the U.S. Attorney's Office investigators were mining evidence against him, his lawyer finally received a response to his request for admission to Eastern Sate.

Finally, Doug was going to have some good news.

Once he was in Eastern State perhaps Deputy Johnson and all the fuckers in Omak would give up on railroading him for shit he didn't do. He didn't even care if he went back to Omak or Pogue Flat any more. He just wanted to contact Clairann.

Everything was about Clairann.

12
A Full Range of Psychiatric Unit Activities

June 8, 1988

Phillip Wetzel
Attorney at Law
921 North Adams
Spokane, Washington 99201

RE: Douglas Perry

Dear Mr. Wetzel,

This letter is in response to your request for information regarding admission to Eastern State Hospital for your client.
You shared the following information with me: Douglas Perry is a single, 35-year-old male currently in jail in Spokane County on a federal offense regarding manufacture and storage of bombs. In early May he was released from jail for a five-day stay at Sacred Heart Hospital in Spokane. Since Sacred Heart was unable to keep him on a locked area, he was returned to jail approximately May 12. He has been in solitary confinement since that time. In the past he has been diagnosed as a Paranoid Personality Disorder. Since May 12, two mental health professionals have seen him and agreed that there is no thought disorder (Axis I diagnosis) present.

They did not find him detainable or committable as a 72-hour Evaluation and Treatment. Reportedly, Dr. Keller at Mental Health has agreed with this diagnosis.

You called today requesting information pursuant to having your client housed at Eastern State Hospital pending his release hearing this Friday and possibly pending his trial date.

Mr. Perry would only be admitted to the Legal Offender Unit under a 15-day order for evaluation of sanity and competency (RCW 10.77). Because he has federal charges, Federal Court would have to order the evaluation and pay for his hospitalization. If Mr. Perry was deemed incompetent, his order staying proceedings time of up to 90 days would likely take place in a federal facility in Missouri.

We discussed the possibility of Mr. Perry applying for voluntary admission to Eastern State Hospital on the adult Psychiatric Unit. Because he has been seen by two mental health professionals who both felt he was not detainable under RCW 71.05, it is highly unlikely that he would be granted voluntary admission. The Adult Psychiatric Unit does have two locked wards, but neither is considered to be a security ward and there would be the risk of Mr. Perry taking unauthorized leave.

Since the Axis II diagnosis of Paranoid Personality is not a disorder which is treatable with psychotropic medications, the purpose of housing Mr. Perry at Eastern State Hospital would only be for (1) his preference over confinement in jail or, (2) protection of society given his current propensity for dangerous activities. Those same two factors must be considered in any discussion regarding his release to the community.

Thank you for calling. Please call again if you need further information.

Sincerely,

Judith W. Coram, R.N., Program Director
Competency, Evaluation and Treatment Program
Legal Offender Unit
Eastern State Hospital

He Said, She Said: The Spokane River Killer

It was over. He was not going to be allowed into Eastern State Hospital either. He wanted to collapse right onto the floor and sob. But such a distasteful action was quite beneath his hidden intellect. He would never give up so easily. If that were the case, he would have done so much sooner than his fourth decade on this planet. He clearly had the means to solve his problems by his own hand and end his miserable life if that were what he ever wanted.

But he would never give in to them.

He was smarter and more clever than they would ever know.

Doug waited patiently near the phone in the common area until finally it was his turn. He phoned Mr. Wetzel and demanded that he appeal to Dr. Keller for another letter ahead of the de novo hearing. His lawyer warned Doug that his gambit was coming to an end; he could not just continue to fight.

But Doug would never quit.

Mr. Wetzel agreed to call Dr. Keller, but he would need to ask the court for a continuance until June 29, 1988 if there were going to be any chance of convincing the court to release him to Sacred Heart again.

On June 9, Dr. Keller filed an affidavit with the court asking (again) to allow Doug to be released to Sacred Heart Hospital since he cannot go to Eastern State:

TIMOTHY KELLER, being first duly sworn on oath, deposes and says:

I am a licensed psychiatrist in the State of Washington and my curriculum vitae is attached hereto and incorporated herein as Exhibit "A."

I admit patients at the psychiatric unit at Sacred heart Medical Center.

In that regard, I admitted Douglas Perry to Sacred heart Medical Center on May 6, 1988. Mr. Perry was in the psychiatric unit until May 12, 1988. I completed a consultation attached hereto and incorporated as Exhibit "B."

Mr. Perry has a paranoid personality disorder. He is not psychotic or schizophrenic.

Mr. Perry did well at the Sacred Heart psychiatric unit. He related well to staff and participated in treatment activities. The staff was disappointed and somewhat bewildered when Mr. Perry was placed in jail.

From every indication that I have, including history from Okanogan Mental Health and Mr. Lang of the ATF, there is no indication that Mr. Perry would be a danger to the community. On the contrary, he has made no threats, but has made it clear that he would do nothing to harm anyone. He has stated that his main interest is in being left to himself. This was given creditability by his performance in the one argument he had at Sacred Heart where his reaction was to simply go back to his room and close his door.

Mr. Perry is certainly not a candidate for civil commitment as he does not meet the legal criteria for being a danger to himself, being a danger to others, or being gravely disabled.

Persons who suffer from Mr. Perry's paranoid personality disorder are typically only unpredictable when they are cornered or threatened. Mr. Perry is capable of dealing with the day to day stresses and problems which he would face with release.

Mr. Perry should be released from custody. Sacred Heart Medical Center will admit him if the hospital is allowed to treat him. That would include enough freedom that he participate in the full range of psychiatric unit activities and the level system.

I would recommend release to Sacred Heart Medical Center. Typically a patient would remain at Sacred Heart Medical Center for approximately 14-days. At the end of that time, Mr. Perry should be released to the community upon the following conditions:

1. That he not possess any weapons.
2. That he report to a probation officer on a regular basis.
3. He should not leave the City of Spokane.
4. He should take medications as prescribed.

5. *He should obtain an apartment in the City of Spokane and refrain from contacting persons in Okanogan County except as may be necessary, in conjunction with counsel, to prepare his defense.*

Sacred Heart Medical Center has staff which can and will assist him in obtaining a residence and whatever further treatment or medication may be necessary.

Upon the completion of his inpatient stay, I would be happy to update the Court on any further relevant findings and recommendations.

TIMOTHY KELLER

* * *

With little warning, the skies, once blue above the pine forested foothills to the northeast of the city, faded to a dull and dreary gray. The unexpected drizzle sent everyone scrambling for cover.

Traffic backed up.

Headlights turned on.

Puddles of runoff splashed along the strip and sang from wet tires as wipers buzzed across windshields. Cars honked. People pulled light jackets, or whatever they had, over their heads as they darted through crosswalks without even looking.

Nothing stirred up the strip like a June thunderstorm.

She just sat under the overhang trying to stay dry. She pulled her handbag from under her arm and unclipped the latch. She only had a few more smokes left. But what else was there to do? Laugh at the idiots who acted like the rain was some sort of acid? Sent down to cleanse this shithole of a place? It was going to take more than a little water from the sky to rinse this place clean.

People are stupid.

She reached her hand down her skirt and scratched her crotch. It was sore. Most Johns didn't know the difference between a thigh fuck and actual intercourse. But that older man in the Corvette sure did. And he was not to be denied. She barely managed to jerk her tampon out beforehand. Thank God it only lasted three or four minutes.

It had been more than a month since she ditched on the funny farm at Sacred Heart.

She remembered the hippy-looking dude with the thick glasses and how he was so sweet on her.

She laughed.

Those were the days.

Until he fucking disappeared on her. She even thought he was pretty cool. But it figured. Men were assholes and he was a man. So why would it be any different.

She had been off of the meds for over a week. She knew she could probably go the clinic and get her scrip refilled. But then she would have to listen to that pretentious old hag try and lecture her about getting help and utilizing the resources available to her. As far as she was concerned, her best resource was between her legs.

And right now it was sore and worn out.

At least she had a couple hundred bucks so she could maybe catch a few days at the Motel.

"The Motel."

That's what everyone called the Spokane Street Motel where she could sign in and pay cash without getting hassled. Unless you considered the constant barrage of pimps and crack dealers trying to get her hooked on crack or offering protection for her weary snatch.

Everybody always wanted to fuck her.

Even the girls.

The Motel was only a few blocks back toward downtown and a couple of blocks off Sprague Avenue on the corner of Short Avenue and Spokane Street.

The thunderstorm made the air smell like dirt and rotting grain from the old silos across Sprague by the train tracks.

It was putrid.

He Said, She Said: The Spokane River Killer

Her heels were half a size too small but she had only traded a couple of packs of smokes for them and they seemed to suit her figure nicely. The mini-skirt she was wearing was stretched near the back from hiking it up too many times in the backs of trucks, mini-vans, and behind the occasional dumpster. She even started to notice the familiar yellowing from semen stains she was unable to avoid.

Men were disgusting pigs when they came.

Some of them bit her on the neck or tried to lick her ears thinking that somehow she was going to be so turned on that she would want to start having regular sex with them because it was *so good for her.* Others pulled her hair and nearly snapped her neck. In her own way, she did kind of like it. Once in a while she would even orgasm. She never could tell what it was that had turned her on though. Sometimes one of the college guys would really get into it with her like he was making love or something. She almost felt bad for these awkward, otherwise good-looking young men. She figured they just had too many insecurities to find regular girls, or they, like her, had a story that no one really wanted to hear. It was for them that she felt something.

They would always ask how she liked it or if it felt good. *Felt good?*

I am fucking you for money, asshole, so I can avoid going back to something I don't want to remember. Or to keep something I can't forget from causing me to go out and kill college faggots like you.

It was truly a love-hate endeavor.

Just as she was about to cross Sheridan Street, a young man whistled toward her from his car. He parked in an open spot and leaned over to open his passenger door. She quickly shifted gears and put on her alternate persona as she jumped into his passenger seat. Her customers knew her only as Joan.

"Hi sweetie, I'm Joan. What do you want? I'm down for whatever. I'll blow you for $40 and—"

The young man cut her off before she could finish and jerked her head toward his. Her elbow smacked into the steering wheel as the young man placed his lips passionately on hers.

Their tongues danced between their mouths and she felt herself becoming uncharacteristically aroused. She reached her hand under the steering wheel and felt the young man's crotch beginning to bulge outward.

She pulled back and stared at the young man.

"Or I can just... give you a hand job... for... like $20?"

Clairann knew he was young— and by his casual clothing she figured he could have been a college student or— it didn't really matter. She just knew a hand job for $20 was far more appealing than having his cock swimming around her mouth for 10 minutes.

She *was* tired.

The young man opened his door and climbed out of the little car. It was obvious to Clairann that if he were going to do anything, it wasn't going to be in the car. The seat would not go back far enough for her head, or hands, to clear the steering wheel.

"How much to fuck?" the young man asked quietly.

She wasn't quite prepared for that. There were plenty of young men cruising the Avenue looking for action, but most of the time they were introverted, closet males who just wanted a blow job. Rarely were college boys looking for sex in the middle of the day. They rarely wanted to risk standing behind a dumpster in broad daylight.

"I want to fuck you right here. Right now. *How much?"*

"We can fuck... we can fuck for a hundred," she finally answered.

She hoped that the $100 price would dissuade the young man from his offer. But it only seemed to arouse him even more. He shoved her toward a stack of concrete blocks and reached his hand forward to her mid-section. With a violent jerk he bent her forward. His belt buckle clinked in the warm summer air. Before she could even catch her balance, she felt her skirt ripped upward over her hips

In the distant whir of the traffic along Sprague Avenue, she thought she could hear voices laughing and telling her to be quiet.

The man's hands thrust upward, grabbing her by the chest. She tried to turn her head to catch a glimpse of her sudden partner, but the man jerked her head back around toward the wall.

"Easy!" Clairann implored.

"Just shut up and take it—"

And with this final order, she felt the man's cock drive upward between her ass cheeks north of her vagina. She grimaced and held her breath. She knew she had to pretend her damnedest that she liked it— or it would only get worse. Some of the college boys were bad tricks. They would beat the shit out of her and not even think twice.

The fake screams of joy when she was in pain.

The feigned attempts to remain silent when she yearned to cry out.

The man's hands gripped her pelvis, and with every thrust, the searing pain grew more intense. She bit her lip and braced herself against the concrete blocks.

The young man panted and groaned while quietly screaming degrading remarks in her ear.

She tuned it out.

She was going to make enough money to chill at the Motel for at least a week now.

It was worth it.

Once again, she was running through the fields of the dairy farm and playing hide and seek with her sister. She was hiding in a pile of hay in the huge barn. Her mother was cleaning milking buckets, and her father pretended to give away her hiding spot. She could hear the dogs playing in the field and the wind rustling the leaves of the giant trees lining the long driveway to the Eberle Farm.

She was far away from an empty gravel lot at the corner of Sheridan and Sprague.

Before she knew it, it was over, and the man unhanded her.

She draped her head down sideways, as the familiar liquid warmth ran down the inside of her leg. She took a deep breath, continuing to grip the concrete blocks. She needed a moment to gather herself.

Again she took another deep breath and then let out a long sigh.

She swiped her hand up along her chin and then over her face, pulling her hair back from her forehead.

It was over.

All she needed was the $100 from her trick and a ride back a few blocks west on Sprague.

When the car door slammed shut, she let out a muffled shriek and raced to get her skirt situated on her hips.

What the fuck?

By the time her skirt was around her hips, the young man had started his car and thrown it into reverse.

"Heeeyyy!!!!" she yelled running toward him while trying to secure one of her heels that had nearly come off while she was fucking.

Before she could get within 20 feet of the car, the taillights raced away throwing dust and gravel.

She had been ripped off.

Again.

13

Once Bristled With Apple Trees

On June 29, 1988, Doug and his legal team convinced the court to follow Dr. Keller's recommendations. He would be allowed to move into his own residence as long as he remained in Spokane until his case was disposed of. Doug had been incarcerated in one way or another for more than two months. He was still receiving his social security payments and had saved enough money to rent a small house on Dalton Avenue between Addison Street and Standard Street. The small house was a short distance north of downtown across the river. He would be allowed to return to Omak to collect his personal belongings and his little red Pinto he favored so much.

On July 11, 1988, in a last-ditch effort to avoid a felony conviction, which would disqualify Doug from possessing firearms, Doug and his legal team filed a motion with the court to suppress the evidence seized during Deputy Johnson's search. They claimed that the search warrant was gained under illegal circumstances and that Deputy Johnson was clearly "out to get" Doug Perry. His legal team submitted a Memorandum of Authorities to the court and hoped for the best.

Memorandum of Authorities

FACTS

DOUG PERRY has lived his whole life with his mother, Ruth, on Pogue Flat, an orchard area outside of Omak.

They both suffer from mental illness and both survive on social security. They live in a small house on a bare twenty acres that once bristled with apple trees.

DOUGLAS has had many contacts with the sheriff's office, many times as a complainant. He has been convicted of two misdemeanors, once for shooting a dog, and once for carrying a pistol. DOUG is a federally licensed firearm dealer and a known gun collector.

On April 25, 1988, the sheriff's department responded to a domestic violence call at the Perry house. Ruth Perry reported that DOUG had hit her. DOUG was in his rented room in the basement. Deputy Johnson asked to talk with DOUG, but DOUG would not respond. Later, DOUG said that he would shoot anyone that came through the door, and that the door was wired with explosives.

DOUG eventually came out and was arrested and jailed for simple assault. When he left his room, he locked the door.

The next day, Deputy Johnson obtained a search warrant to find and seize the explosives PERRY mentioned. (Attached and incorporated herein as Exhibit "A").

The search produced 53 legal firearms. In addition, at the bottom of a dust covered trunk, in a different basement room from where DOUG'S guns were found, the search produced five short pieces of pipe, capped, containing smokeless powder. The trunk also contained a substantial amount of clothing and some rifle ammunition.

ARGUMENT

The issue is narrow. The affidavit must show on its face whether probable cause exists that contraband or evidence of a crime will be found at a particular place. Illinois v Gates, 462 U.S. 213, 103 S. Ct. 2317, 76 L. Ed. 2d 527 (1983). In addition, a reasonable good faith belief in the propriety of the warrant saves an otherwise invalid warrant. United States v. Leon, 468 U.S. 897, 104 S. Ct. 3405. However, deference to the magistrate's decision is not boundless. Leon at 914. An officer is not entitled to rely on a warrant based on an affidavit so lacking in indicia of probable cause as to render official belief in its existence entirely unreasonable. Leon at 923.

This case fits into the exception Justice White carved out of the Leon holding.

DOUG PERRY was in his home. He had a right to be there. He had a right to be secure from warrantless arrest there. Payton v. New York, 445 U.S. 573, 100 S. Ct. 1371, 63 L. Ed. 2d 639 (1980). Officer Johnson had no right to enter DOUG'S room without an arrest warrant and he didn't have one.

DOUG PERRY would not respond. He didn't have to. He warned the deputy to stay away. He exerted his constitution right to be free from warrantless arrest in his home. He exerted this right reasonably. If Johnson had entered, the entry would have been illegal.

It is this context which reveals the objective unreasonableness of Johnson's claim of the existence of probable cause. The affidavit is the bare-bones type criticized in Leon. The only fact which is even relevant to a conclusion that contraband or evidence is in the house is DOUG PERRY'S statement. The statement was made to a police officer by a man in his own residence while the officer was attempting to effect an arrest without a warrant.

No objective officer would believe probable cause existed to search the residence for explosive devices. If Johnson did, his belief was unreasonable.

In the same context, the magistrate erred in finding the affidavit facially valid. There are simply insufficient facts to produce a conclusion that illegal explosive devices would be found in the PERRY residence. The speciousness is seen again in the fact that the warrant authorized the seizure of legal weapons and ammunition which were totally unrelated to the suspected crime.

CONCLUSION

Deputy Johnson seized upon a single angry threat of a paranoid man who was total within his rights, It was not reasonable for him to conclude that he would therefore find evidence of illegal explosive devices within PERRY'S room.

The evidence should be suppressed. All legal firearms and ammunition should immediately be returned.

RESPECTFULLY SUBMITTED this 11th day of July, 1988.

Phillip J. Wetzel
Attorney for the Defendant

After considering all of the facts in the case, the judge refused to suppress the evidence.
Doug was devastated.
He knew that a felony conviction was going to complicate matters with his guns. They were like his children, and there was no way he was going to willingly give them up.
But his options were deteriorating before his eyes.
Doug's lawyer conceded that with the evidence mounting against him, Doug would most likely be convicted of the charges he was facing. If he exercised his right to take the case to trial and was, in fact, found guilty, it was very likely the judge would sentence him to at least 3-5 years in Federal prison. A plea bargain, Mr. Wetzel argued, was his best scenario.
Doug knew that his lawyer was probably right. Even though they all acted like the outcome was some "grand mystery" — Doug knew the system.
The fix was in.

He Said, She Said: The Spokane River Killer

On July 19, 1988, Doug and his lawyer appeared before the court.

Mr. Wetzel looked toward the judge, "Might I approach the bench your honor? There are a couple of documents: a plea agreement and a stipulation."

Ms. Johnson, the prosecuting attorney, looked annoyed.

"Your Honor, that agreement isn't signed by the United States. Essentially, those were the terms of the agreement, but I didn't like some of the wording so we didn't sign it. But those are essentially the terms of the agreement."

Mr. Wetzel glanced back at his opposition with a look of disdain. The judge flipped through the documents and removed his glasses.

"All right. Well I have some difficulty with the language in that it appears to be an attempt at an 11(e) sentence to the effect— as to what the sentence will be," the judge leaned back and placed his glasses back on his face, "It's not my policy to accept such pleas. Apparently all this is, is that the Government will recommend that there not be any further jail time. Is that what this all amounts to?"

Ms. Johnson looked toward the bench, "That's correct your Honor. Apparently, essentially what it is— is the United States will not make a recommendation with regards to jail time or fine; however, if the court were to impose conditions, we would agree that a ten-year probationary period would be appropriate."

The judge sighed and looked at Ms. Johnson somewhat surprised, "I can't impose probation for ten years."

"It's merely a suggestion to the court, obviously" she replied.

"Well, the maximum probation I can impose is five years, unless there is something I don't know here. Have you ever heard of any more than five years, Mr. Grunte [court clerk]?"

"No."

Ms. Johnson seemed unprepared.

"Then the United States would recommend five years, Your Honor," she continued.

The judge looked back down at the documents in front of him, "All right."

Doug shifted nervously in his chair. After all of this, he just wanted to get out of jail. He had agreed to everything they wanted and now the judge was reluctant?

Ms. Johnson turned to the desk behind her and pulled another document up in front of her.

"And there are numerous conditions, Judge, that are not listed in the plea agreement, but there are some additional conditions that should be noted for the record," she added.

The judge looked even more surprised.

"What are they?" he asked, shaking his head.

"One of the conditions, Your Honor, is that the defendant would allow whoever the seller is of these firearms to provide ATF a list of the firearms and serial numbers so ATF can track those weapons and make sure that none of those weapons go back into the defendant's possession or go to a prior felon who has been convicted of a felony. There is also—," Ms. Johnson paused awkwardly and continued, "and the defendant."

The judge could sense that Ms. Johnson was confused.

"I'm not sure I understood," he began, "I thought these weapons were in Mr. Perry's possession?"

"No, Your Honor. Firearms were seized by the Okanogan Sheriff Deputies, I've talked to them, as a result of a search. They don't have any pending charges. They don't have a plan to forfeit any of those items, and I'm not real sure why they are holding the firearms, but as I understand it, they are going to release these firearms."

The judge appeared somewhat shocked at what he was hearing.

"But you said they wanted to check to see if they *go back to the defendant?*" he asked in a condescending tone.

Ms. Johnson realized she was not communicating entirely clearly.

"What the plea agreement is," she began, "is that the defendant will liquidate those firearms and they will have to be sold and mutually approved by the United States and the defendant. For instance they can go to a firearms dealer. He would then sell those weapons and the proceeds from those weapons would go to the defendant. ATF merely wants a list of the weapons sold and who they are sold to and serial numbers."

She turned and took another stack of documents from the desk behind her.

"There was also ordered by Magistrate Hovis that the defendant surrender his federal firearms dealer license to ATF, and as of this time we don't have information that he surrendered that license. He's agreed to do so, as previously required by Magistrate Hovis."

She stood, reading through the document and flipped to the next page. Agent Hearst stood and whispered something into her ear before he sat back down.

She nodded.

"Your Honor, the wording on... I believe it's the last condition, I don't have a copy of the plea agreement, provides that the defendant shall participate in a debriefing by ATF agents. The United States will provide use immunity with regards to that information; however, of course, if there was independent information, the United States would reserve its right to prosecute for any other violations of law that occurred independent of the— who received information from independent sources from the defendant's statements."

The judge looked at her strangely again, "What is this debriefing to consist of?"

She could sense the judge was not impressed with how poorly organized they were.

"Judge, all we request merely is that the defendant come to the ATF office or the officers have an opportunity to speak with him. He can have his attorney with him. ATF agents merely want to ask him some questions with regard to any other firearms or explosives that he may possess or that he may have in his custody, possession or control."

Doug shook his head and leaned back in his chair.

"There was an additional search warrant executed in this case, " she continued, "and at that time a machine gun was discovered. There were also some statements the defendant made to the Okanogan Mental Health people which indicated that he had other firearms. We merely want to explore those alternatives. If he does in fact have any other firearms, we would like to confiscate those firearms and have them, if it's appropriate, or if they are illegal we would seize them."

"So I take it the debriefing portion of the plea agreement is that Mr. Perry will dutifully respond to questions from the ATF agents as to; one, the source of the firearms that had been picked up, and: two, his knowledge as to any other firearms that he may have possession, actual or constructive possession of. Is that correct?" the judge asked.

Doug's right knee started shaking and he leaned over to his attorney and whispered in his ear. His attorney put his hand up toward Doug, admonishing him to remain quiet. Doug slumped back in his chair again. Removing his glasses, he wiped his arm across his face and placed them back on.

"That's correct, Your Honor, I don't believe there are any other conditions, Your Honor, to the agreement. As I said, some of the wording in the agreement is why I didn't sign it, but I think the terms are essentially what we've agreed on."

The judge leaned forward and focused his attention toward Doug and his attorney.

"All right. Mr. Wetzel and Mr. Perry? Before I proceed with the formal arraignment, Mr. Wetzel, has Ms. Johnson correctly set forth the understanding?"

Doug shook his head while his attorney stood up.

""I believe so, Your Honor; however, Mr. Perry did indicate some hesitancy as to the debriefing, and earlier, you know, he basically had agreed to do that. But just when we were sitting there, there was some hesitancy expressed and—"

"Well, as in the case I was just proceeding with," the judge interrupted, "I'm not going to accept a plea unless it's an unequivocal plea. We have jurors coming in. This case is ready to go to trial next Monday and I'll be here ready to try it, and I assume Ms. Johnson will also."

Doug leaned forward and pulled at the tail of Mr. Wetzel's jacket. He leaned toward Doug while Doug whispered in his ear again. His attorney dismissed whatever it was Doug said and continued.

"We're ready, too, but I'm not sure that it isn't a—"

Doug leaned back in his chair and threw his hands in the air. The judge did not appear pleased.

"Why don't— we'll move right along to the case we were on before, and you and Mr. Perry should take time to discuss this further. We are in recess."

He struck his gavel onto the desk and Mr. Wetzel followed Doug and the bailiff into the small conference room to the side of the courtroom.

Doug dropped his tiny frame into the conference chair with a thud.

"Doug, this is the best we are going to get. I told you that once we were unable to get the search thrown out— that was it. We either take a plea, or next week a jury is going to find you guilty."

Doug laid his head down on the table face down.

"God dammit!" Doug yelled and smacked his fist into the table.

"We tried to get you into Eastern; we tried to get you into Sacred Heart. There is just not much room to maneuver here, I'm sorry. But I think the judge will be lenient."

Doug started shaking his head and looked up, "If I rat out the people... the people that I got those— they'll fucking kill me. You don't under... you don't understand."

Phillip sighed.

"Look, I know how tough it can be. I really do. But I'll be there when you talk to the ATF guys— I can do everything I can to keep the questions to a minimum. But the fact is— this is the best you are going to do. Unless you want to risk a substantial amount of jail time. I'll try this case, Doug; I'll do my best to convince a jury that you just want to be left alone and that the Okanogan Sheriff had no right to enter your room— but if they disagree with us on that— you will most likely be found guilty."

Doug sat in silence and stared at the wall. Every few seconds he shook his head and stared down at his feet under the table.

"Are you sure I won't... sure I won't get any more jail? I have to get... get out of here. I can't take... take any more... more of this."

"I think we have a good shot, Doug. The judge just wants to make sure we know that he is not bound by the terms of the agreement. He can impose whatever sentence is allowable by law. It's the principle."

Phillip notified the bailiff that they were ready to continue. A few minutes later, the bailiff led them back into the courtroom.

"Can we move back into Mr. Perry's case here?" the judge began.

Doug's attorney moved forward, "Yes, I believe so, Your Honor. Yes, we did go over Paragraph E of the plea agreement, and Mr. Perry doesn't have any problem with that, Your Honor."

"Well, but I want to make certain that there is an understanding as to what the agreement is, and as I read the agreement, the debriefing will require Mr. Perry to fully and truthfully respond to the agent's questions as to his knowledge of other firearms and location of any other firearms and the source of firearms that, as I recall, were at the residence, were they? Were they all at the residence?"

Doug's attorney nodded, "Yes, they are all at the residence, and you're going to do that, Doug?"

Doug nodded also, "Yes."

The judge leaned forward again, "Now, does that clarify, while it's not a plea agreement in that it isn't agreed to as such, but as to that portion referred to in Paragraph E, Subparagraph 2(E)," the judge turned to his left and looked deliberately toward Ms. Johnson, "is my statement, Ms. Johnson, correct as to what the agreement is?"

"Yes, Your Honor, except when we spoke about it, I think that would include both actual and constructive possession. There were some allegations that maybe he didn't have these weapons in his home; that maybe they were located in another area," she replied.

"Yes, that would be my understanding that Mr. Perry has agreed to dutifully respond to any questions that might be propounded to him concerning any knowledge he may have as to the location of other weapons," the judge said.

Mr. Wetzel nodded, "Yes, that's correct."

The judge turned his gaze directly onto Doug, "And is that correct, Mr. Perry?"

"That's correct."

"All right. Does that cover it?" the judge asked.

Ms. Johnson nodded, "Yes."

When Doug's attorney began speaking again, a collective sigh seemed to erupt.

"Your Honor, I also wish to make it clear, " Mr. Wetzel began, "for the record, that this plea, you had stated earlier that it is not your policy to accept a plea pursuant to Rule 11(e) (1) (c), and there is a stipulation that we passed up that makes this plea under 11 (e) (1) (c). Ms. Johnson hasn't signed it because she has a problem with the wording, but that essentially is our understanding."

The judge leaned forward and brought his hands out in front of him while he shook his head.

"Well, if this is an attempted agreement to bind the court to any specific sentence, then it's not my policy to accept such pleas," he repeated.

Mr. Wetzel looked visibly frustrated, "Well, I guess, I understand that. I would ask, however, that you consider doing that, and, in fact, consider either making a decision on that after completion of the PSI [Pre-Sentencing Interview] and it is not an ill-considered agreement. It's been an arduous procedure to set it out, and I think it's one that makes a lot of sense in this case."

"Well, obviously I accept pleas where the Government has agreed to make recommendation or no recommendation, as long as that is set forth. But I, in these last nine years, have had a policy strongly urged upon me by other judges when I first came on the bench not to accept such pleas because it takes away the court's discretion. If that's the proposal, then I'll just have to reject it and we'll let the jury decide guilt or innocence, and then I'll impose what I feel is the appropriate sentence."

Doug felt his knee beginning to shake again. These people, all of them, his lawyer, their lawyer, the judge — they were out to railroad him. He could feel it.

"All right. Mr. Perry tells me that he is willing to —" Mr. Wetzel began.

Doug leaned in and whispered to his attorney.

"What?" his attorney asked with a shocked look on his face. This was beginning to unravel. He and Doug whispered back and forth.

"Okay," Mr. Wetzel sighed, "Then we don't have a plea then."

The judge sat back in his chair abruptly while Ms. Johnson stared at the opposing counsel with a blank stare.

"All right," the judge stated sternly.

Doug started shaking his head and ripped his glasses from his face. He drew his hands up through his hair and slapped his hands down on his trembling knees.

"I would state this— we intend to waive our right to a jury trial and try this case to the court," Mr. Wetzel argued.

Ms. Johnson looked at the judge and then over at Mr. Wetzel, and then back to the judge. She shook her head. The judge raised his hand toward her, motioning her to remain silent for the time being.

"Well, it isn't just your right; it's the Government's right, too," he reminded Mr. Wetzel.

Doug and his attorney were visibly upset.

"Well, I believe... well—" Mr. Wetzel muttered.

The judge looked over at Ms. Johnson, "It's set for Monday."

"Yes, I'm aware of that, Your Honor," she answered, "Originally, there was a motion to suppress scheduled for today."

Doug reached over and pulled again at his attorney's jacket.

"Oh, excuse me. Excuse me," Mr. Wetzel stated to the Court and turned to kneel next to where Doug was sitting.

For a few seconds, he and Doug whispered back and forth. Mr. Wetzel stood back up and turned to face the judge.

"I guess I misunderstood. Mr. Perry, for the record, when I asked him previously what he wanted to do, he said he wanted to go with the agreement. I asked him if that meant that he wanted to bind Your Honor, and he said, 'Yes,' and when I stated that we would go to trial, Mr. Perry said, 'I want to go with the agreement,' and what he just told me that he meant by that is that he will— basically the prosecutor's recommendations will suffice and that he will agree to plead guilty where you are not bound, Your Honor."

The Judge looked directly at Doug.

"All right. Just so you understand, Mr. Perry, if you plead guilty, even though the Government may recommend probation and no further jail time, that I'm not bound by that recommendation. Do you understand that?"

Doug did not want to go back to jail. But what choice did he really have?

"That's correct, yes," Doug answered, somewhat subdued.

"If you plead guilty to Count II, the maximum possible sentence which may be imposed, and you might check me, Miss Johnson and Mr. Wetzel on this, is incarceration for any term that I might feel is appropriate up to a maximum of ten years and/or a fine of $250,000 or both. That's the maximum possible penalty that could be imposed. Do you understand that, Mr. Perry?"

Doug just wanted it over with. He knew how the whole damn thing worked. He wasn't going to get no 10 years or $250,000 fine.

He knew it.

Everybody knew it.

Why did they have to act like it might happen?

Was it supposed to scare him?

"We are ready to enter the plea, Your Honor," Mr. Wetzel spoke up.

Doug let out an audible sigh — indicative of his utter contempt and disdain for this whole thing. All because Deputy Johnson had some sort of hard on for him.

The judge removed his glasses and stared Mr. Wetzel down again, "I want you to understand that if you wish to talk further with Mr. Perry, I want you to take the time. I'm going to be here. I have other matters that I can work on in chambers, and, Mr. Perry," he fixed his gaze toward Doug, "if you wish any more time to talk with Mr. Wetzel, I want you to take that time."

This was becoming painful.

"No," Doug quipped.

"You're ready to proceed?"

"Yes," Doug said, tersely.

Doug knew what was going to happen. As much as they tried and tried, the system in Spokane was just as easy to read and manipulate as it was up in Okanogan County. In some ways it was even easier.

They had let him out and move into the small house in the neighborhood just north of downtown across the river and up the hill.

Sure, it was crowded, and not anywhere as scenic as Pogue Flat. But it was a home. A home away from the perpetual insanity of his mother. There was no way this judge was going to do anything other than give him some jail time, suspend it, place him on community supervision, and require him to go to counseling.

He had spun this record before.

And the judge did exactly as Doug knew he would.

Omak and Okanogan were rid of Doug Perry.

For now.

Rightfully or wrongfully so, the actors and conspirators in Okanogan County had finally rid themselves of a festering lesion.

Doug Perry had been flushed into the sewer pipe.

And that pipe led right into the heart of Spokane.

Sprague Avenue.

Jon Keehner

Part II:

Clairann

14
Weed Infested Alleys

By the light of day, exhaust fumes from the Interstate descended downward onto the strip during the sweltering heat of summer, turning the asphalt jungle from hellfire to brimstone. And the sun the prison warden.

No shade.

No cool breezes.

Nothing but weed-infested alleys and sterile concrete structures. Anybody who was here wasn't here by choice. Some sort of inconvenient circumstance had drawn them here like emaciated horseflies to a wet pile of bloody stool.

Festering and vile.

Doug's reunion with his mother and brother on Pogue Flat was, by court-ordered design, very short-lived. He retrieved his personal possessions and his Pinto and made the three-hour drive back to Spokane in short order.

In a lot of ways the move felt good.

Most of his free time was spent pondering how he could find the girl from Sacred Heart, Clairann.

She made him believe the world was a better place.

Within a few weeks of his release he moved into a tiny two-bedroom in one of Spokane's older and more humble neighborhoods just north of the river and east of Division Street. The little gray house on Dalton was perfect for him. He had just enough room to live by himself in modest comfort but enough room whereby he felt he needed to tinker with projects.

That changed quickly.

Even before he received payment for the guns he was forced to surrender and sell, he was scouring the Little Nickel want ads in search of a cheap pistol to protect himself. Now that he had finally received the proceeds from the sale, he was even more impatient. He knew that if he were caught with even a .22 caliber handgun, he would be sent directly to prison for violating the conditions of his plea agreement.

But Spokane at night was not a comforting city.

The wailing of sirens, the screeching of brakes, and the dull roar of a big city were always at the forefront of his senses. His paranoid disposition was not going to be miraculously cured by his presence in Spokane. He could treat the symptoms, but underlying all of his deviant and skittish behaviors was the core belief that if he were not prepared to defend himself with a gun from violent acts perpetrated on him by others, it was only a matter of time before he met his doom.

Guns were an integral part of his very being and fiber.

He was NEVER going to give them up, no matter what the court said he had to do.

It did not take him very long and he was able to find a Makarov pistol chambered in a .22 long rifle. It certainly wasn't optimal for personal and self-defense. But a .22 was more than capable of killing a human being, especially at very close range with proper bullet placement. Not surprisingly, the .22 long rifle is considered one of the most dangerous and deadly weapons simply because there are so many of them in circulation and because so many have underestimated their killing power and not given them the healthy respect they deserve when handling, thus hurting themselves or others close by from their carelessness.

A .22 bullet to the head is nearly always fatal.

The Makarov felt good in his hand. Just like his dad's old pistol did. He was sad he had to get rid of it. He held it out in front of him and looked down the sights. Sitting in the driver's seat of his Pinto did not give him much room to maneuver, but the comfort and familiarity painted a broad grin on his otherwise expressionless facade.

It was nearly noon, and he had scheduled his counseling appointment for 10 a.m. just so he could get it over with early. The guy who sold it to him did not seem to ask too many questions and seemed happy to just get rid of the old pistol.

What a fool.

He still had a couple of thousand dollars left, and he needed to get some stuff for his house. He stopped in to 7-11 and procured a Super Big Gulp full of Coke and searched for a good rock station on his car radio. His counseling seemed to be going well, and his meds were finally leveling out.

The drive downtown took him south along the multi-lane Division Street and eventually dumped him into downtown near Riverfront Park. The past couple of weeks had been unseasonably warm even for Spokane in August, but a cool breeze seemed to be sliding in from the foothills to the east near the Idaho border and cooled things off a bit. As he came into downtown and began looking for a parking spot, the buildings fell into a creeping veil of darkness as a giant dark cloud blocked out the sun. When he finally parked and jumped out of the car he had to dart toward the sidewalk to avoid the giant raindrops from the approaching thunderstorm.

It smelled like dust.

His first stop was the small electronics store across from the 24-hour cafe he found a couple of weeks earlier when his insomnia took over his lonely nights.

Diesel smoke.

Uncharacteristically wide sidewalks.

Clans of street people with no good intention —

"Doug?"

It was the softest and sweetest voice he had ever heard and knew it in an instant. He spun around and stared past two larger men, each wearing more poorly fitting clothes than the next.

And there stood Clairann.

She was smiling and giggled as she wiped a little blood from her lip. He was surprised at how much more of a sophisticated woman she looked than when they were in Sacred Heart together. Her hair was curled and pulled upward, enormous hoop earrings dangled from her lobes and her eye make-up made her look like an Egyptian goddess. Her red lipstick was somewhat smeared where she had been wiping the blood from her cut lip.

She smelled like baby powder, fresh laundry, and what he imagined a Caribbean vacation must smell like — all rolled into one.

For a moment he just continued to stare.

Her white miniskirt and pink bikini top resembled outfits had seen girls wear in music videos. He felt his jeans grow tighter-- so much so he had to casually place his hand in his jeans pocket to adjust himself, lest he become more outwardly aroused.

"Cat's still got you tongue, I see," she quipped, still smiling like an angel.

"Uh… Clairann. Hi!" was all he could say.

The two thugs standing to either side gazed down upon him like gargoyles near the gates of some demonic lair.

She stepped between the two men toward him and outstretched her arms hoping to embrace him.

183

As was often the case in her presence, he had to remind himself to breathe.

"What are you… are you doing down… doing down here?" he asked as he pulled her into his arms and against his chest.

He turned his head ever so slightly to the side and the softness of the skin on her neck and shoulders as it rubbed on his unshaven cheeks doubled his bulge.

She placed a tissue from her handbag up to her lip, "Oh, just trying to make my way. You know. Like everybody."

Doug stood awkwardly with little to say.

"Would you like to go grab some lunch? I was just headed to the cafe," she asked and pointed across the intersection to the 24-hour cafe.

Doug swallowed.

He licked his upper lip and swallowed again without so much as a response. He had no idea how to respond or react to her.

Her beautiful likeness had occupied so many of his pre-slumber fantasies that he could hardly fathom seeing her again.

"Come on," she grabbed his arm and threw it up and under her elbow so he could escort her across the street.

Doug felt like the luckiest man on Earth.

As they sashayed through the crosswalk she continued, "So how have you been? Still pouring your heart out to the 'ones in the know?'"

The 24-hour cafe looked out across the Spokane River. It's enormous glass pane windows and spongy, baby blue and orange interior felt like a 1970s diner. The polished stainless steel and well-seasoned breakfast stools gave the cafe a quaint feel.

A pleasant-looking woman in her midthirties showed them to a booth in the back corner near the restrooms. Doug slid in, and before he could turn to look, Clairann slid in next to him and gently patted his thigh. As the menus dropped in front of them Clairann gave Doug a bright and seductive smile.

He could not believe his good fortune.

"So, tell me what you been up to," she asked and perused the menu.

Doug flipped the menu upward toward the window and poked his glasses back up the bridge of his nose from where they had slid down.

He sneezed.

"Bless you," she said without looking up from the menu.

For a moment they sat in silence.

"Well, I got my case thrown out," Doug began, unsure of what to talk about.

"Really?" she asked, seeming thrilled at his every word.

"Well, actually, I was going to take it… to take it to trial. But they knew I would win so they dropped… so they dropped it," he said uncomfortably.

Clairann seemed really impressed.

Doug was used to lying.

"I'm not surprised," she began, "you seem like a really good person. I bet you would make a good dad someday."

Doug swallowed hard and nearly choked.

"No. I mean it," she continued and put her hand on his thigh, "you seem like a really good guy and I just— I just know men pretty well and you seem like a good guy."

Doug looked right into her eyes. She was so beautiful.

"How did you get the… get the bloody lip?" he asked.

"Oh, nothing. No big deal. I just… I just tripped into the corner of the car door. It's nothing," she replied.

"So I remember you said you grew up on a farm or something?" Doug asked.

The waitress interrupted them and asked for their order.

"I'll just have water," Clairann answered.

"I'll get it," Doug insisted, "Get whatever you want— I owe you for missing your session like I .... session like I promised."

"Ok. Fine. I'll just have what you're having," she answered politely.

Without warning a mild buzzing sound began to emanate from her handbag. She reached in and pulled a little digital pager from her purse. She flipped the tiny electronic box around so she could see the digital display of the phone number someone had just called her from.

"I have to go use the phone real quick; I'll be right back," she said as she slid out from the table and stepped toward the pay phone near the restroom hallway.

The pay phone was just out of earshot, but Doug could see she seemed to be arguing with someone. For almost 15 minutes she stood with the receiver to her ear, and every once in awhile she apologized and then called whoever was on the other end a lying asshole. She eventually slammed the receiver down and returned to the table. Her food had already been placed on the table.

"Guess I was gone a little longer than I thought," she giggled.

The waitress on duty and the hostess stood near the cashiering counter and glared at her.

She knew.

They knew.

"So, do you have any... do you have any kids?" Doug asked as he finished eating the stack of pancakes the waitress had brought over.

Clairann kept eating.

"I had a daughter. And a son. But they don't live with me. They are— well one is with—" she stopped herself. "Well my little boy, he is with my parents back in Sequim."

"Oh that's right, you said you grew up on a farm?" Doug asked trying to move the subject to something she was more comfortable with.

She recognized his attempt to ease the conversation, and her heart felt just a little warmth toward him.

What a sweet guy.

"Yeah, I grew up on a big farm that my grandparents started; my dad was born here, but his family was from Switzerland, but my mother actually moved here from Switzerland. She was brought here like a breeding cow," Clairann began, her voice changing drastically.

Doug could tell that home was not a happy subject for her. He tried to change the subject.

"Yeah, so... I don't have to do any... do any jail time."

"I thought they dropped the charges?" she quickly retorted.

Doug had been caught in his lie.

For nearly a minute both of them sat in silence. The clanking of glasses and small talk hung above the scraping of silverware on the plates. They each had their own shortcomings— no need to bring them under such heavy scrutiny.

They were having such a good lunch.

"It's no biggie," Clairann finally laughed, "I've been arrested so many times I can't really even count them."

Doug laughed in surprise thinking that was what she wanted him to do.

"Do you think you could give me a ride up the hill toward Deer Park?" she asked as the waitress cleared the table.

"A ride? In my... you mean in my... yeah... yeah I can do that," he answered.

After taking care of the bill they skipped and giggled their way through the streets of downtown to Doug's car. Her pager buzzed at her nearly every 5 minutes but she tried to ignore it as much as she could. Even as socially encumbered as Doug was to the ways of the fairer sex, even he could tell she was getting irritated every time the pager went off. Finally she asked Doug to pull the car into the parking lot at the 7-11 where she could use the phone booth. With her pager in hand she threw open the door of Doug's car and marched toward the phone. Thirty minutes later she returned.

Annoyed.

"Well," she sighed loudly, "looks like I'll need to go to a motel or something. Can't go home tonight—

"What?! *Why?*" Doug asked her intently.

"I don't want to talk about it," she quipped back.

Doug felt confused.

She just stared out the side of the car and sighed.

"You could stay at... stay at my house?" Doug offered innocently.

With a brisk purpose, Clairann turned toward him grinning from ear to ear.

"Are you sure?" she asked, almost mockingly.

"Of course. It's my... it's my house!"

Doug started the engine and slipped back onto Division and headed back toward Spokane. Like an orphan waiting to see her new-found family, Clairann stared at row after row of the small, two-bedroom homes in north Spokane, wondering which one was his. Finally, he slowed the little car down and pulled into a driveway leading a few feet to a tiny square house.

It was wonderful.

"This is *your house?*" she asked, bemused.

Inside, Doug showed her where the bathroom was and let her know he could sleep on the sofa if she felt more comfortable. She smiled at his sense of chivalry or perhaps (she thought) his deluded innocence. Either way, she wasn't sleeping in the Spokane Motel with two other whores and a pimp who wanted to beat the shit out of her for not giving him his cut of a night's worth of blow jobs and thigh fucks.

Doug spent most of the afternoon and evening showing her his Makarov pistol and his enormous collection of VHS movies. He entertained her with stories from his childhood playing in the meadows and valleys surrounding the orchards of Pogue Flat. How his lovely mother could bake the best apple cobbler ever tasted and how his older brother, Larry, had introduced Doug to a small organization of gun buyers and how Doug was going to be their sole consultant on gun purchases. He explained how the community in Omak wanted Doug to run for public office some day and how respected and liked he was among his neighbors.

Eventually Clairann grew tired of Doug's endless stories about government conspiracies, liberty, and guns. She just wanted to get the inevitable payment for her night's lodgings out of the way so she could go to sleep.

She hadn't slept in nearly 48 hours.

Without warning she pulled him to the sofa and reached over to turn off the lamp on the end table.

Doug was confused.

He seemed a little on the shy side and she could quickly tell that this was probably his first time.

"A virgin, eh?" she laughed.

Doug looked at her with a cumbersome glance.

"No... no, not at all. I... I—."

"Whoa!" she giggled again, "It's ok, it's no big deal. I just mean, where—"

She reached over and slipped her hand in between his pants and abdomen. Most guys knew to draw their breath in a little bit to allow her hand to slip down where it needed to be.

He did not.

"I've done it... done it lots o' times," he continued, nearly losing his breath.

She knew better.

Doug just sat there with a blank stare on his face. It was all happening so fast.

She shifted sideways in the sofa and turned her hips toward Doug so she could gain a little more leverage to get her hand down his pants. As she did, her skirt slid up further exposing her thighs. He noticed how smooth and soft they were, and he just wanted to reach over and slide his hand along them and up to her hips.

"It's ok. Just relax. I'll do all the work, honey," she reminded Doug as she forced her little hand down onto his cock. He was already rock hard.

"Can I....uh," Doug swallowed hard and nearly choked he was so nervous, "Can I... can... I touch your thigh?"

As the last words trailed out of his mouth he was nearly whispering.

She flipped open the button fly on his pants and pulled his member out of his underwear. It was already glistening from his secretions. Stroking his cock gently, she leaned forward and nodded her head yes, he could touch her if he wanted.

As the tip of his cock slid into her mouth he gasped. Somehow he managed to reach over and slide her white skirt further up her thigh almost exposing her ass. Her thigh was bruised, black and purple, nearly the size of a fist.

Within a minute, and with little effort, she worked Doug to climax. He groaned and shuddered. She spit the fruits of her labor into a little plastic cup she pulled from her purse.

Doug could not believe what had just happened.

He wanted to fuck her so bad — but it was over so quick.

Without a word she pulled the blanket off of the back of the sofa and cuddled herself into Doug's arms as he still lay there wondering how life had gotten so good. She pulled the VCR remote off of the end table and pushed play.

Before long they were both fast asleep.

When Doug awoke the next morning he felt the emptiness of the blanket where Clairann had been sleeping.

Where was she?

Slowly he rose from the sofa and quietly walked toward the bathroom to piss.

She must have slept in his bedroom.

He flushed the toilet, stared at himself in the mirror and wondered whether he should wake her up or not. It was nearly 10:30 a.m. Without a sound he slowly turned the doorknob to his bedroom door. As tightly as he could he pressured the door open ever so slowly so as not to make so much as a squeak. He peeked inside.

She was not there.

"Clairann," he said down the hall, raising his voice just a little.

The house wasn't that big.

Had she gone out on the back porch for a cigarette?

He slipped through the small kitchen and peered through the glass window in the door leading from the kitchen to the back yard.

Nothing.

He turned and quickly went to the front living room window and looked out onto Dalton Avenue.

Clairann was gone.

And so was his little red Pinto.

15

A Night He Would Never Forget

Fucking bitch.

He could not believe she stole his car. He clenched his fists and raised them to his face.

He wanted to scream.

He wanted to throw a chair through the front window.

He couldn't even think right.

He had to call the cops, but she knew all about his Makarov pistol and could quickly make life an absolute chore.

"FUCKKK!!" he screamed as he strode into the kitchen, changed directions and paced down the hall, and then back toward the living room.

Women were all the same.

Fucking cunts.

They smile at you and they bat their eyelashes at you and they smell good.

They destroy you and they torture you.

He had to think.

There had to be something he could do.

Without warning the back door leading from the porch into the kitchen sprang open with a slam into the counter.

There stood Clairann with a bag of groceries in her hand.

She dropped Doug's keys down onto the table as she wrestled with the bag of groceries.

"Good morning!" she smiled, "I didn't think you'd be up yet. I hope you don't mind I took your car to the store. I wanted to make breakfast— it was the least I could do."

She reached up and rubbed her nose.

Doug drew in a deep breath and let it out with a sigh.

He should have known he was being paranoid. He and his counselors had discussed his obsessions for years. But it did not matter. Even with the meds he was just never going to be normal.

She was gorgeous.

Clairann took off her sun glasses and clumsily dropped them toward the floor. She tried to reach and grab them real quick, but she could not quite get them in her grasp. She nearly fell down with them.

She sniffed and rubbed her arm across her nose again.

"What?" she asked, shaking her head.

Doug looked at her, puzzled.

She started unloading items from the bag. Cupboard doors slammed and the refrigerator door squeaked open and closed.

Doug stood in the living room near the entrance to the kitchen. He fantasized that she was his woman, performing her domestic chores for him. After cooking his breakfast she would freshen herself up, look pretty, and have sex with him.

He imagined that she would be his lover, his best friend and companion forever.

She was so beautiful.

"What do you want to do today?" she asked, snapping Doug from his daydream.

He looked outside the window at the warm summer skies.

"Hold on, let me go pee first," she said as she slipped past him toward the bathroom.

Doug sat back on the sofa and turned on the television. Without much of interest on TV, he fetched the newspaper up from the end table and slowly began thumbing through the pages.

Spokane was a bustling city. So much happening and so much to do. It seemed everywhere in town there was stuff happening. Crime. Politics. Sports. Spokane had it all.

What is taking her so long?

Doug stood up from the sofa and carefully folded the newspaper marking where he was reading so he could lay it on the coffee table. He slipped down the hall and could hear Clairann sniffing heavily through the door.

"Are you OK?" Doug asked.

"Oh yeah, sorry. Sorry I'm fine. Just give me a minute. Woman things, ya' know?"

Doug remembered that his mother often had odd, extended liaisons in the bathroom. Exploring their meanings and ramifications was never of interest to him.

Doug returned to the sofa and continued to read the paper. Outside on the street he could see neighbors pruning their landscaping, washing their cars, and enjoying other activities. He loved the little neighborhood.

"Sorry," Clairann said as she stepped through the living room and back into the kitchen.

She drew in a deep sniff through her nose and wiped her arm across her face again. Doug thought he saw a small chunk of white powder-like stuff fall from her face as she wiped.

He paid it no mind.

After breakfast they decided to go down to Riverfront Park in Spokane for the afternoon. Clairann wanted to get all "dressed up" for him and asked if he would take her to a friend's place who was staying at the Spokane Motel. The motel was only a few blocks east of the park, and he could drop her off and then pick her up an hour or so later.

"I'll be back around one," Doug smiled as she opened the door to hop out of his car.

Clairann wiped her nose and smiled as she got out of the car without saying a word. He was hoping she might kiss him goodbye, some sort of sign as to where things were heading, but he did not want to push it.

He still needed to obtain some better cookware, and after running into Clairann the day before, he needed to resume his errands. The downtown district holding all of the shops he needed was just across the river from the park. The convenience of living in a bigger city like Spokane was beginning to brighten his spirits.

And so was the love of a pretty girl like Clairann.

And he loved her, too.

Inside the kitchen wares and cooking shop he found himself surrounded by hanging pots and pans of all shapes and sizes. Wire baskets, spoons, serving ladles and all manner of utensils adorned the walls and ceiling racks. Stainless steel, chrome, bronze, and Teflon.

It was everywhere.

The air-conditioned shop felt good. It smelled like Moroccan leather and lavender oil with a hint of bold citrus. He knew he was in the right place. As he browsed the cooking wares he imagined Clairann clinging to his arm next to him, lovingly advising him on what to buy — wanting to give her input as well.

He could see himself living with her.

Part of him was sad that she was not there to help him choose what to buy. He thought for a moment that maybe he should wait— that this could become part of the date he had planned for the rest of the afternoon?

No. Why would she want to be saddled with the task of outfitting his tiny little kitchen at this stage of the relationship?

But he wanted her so badly.

He strolled up and down the aisles of the shop searching for the best deal he could find. He wanted cookware that showed her he was sophisticated and stylish, but neither too frugal— nor too extravagant. Something that would impress her and show her that he was the one for her as well.

Finally, he found it. The perfect set of black Teflon with stainless steel handles and accents. It was contemporary yet refined. It had class and charm as well as utility. It was as perfect as she was.

399 dollars?

For a second he hesitated. Spending that much money on a cookware set might be foolish. But she would love it. He could tell she loved to cook.

But 399 dollars?

He stared at the box, flipping it from end to end, reading every word.

Fuck it.

He wrestled the box up under his arm and nearly knocked a display of new glassware off of one of the shelves as he navigated the aisles toward the cashier counter. He plopped the big box up onto the counter and pushed his glasses back up his nose while he brushed the hair from where it had fallen in front of his eyes. He reached back into his jeans pocket and removed his wallet.

He opened it carefully and thumbed through the stack of hundred-dollar bills as he counted them.

1600?

He immediately counted them again.

"Take your time," the young woman standing behind the counter politely said.

13…14…15…16.

16?

He was sure the day he went to the bank he pulled $2000 from his account.

Had he dropped some when he paid for lunch at the cafe?

Not wanting to cause a stir he gave the clerk $500 and waited as she counted out his change and handed him the receipt. She pulled a large, wide mouthed bag from beneath the counter and carefully placed the box of cookware into it and handed it to Doug.

"Thank you," she said.

Doug turned and slipped his wallet back into his back pocket.

He was positive he had $2000. How could he have lost $400?

The 24-hour cafe was only a few blocks away, so he opened the rear hatch of his car and set the bag containing the box of cookware into the rear cargo area and closed the hatch. He looked at his watch; he still had at least 40 minutes remaining on his parking meter, and Clairann would not be expecting him for at least another half an hour.

He drew in a deep breath and sighed. He reached back and pulled his wallet and counted the money again.

He was short by $400. He knew it.

The streets of downtown did not seem too busy, and with a little time to kill, he decided maybe there was a chance the money had fallen out of his wallet and one of the waitresses had picked it up and was just waiting for someone to come and claim it.

As he approached the cafe he was relieved to see the same waitress working the tables near the back foyer. He could see her through the giant glass windows, and he gave her a pensive wave as he walked to the front entrance.

She smiled and nodded back.

Whew.

"Hey, how are you? I was just... was just in here last night... night with my *girlfriend* — and I —" Doug began.

The girl working as a hostess the day before laughed out loud as Doug said girlfriend.

"*Girlfriend?*" she blurted out, "Is that what you call 'em now?"

The older waitress looked at the young girl with stern disapproval. The younger girl knew she was being rude and quickly removed herself from the front counter area.

"I remember you, yes. Yesterday. What can I do for you?" the waitress asked as she turned her attention back toward Doug.

"I think I might have... I might have dropped some money... money when I paid the bill?" he asked.

The waitress wanted to laugh out loud herself. She knew exactly what had probably happened. She had seen it all working in this 24-hour cafe. But the girls were some of her most loyal and regular customers. She learned early not to judge. They were paying customers just like everybody else — and as long as you gave them some respect and tried to treat them like the human beings they were, they were pretty good tippers.

"Sorry, hun," she simply shook her head.

Doug looked under the tables near the booth they were sitting at the day before, and satisfied that his $400 was not to be found, he resigned himself to his loss and walked back to his car.

How the hell did I lose $400?

When Doug arrived back at the Spokane Motel he parked right out across the street from the entrances to the rooms. He was a little earlier than he had told her, so he figured he should just wait patiently until one o'clock, and then she would probably be right out.

The afternoon was getting hot, and sitting in a parked car along the asphalt jungle wasn't helping.

A few minutes after 1 p.m. he tapped on the horn to let her know he was out front. He thought back to when she got out of the car, but he was so distracted by whether or not she would kiss him goodbye he forgot to pay attention to which room she had gone into.

At 1:15 he honked a little longer.

At 1:20 he was getting impatient and honked three times in a row for about 10 seconds each. He was sure she would have heard that.

Finally, the door from unit #3 opened and a large man in a white undershirt and tight track shorts emerged from the doorway and stared right across the street at Doug. He was nearly bald, and tufts of jet-black hair that matched his enormous mustache braced the side of his head like bad breath. Every space of bare skin that was visible was covered in the most horrendous tattoos.

He looked downright mean.

"Honk that fucking horn again, and I'll beat your little faggot ass!" he hollered toward Doug.

Doug gulped.

Who the fuck was this guy?

It did not really matter. Doug started his car and prepared to flee as fast as he could.

But Clairann?

He took a deep breath and felt for his backpack on the seat behind him. He could feel the pistol inside the pocket closest to him and he relaxed just a little.

The man stared at him for another moment and turned back inside.

Just after the man disappeared into the motel room, the door to unit #4 opened and out stepped the hottest-looking woman he had ever laid eyes on.

It was his Clairann.

She was wearing pink spiked heels, jean shorts, and a sleeveless white blouse with huge pink buttons. Her makeup looked refined and not over the top like he had seen her the night before. Her perfume reminded him of the girls on the ceiling back on Pogue Flat.

"Sorry, I'm late," she said as she slid into the passenger seat of his car. She slipped her hand onto his cheek and kissed him gently on the lips, "the wait will be worth it, *I promise.*"

Doug could hardly hold himself back.

"Where are we going?" she asked and played with her hair while looking in the mirror.

"Have you ever taken the gondola over the falls?" he asked.

She had been on more than a dozen dates over the falls.

She had *fucked* Johns in the gondolas.

She had *blown* Johns in the gondolas.

She even fisted a Jane over the falls on a date once.

"No!" she exclaimed with glee, "I have always wanted to though!"

Everywhere the two of them walked, Clairann hung on his arm like a candy cane on a Christmas tree. She knew how men needed that every once in a while. It was part of their masculinity. She knew how to use it to her advantage.

Every few minutes she needed to stop in the ladies room and freshen her makeup. For some reason she could not stop wiping her nose. Doug wondered if she had gotten a cold or something.

As they strolled around the park watching young families with strollers and leaping children chasing the ducks and geese around, Doug told her stories of growing up on the orchard and how he just wanted to live a simple life and be left alone. He rubbed the side of her index finger as they held hands and walked along the path beside the river. Whenever they stopped he stood behind her and pulled her into his arms so her hair rubbed below his chin.

It felt so soft.

Every time she left his embrace to keep walking, she purposefully pushed her ass into his groin and wiggled it just a little, teasing him.

And it was working.

He could feel the wetness inside his underpants.

It made his blood tingle.

After an hour of lust-filled meanderings and sexual innuendos they made their way to the gondola entrance. The gondola was built for the Spokane Expo of 1974 and carried up to 4 passengers out along the river, over a series of staircased falls next to the old electricity power house and then back. It took about 20 minutes to make the round trip. It was one of Spokane's more popular attractions.

A gentle breeze up the river created a bit of a spray of water as they crossed the falls. Clairann giggled and pointed like a schoolgirl.

Doug loved her.

He wanted her.

Clouds were whiter and the sky was bluer when she was with him.

After they had passed the falls she looked over at him and began kissing him excitedly on the lips. Her left hand caressed his rough cheek and her right hand reached down and felt him through his pants.

She smiled broadly at him and her eyes twinkled like stars.

He had no idea how to respond. The only experience he ever had of this kind were the fantasies that played out nightly in his imagination before bed.

This was new.

He could not wait to get her back home to his little house and make love to her. They would make love, and watch movies on his VCR and cuddle in his bed. She would wake up and make him breakfast and they would spend Sunday afternoon together.

And Sunday night.

And the next day.

He would ask her to move in and they would be together.

She tried to unbutton his pants and he pulled her hand back.

"Wait until we get home," he begged with a smile.

"*Home?*" she smiled widely, "That's fine. But, we need to stop back by Marilyn's motel room, OK?"

"Who's Marilyn?" he asked still trying to kiss her.

Clairann pulled back and adjusted her hair. It was obvious he was not going to fuck her on the gondola.

"My friend at the Spokane Motel. You saw her. She's *black?* You don't have anything against black people do you?"

Doug was mortified. He could not tell her how he really felt; that would ruin everything.

"No... no... of course not," he laughed.

"Good!" Clairann continued to smile, "Her real name is Yolanda, but just call her Marilyn when you meet her. And never use her real name, Yolanda — *never.*"

Without realizing how much time had passed they realized they were back at the end of the ride. Doug jumped out and took her hand like a prince leading his princess from a stagecoach.

This was going to be a night he would never forget.
In so many ways.

16
The Chaos and Carnivàle

The intersection of Short Avenue and Spokane Street was becoming comfortably familiar to him. The incessantly flowing streams of dust, smoke and utter foulness worked to clog out any hope of those who found themselves washed up on Sprague Avenue.

Or any of the adjoining rodent-infested streets and dead alleyways.

Tonight, however, the atmosphere surrounding the motel bristled with activity.

It felt like a street fair.

She jumped from his car nearly even before he had stopped moving as he parallel parked on Short Avenue.

"I'll be just a minute!" she hollered over her shoulder with a grin.

He watched as she crossed the roadway and disappeared into unit #4. He turned the key to his ignition all the way back so he could listen to the radio while he waited. He knew she wouldn't be long. This was going to be a night like he had only imagined before. These kinds of things didn't happen to people like him.

He was surprised to see so many people going in and out of all the units — even for a Saturday night. Surprisingly, people were going into unit #4 where Clairann went.

Maybe her friend Marilyn was hosting a party?

After nearly an hour the situation was becoming alarmingly reminiscent of the day's earlier events.

He dared not honk the horn.

He leaned forward, pressing the steering wheel into his chest as he struggled to look through all of the people loitering in front of the units.

Street pimps. Gangbangers. Drug dealers.

The typical Rogue's Gallery of thugs and ruffians.

Despite the obvious danger, he had to go see what was going on.

Was Clairann in trouble?

As he approached the small group of people gathered around the front of the motel he could see that most of them appeared vagrant or otherwise homeless. Some of them seemed to be wearing clothes that were so oddly out of character that the garments must have been donated.

Gently he tapped on the door to unit #4. A few moments later the door swung open and there stood a pretty, black woman.

Doug smiled, "You must be Marilyn?"

His polite greeting did nothing to change the expression on her face or her posture blocking the doorway.

She looked unamused.

Inside the motel room Doug was shocked at the cloud of thick smoke permeating the air. It didn't smell or look like any cigarette smoke he had ever seen before.

And it smelled like diesel or ether.

He could barely see the opposite wall clearly through the smoke. In the dim lighting he could make out nearly five or six figures standing in what he surmised was the kitchenette portion of the motel unit.

"I'm here to get Clairann," he struggled saying as he tried to peer around the woman blocking the doorway.

"She decided she gonna stay," Marilyn answered, still expressionless.

This was not what Doug was expecting.

He struggled with what to do next.

"Can I just talk to her for a second?" he asked as he tried to gain entry to the motel room.

Marilyn stepped into his path and put her arm up on his chest. As she did so, a taller, thin, black man wearing what seemed like five or six gold necklaces stepped out from the darkness and shoved Doug back into the entryway.

"You got a fucking problem, *little man?*" he yelled at Doug, "Boy! I beat yo' ass you come 'roun here with that shit. You feel me?"

Doug was horrified.

His Makarov was back in the car.

The small crowd of people outside had suddenly focused their attention on Doug and the big man who was about to beat his ass. Everyone loves to watch a train wreck.

Doug knew there was no way he was going toe to toe with this guy. His best bet was just to go back to his car and wait.

Whack!

Doug's face felt like it was on fire and frozen at the same time. His glasses went flying off of his face, and he nearly spun himself into the bushes. The man had slapped him with an open palm like Doug was some kind of bitch.

"Now you know," the man yelled and came toward Doug again.

Doug's blood was beginning to tingle.

"GET THE FUCK OUT OF HERE!" came the black woman's voice as she flew out the door of her motel, "I don't need that shit!"

He Said, She Said: The Spokane River Killer

The man who was going after Doug looked at her with disgust.

"I gotta' be back in Tacoma anyways. You all fuck this shit," he retorted back and strode across the street.

Doug had been granted a reprieve.

He felt around the gravel for his glasses and tossed them back onto his face.

"You run along now, ya hear?" Marilyn looked at Doug, "Joan is done with you for the night."

"Joan?" he said, confused.

"Clairann, Joan… Joan, Clairann— whatever you call her. SHE AINT COMIN'," Marilyn commanded as she turned back for her door, "Beat it. Or you get yo ass beat fo sho."

What a shit show.

Doug knew when a situation was out of his control. He was not completely naive to the chaos and carnivàle of street life.

Plans and maneuvers filled his thoughts as he crossed the river on Green Avenue and motored back up the hill toward his house.

He could kill them all and go in and get her. He had extra magazines and more than enough ammo.

But there were so many people around.

He would never get away with it.

Maybe he would go track that dumb nigger down that had bitch-slapped him. And kill him.

How had a day going so well gone so bad, so fast?

He raised his fists and smashed them both against the steering wheel as he let out a loud scream of frustration.

He could go back down and park around the corner?

Perhaps she would come back out and he could at least talk to her. Something had to have happened. Most of her boyfriends probably got mad when she did this— but he wanted to be different than her other boyfriends. He wanted to be supportive. He was OK if she had to do things a little different. No one was perfect. She just needed to know that he was ok with her.

He had to let her know.

He could call the police and say that a bunch of illegal shit was going down and they would raid the place and then he could talk to her.

He slid the little car into a spot on the street out front of his house. There had to be something he could do.

For hours he sat inside the house with the lights off and stared out the window. He palmed his Makarov like he was making love to it.

He knew he should have asked for her pager number. But why? She was coming up to the house for the night with him.

This was so fucked up.

A plan.

He had to come up with a plan.

It was what he was good at.

Even as a kid growing up on the Flat he was always the one who came up with the best tactics and strategies for whatever objective he and Dwight were seeking.

But what to do about this eluded him.

Women.

Can't live with 'em... can't kill 'em.

* * *

Bam! Bam! Bam!

"Doug?" her voice called out quietly.

The banging on his back door startled him awake. He had fallen asleep on the couch trying to figure out what to do.

Clairann?

It was nearly 4 a.m.

He flipped the switch turning on the back porch light, and there stood Clairann, softly crying at his back door. Her lip was cut open, one of her eyes was nearly swollen shut, and the left side of her forehead was bruised black and purple.

Someone had obviously beat the shit out of her.

Through all of the disfigured swelling, she managed a smile as Doug opened the back door and pulled her into his arms.

She started to sob.

He didn't care what had happened. He just had her now. There was no way he could be mad at her. There had to be a logical explanation. And even if there wasn't, he could pretend there was, just to keep the peace.

He pulled her in tighter.

She looked up at him as though she wanted him to kiss her. As he moved toward her lips she turned away and dropped a laugh of pure denial.

"My mouth hurts," she giggled.

He pulled her back into his arms.

My Clairann.

Her blouse was stained with soil near the collar, one of the over-sized pink buttons was completely missing, and another was dangling by a thread. Her ear was even bleeding where it looked like one of her hoop earrings had been torn from her earlobe.

She was a mess.

Both of her knees had been bleeding, and a dried stream of blood ran down her left calf clear to her ankle. Her feet were bare and covered in the detritus of a long walk through the asphalt, weeds, and gravel of Spokane's deliverance into legitimacy.

Doug led her into the bedroom and retrieved a wet washcloth from the bathroom and handed it to her. As she began cleaning her feet and legs he fetched a larger towel. He sat down on the bed next to her.

"I know you wanted to fuck... but... I just..." she began.

Doug was caught off guard by her direct nature.

As she tried to wipe her forehead, he placed his hand over the top of hers and helped guide the washcloth to where it might do the most good.

She smiled and gasped in pain at the same time.

"There is so much about me you don't know," she said quietly.

She leaned backwards and fell onto the bed.

Doug helped pull her jean shorts off of her, and she took off her blouse. In one fluid motion she slipped under the covers.

Her naked body, in view for a brief moment, beautiful in its shape and form, was covered in scars, bruises, and welt marks.

He felt like crying with her.

"Cuddle with me," she softly suggested as she rolled away from him onto her side, "and I'll tell you things."

Doug quickly undressed and climbed under the covers with her.

"So... remember when you said you were going to come to my session at Sacred Heart?" she began.

Doug felt a wave of guilt and shame swell over him even though missing her session was out of his control.

"Well... that was multiples meeting to try and introduce you," she continued.

She pulled herself from his embrace and rolled over onto her back and slid up toward the headboard, placing a pillow beneath her head. Doug did likewise.

"Multiples?" Doug quizzed.

"When I go off my meds, they start to come out. Without my meds, I can have more than a dozen personalities. I can't control them all."

"But you seem normal to me—"

"Watching you struggle with the obvious, is... well... cute," she said.

"I'm a Sprague Avenue whore. It is what it is. I can't go back to Sequim. My ex-husband— well— I can't. My kids—"

Doug fell silent.

A prostitute.

"If I don't do what needs to be done, then this is what happens," she continued.

She turned her head away from him and groaned. A few seconds later she started to sob.

"I don't know what to do!" she cried.

Doug put her hand into his.

"You can stay here, with me? You never have to go back to that life, ever. I can pay the rent, and you can get back on your meds, and we can go to group. It will—"

"Shhhh..." she interrupted him.

"No. I *mean it*," Doug argued.

He sat up and looked right at her.

"You can stay here. None of them ever have to know where it is. This can be your hideout. Your place away from it all. I'll get you a key, and you can decorate and do whatever you want to. It will be your house also!"

Clairann had seen this routine a hundred times before. If she had a dime for every new trick that wanted to save her from the streets... problem was, how were they going to save her from herself?

"That sounds... really nice," she sat up and looked affectionately into his eyes, "Do you really mean it? Because I have heard this before..."

"Yes!" Like I said, this will be your hideout. You are safe here. No one will ever know where you live. None of your—"

"Pimps," she filled in his thought for him.

"Yeah— your pimps. No one! No one can ever know. You'll be safe here. And I'll be here waiting, always... to help you with whatever you need. We can go to group together... and we can—"

"Enough. *I get it*," she finally acquiesced, "I would love to live here. It will be wonderful!"

"You mean it?" Doug asked emphatically.

"Yes!" she laughed, "It will be my little retreat away from all the bullshit."

Doug wanted to pull her into his arms right there and make love to her. But she was in such pain and discomfort. He would have to wait. But she was moving in with him and leaving that life behind.

What a night.

In the morning he awoke, and he felt across the bed, and she was not there. He flailed across to the other nightstand and grabbed his glasses. He could hear the water running.

She was in the shower.

The splashing of the water against the curtain, the screaming of the pipes and the rattling of shampoo bottles was a beautiful sound to him.

He had cuddled her all night as she slept in his arms.

It was all he could do not to join her in the shower.

Patience.

He pulled on his underwear and slipped quietly down the hall toward the kitchen to surprise her with breakfast when she emerged, renewed, from the shower.

As Doug came around the corner he gasped in fright.

"Morning. You must be Doug," a woman with a gravelly voice said and stood up from his kitchen table.

What the fuck?

"Who the fuck are you! And what are you doing in my house?" Doug yelled.

She put her cigarette out in the coffee cup and waved away the cloud of smoke hovering in his kitchen.

"I'm Clairann's friend, Shannon," she said extending her hand.

Doug heard the bathroom door open and Clairann emerged wrapped in a blue bath towel.

"I see you met Shannon," she smiled.

"We just did," Shannon quipped as she sat and lit another smoke.

"Could you do that outside?" Doug implored looking back and forth between Clairann and Shannon in utter amazement.

"Oh. Yeah. Sure," Shannon said.

"NO," Clairann piped up, "This is my house too, and she can smoke in here."

Doug looked at her somewhat dismayed. But she was right. If he was going to share his home, she had the right to make the rules as well.

Shannon froze and looked at them both, "Look. We need to get going as soon as you're dressed. So I'll just wait outside, eh?"

Doug looked back at Clairann.

"Get going?" he wondered aloud.

"Yeah, I just... I mean... yeah I just got to get some things, you know? I'll be right back."

By now, he knew better.

*   *   *

It had been weeks since he had seen Clairann. Having finally gotten her pager number, he had paged her numerous times and even gone over to the Spokane Motel hoping to find her. At first he would knock on the door and explain that she was expecting him. But every time 'Marilyn' or 'Yolanda' or whatever her name really was would rebuke him. He even parked across the street and waited and watched hoping to see her— but the guy in unit #2 had seen him so many times that he told Doug if he saw him again he would beat his ass.

Doug fantasized that he could just kill the fucker, but he didn't want any trouble while he was on probation. He even tried leaving notes at the door. Once he even had flowers delivered.

Nothing.

As the loneliness of Spokane started to set in and eat at him, he started trolling Sprague Avenue for prostitutes hoping he would see her. He would get tricks and pay them for hand jobs and blow jobs and obsess if they knew Clairann. He eventually met a whore name Shelley who claimed she knew where to find Clairann. He took her back to his house to fuck for $40, but when he went into the bathroom to piss, he returned to find that she, along with all the cash in his wallet, was gone.

He hated these whores with a passion.

They were liars and thieves.

If it weren't for them he would have his Clairann.

If it weren't for them he could live his life in obscurity and peace with his love, his best friend, his beautiful Clairann.

He just had to find her.

In August of 1989, Doug was cited for patronizing a prostitute. He agreed to deferred prosecution and a recommendation of 12 months of community supervision. He was now on state probation as well as federal probation.

Rather than place him in jail, both the United States of America and the State of Washington had taken responsibility for supervising his activities.

But he had to have Clairann.

And he had plenty of time to think about how.

He had a plan.

Nothing, or no one, would get in his way.

Ever.

17

The Darkness and Frigid Air

Within a few months, Clairann started showing up on Doug's doorstep like a stray dog. Of course, Doug took her in hoping he would finally have the storybook life he wanted. Sometimes she would stay for a day and sometimes she would stay a couple of weeks. But in the end she always disappeared under some unforeseen and tragic circumstance.

A circumstance she could not control without medication.

Her medication took the form of cocaine, heroin, or whatever en vogue substance lined the pockets of Spokane's drug dealing establishment.

He made her promise she would not interact with Yolanda or Shannon or Wiggy or any of the stupid whores who always seemed to be there in her moments of weakness. Doug begged and pleaded with her to stay off Sprague.

He demanded it.

Regardless of his pleadings to the contrary, Clairann would never stay on her meds or take her treatment seriously. Despite her occasionally normal outward behaviors and appearance, she was severely mentally ill, and no amount of good will or positive affirmation was going to change it. Much like Doug, the criminal justice system was as close as she could get to an effective intervention on her behalf.

The blind leading the blind.

In late October of 1989 she showed up at Doug's doorstep strung out and needing to convalesce. She had been beaten rather brutally by a cocaine dealer from Seattle, and the dealer made it very clear that if he had to come looking for her again, he would not allow her to survive the next beating.

She believed him.

Fear can become an effective motivator when properly applied.

Unlike other times, Clairann finally started to pull herself from the brink of the abyss. She and Doug settled into as normal a routine as two severely mentally ill people with limited resources could do.

As winter settled into the Inland Empire of eastern Washington, the snows so prevalent in Spokane made it more difficult for them to get down off the hill, across the river, and downtown to their appointments. Doug decided they needed a four-wheel-drive vehicle — but they had little extra money considering his continuous additions to his firearms collection. Eventually he found a white, 1969 International Scout 4x4.

It was cheap and along with his little red Pinto, gave him enormous utility.

Besides having four-wheel drive to get them around Spokane in the snow, he could open up the back tailgate and haul trash to the dump, pack in bags of groceries, and when it was all said and done, because the vehicle had no carpet-- he could clean it by hosing out the rubber interior.

Although Doug had oft been played the fool by Clairann, his expectations were guarded, and he slowly began to assert a small amount of dominance over her.

And it seemed to be working.

By Thanksgiving she had not slipped back even once. Doug was regularly meeting with his counselors and maintaining his medication regimen.

Clairann was doing the best she could, given the circumstance. Her meds made her feel "horribly unfamiliar to herself," but she and Doug were making it work. She kept her pager so that Doug could communicate with her when he needed to, but the pages hailing from Sprague Avenue and the surrounding streets continued to wane as Christmas approached.

No calls from whores needing rides.

No calls from whores needing a place to hide from their pimp.

No calls from whores missing their friend they called "Joan."

As the 1980s came to an end, Doug and Clairann spent New Year's Eve with each other. Clairann's counselors had suggested she might start going to Narcotics Anonymous (NA) meetings again. Doug, who rarely partook in the types of drugs that plagued Clairann, supported her in every way he could.

And that meant learning to trust her.

Slowly at first.

As she began to venture out more and more on her own, that little, nagging feeling that this might be the time she goes "on a run" for a few days or weeks, reared its destructive head less and less. Clairann even began taking the bus downtown as she needed. The 1990s were going to be a decade of promise and hope.

Her NA meetings were held a few blocks away from the house in the basement of a community church. It was so close that when Doug was out running errands or napping, she could quietly slip out the door and take in the bracing air of the Spokane winters as she slowly paced her way through the old neighborhood.

As she walked along the sidewalk, she became more and more familiar with the neighbors. Which ones were old and retired. Which ones were new, young couples with kids. Which ones were rented from folks with poor intentions.

They were all there.

But she was free of the life.

Sprague's tentacles had been severed.

In early February, an enormous snowstorm dumped almost 24 inches of snow on Spokane over a week-long period. It was nothing out of the ordinary for the people of Spokane. The city and county were always prepared for the winter weather, but in February of 1990, the snow storm was followed by a few weeks of brutally cold and clear weather. The piles and berms of snow plowed into parking lots and street corners froze into giant mountains of ice.

On Tuesdays, Clairann regularly volunteered to show up early, unlock the church basement, and make coffee for the regular 5 p.m. meeting.

She had hoped that Doug might drive as it was bitterly cold out. The little thermometer he had hung outside the living room window showed that it was 5 degrees Fahrenheit.

She slipped down the hallway and opened the bedroom door. Doug was fast asleep having spent the weekend battling the flu. He finally came to mend on Saturday, but she knew how good the sleep would do him.

She closed the bedroom door as gently as she could.

Inside the hallway closet she removed her down trench coat, her knit hat and gloves, and the scarf Doug had surprised her with on Christmas.

The walk to the church was not as bad as she thought it might be. Most of the neighbors had shoveled the snow away from the sidewalks in front of their homes easing her passage.

The sun set fairly early in February, but the street lights and evening commute traffic kept a strange menagerie of shadows dancing across the piles of snow.

Leafless trees and chain-link fences.

Utility poles and power lines.

The grounds maintenance people had done a wonderful job of shoveling the sidewalks at the church and the parking lot was clear of snow. She pulled the church key ring from her pocket and slipped the biggest key into the deadbolt lock. With a little force, the door swung inward, and the warmth from the furnace washed over her face.

It felt good.

She flipped the three switches near the entrance and the small utility room adorned with tables and chairs for the meeting sat exactly where she had left them the week before when she closed down. There was comfort in knowing it would be as she left it each week.

As she began setting up the coffee pot, some of the attendees for the night's meeting began showing up.

Quiet and demure.

Some of them she recognized. Others she did not.

Some of them recognized old friends and embraced while exchanging pleasantries.

Some of them sat in the corner and picked scabs off their faces.

All of them were searching for answers to the maladies which plagued them.

"Clairann?" came a voice from the entry way.

She turned to look.

She knew that voice.

With a huge embrace their stood her friend Nickie.

"What are you doing here?" Clairann asked.

But what was anybody doing at an NA meeting?

She knew.

Nickie had been trying to quit dope as many years as Clairann had known her. Every once in a while she might string a few days or even a week together. But eventually the monkey would get too strong and she would fall, taking as many with her as she could.

"Clairann! So glad to see you. It's been months!" Nickie screeched, "We have so much to catch up on."

*   *   *

Doug rolled over as he awoke, and the emptiness of his bed beside him gave him pause.

Clairann?

He looked over at the clock, 3 *a.m.*

"Clairann?" he hollered, thinking she might be up late reading on the sofa or watching a movie.

He pulled his underwear up over his knees and grappled with a t-shirt.

"Clairann!" he hollered again, pushing the bathroom door open.

The living room was empty and she was nowhere to be found.

Immediately the worst case scenarios ran through his head. But he and his counselors had been working on his trust issues. Letting the worst case scenarios into his head first did nothing to alleviate his concerns. He tried to think of all of the rational explanations for why she might not have come home from the meeting hours earlier.

Was she running errands?

At 3 a.m.?

Maybe she was sponsoring someone and had gone to coffee.

Doug was concerned.

He slid to the end of the sofa and dialed her pager number. After entering in his "code" for an emergency so that she would call back right away, he sat and waited.

As his imagination began to get the best of him, he realized he needed to get dressed and go look for her. It was almost zero degrees outside, and in this weather someone could freeze to death in the right circumstances.

But if he left the house and she called back because she was just at a Denny's talking about recovery or something?

He was torn.

What if she was lying on the sidewalk between here and the church freezing to death having been hit by a car?

What if someone she owed money had unexpectedly found her?

Things were unraveling fast.

If she was having coffee and she called and he missed the call— at least she was ok. If she was lying along the sidewalk in the freezing cold she could be near death.

He quickly put on his winter clothes and dug his gloves out from under the sink in the kitchen. He thought he might drive to the church, but if she was hurt somewhere he might not see her. He grabbed a flashlight from under the back seat of the Scout and took off down Dalton toward Nevada Street.

For nearly an hour he fought off the frigid cold and searched behind garbage cans and parked cars for his beloved Clairann. Something was wrong. He could not fathom losing her again. So many times she had gone away and come back. But finally, these last few months had turned things around. Things were going so good for them.

At 4:30 a.m. he arrived back at his little house, having walked all the way to the church and back.

There was no sign of her.

How could this be happening?

Had she gone back to the life again?

The scenarios he had hoped to avoid popped back into his head like a redundant radio ad.

It just made no sense.

Doug sat in the living room and paged her over and over. He considered calling the police and reporting her missing but he knew what the police would say when they realized a Sprague Avenue whore "on the mend" for three months was the subject of the call.

He could hear their laughter now.

By 9 a.m. he was beginning to believe someone had taken his Clairann away from him. He threw his bottle of meds at the kitchen wall so hard it shattered, and the little pills sprinkled themselves across the counter and the top of the refrigerator.

Whenever stressed, Doug returned to his normal patterns of comfort. He wanted his Makarov, his backpack, and as much ammo as he could fit in the bag. For whatever reason, his guns were his support. He knew he could not shoot his way out of most situations, but they made him feel as though he had control over something.

And control was what he seriously lacked right now and wanted to get back as quickly as was humanly possible.

He also grabbed his new Walther 9mm pistol and slipped it into his backpack.

But there was no replacing his Makarov .22 pistol.

It was his favorite.

He hadn't handled his guns in quite a while — not since Clairann had more or less moved in and stayed for good. The reunion with his weapons made his blood start to tingle, just a little.

A wry smile crept across his face.

He had to find Clairann and protect her.

However he could.

By now Wednesday morning was quickly becoming Wednesday afternoon. He spent a better part of the morning staring at her side of the bed where she had been sleeping, regularly and peacefully, for the last few months.

He began to sob.

He knew exactly where she was and what she was doing.

He also knew that searching for her in the cold of the night was nothing more than putting off the inevitable flood of desperate pain and agony that was coming.

This is what it was to love a drug-addicted, mentally ill whore.

Had there been signs?
Did he miss something that could have helped her?
Not knowing was killing him.
How could he formulate a plan to fix it if he didn't even know what had gone wrong?
He dried his eyes and stood in the bathroom staring at himself. He would be strong. It was going to be all right.
Was it?
He couldn't keep his eyes from tearing up again.
Why couldn't he just have her and live a life?
Why did it have to be all of this bullshit?
He thought he could just pull the Makarov out and blow his head off.
Right there in the bathroom.
That would teach her.
That would prove to her that he loved her more than she loved her drugs.
He began to sob uncontrollably.
Why me?
He went into the living room and paged her again.
He waited.
Nothing.
He grabbed a wool Army blanket he had bought at the surplus store and bundled it up along with a white floral blanket that had been left in the bedroom closet by the previous renter and tossed them into the back of the Scout along with his backpack.
He knew her regular haunts
He knew where he would probably find her.
He had just hoped for something better.
He drove the loop around Sprague nearly a dozen times. Each time he became more and more frustrated.
She was nowhere.
The frigid weather that had been plaguing the strip for the last week was finally starting to break. For the first time in almost 2 weeks the temperature rose above freezing.

It was 34 degrees out.

It was almost tropical for a whore trying to earn a living in the frozen hell of Sprague Avenue.

Near Pacific Avenue and Spokane Street he saw a group of women he recognized. He knew none of their names, but he knew who they were and what they were hoping to accomplish standing out in the cold dressed like they were.

He slowed down and one of the women rushed up to his Scout and opened the door to climb in.

"What would you like, sweetie?" the woman asked.

"Do you know Clairann?" Doug asked.

She smiled and reached for his crotch, "You can call me Clairann—"

"No— I mean it! I am looking for her. She is what I want— she is all that will do. A twenty in it for you."

Doug knew by now how to get what he wanted from the women on the streets.

She would not be swayed.

Doug grabbed her by the hair and jerked her head back violently. She gasped in fright.

Doug's voice changed, low and dark, "Listen. You fucking cunt. I'll rip your fucking head off. Do I have your attention? *Clairann.* No one else. Have you fucking seen her?"

She scratched at Doug's arm and threw the door open as she jumped out.

"Fuck you. *Freak!*" she screamed.

Three other women, including an older one, saw the commotion and ran up to the door. If they were going to survive Sprague, they had to stick together.

"What the fuck is your problem?" one of them yelled at Doug.

"Clairann! I am looking for Clairann!" he yelled without even looking toward the gaggle of screeching banshees.

"I don't know no fucking '*Clairann*'" one of them wailed back.

"Joan, then! She goes by Joan!" Doug yelled as he turned and looked at them.

"Ah shit. Yeah— Joan. She got popped, boy. She in jail. Her and Marilyn," the older woman finally said.

"*Marilyn?*" Doug inquired.

"Yeah. But she didn't go downtown. Jus' Joan. Some shit went down 'tween the two of them. I dunno—"

Before she could even finish what she was saying, Doug took off into the darkness and frigid air.

* * *

By Thursday morning, February 22, 1990, most of the snow was well on its way to melting. It was nearly 7 a.m., and Doug had been waiting out front of the jail for Clairann to come out for more than an hour. He had posted her bail at 6 a.m., but the morning shift change had caused some delay.

He wasn't sure what he was going to say.

His blood tingled like it never had before.

He loved her and knew that this was not her fault. Obviously something had happened to draw her back.

She would never have done this on her own.

Unlike all the other times, this time she had help. She was talked into it or something. It had to be as he imagined.

But he just needed to see she was okay.

He just wanted to hug her and tell her it was going to be alright. They could go home and make love and pretend that it never happened.

Slip-ups were bound to happen but—

When the glass door swung open, she stepped out and into the courtyard surrounded by all of the Spokane County buildings.

She was wearing her long coat and her hat and gloves.

The scarf he had bought her for Christmas protected her neck from the cold.

She walked toward Doug slowly.

He could see that she had been crying.

He tried his best to give her a genuine smile as she fell into his arms.

"I am so sorry," she whispered as her face fell into his chest.

"It's okay," he consoled her, "I know there are going to be bumps in the road—"

She pulled back from him in shock and utter delight. She could hardly believe what she was hearing.

"Do you mean it?" she asked wiping the tears from her eye.

He just smiled and gazed lovingly into her eyes.

She started crying even harder.

"Of course I do. It's not your fault. I know why you did it," he told her.

She looked at him with a puzzled look.

"You're an addict. Relapse is part of it. I know that," he replied.

She fell back into his arms.

She could not believe she was so lucky as to be loved by such a warm and caring man.

"How did you know I was in jail?" she asked as he comforted her in his arms.

"I was worried so I went looking for you; finally, at about midnight, a couple girls said they saw you got popped earlier. So I knew."

"Did they say anything about Nickie? Did she get popped, too?" Clairann asked, her eyes still watery and subdued.

Doug looked surprised.

"No one mentioned Nickie, no."

Clairann shrugged.

"She must not have then," she surmised.

"I couldn't speak to it. No one said anything about her. Was she with you or something?" Doug inquired.

Clairann was too tired to get into it.

225

"I just want to go home and sleep in our bed, is that ok? We can talk about it all when I ain't so tired." she asked.

Doug turned and led her toward the Scout.

"So, if you found out at midnight that I was here, why did it take until now for you to bail me out?"

Nickie?

18
Swirling Pools of Splashing Green Water

She hadn't been able to take her regular walk for almost a week. The bitter cold weather seemed to be subsiding a bit, and the snow had finally melted off enough that she could make her daily round trip along the river. She loved seeing the river in its different seasonal stages. Winter was beautiful to her. At 67 years old, Mrs. Catherine Crisler had learned to appreciate the little things in life. She liked to leave at about 8:00 a.m. so she could be back in time for some of the morning television shows.

Upriver Drive paralleled the north side of the Spokane River from where it diverged off of Mission Avenue less than half a mile northeast of the Gonzaga University campus. The road meandered north and east, winding its way underneath the Greene Street Bridge. A few miles upriver the road jogs off to the north of the river and eventually rejoins the river near Myrtle Point, where the road then becomes Wellesley Avenue in what was unincorporated Spokane County.

As Mrs. Crisler walked along the path overlooking the shallow bank running 50 or 60 yards down to the river, something caught her attention as she approached the 4100 block of East Upriver Drive. The snow was nearly melted away exposing green grass underneath. A white blanket with a floral pattern was 20 or 30 yards below the trail toward the river.

The morning was remarkably quiet given the recent spate of cold weather. The river itself made hardly a sound as it wound its way through town.

Swirling pools of splashing green water.

Further down toward the river she saw a wool green blanket like she had seen used in the Army-- and *someone sleeping? In this weather?*

She immediately gasped and darted off the trail.

It looked like someone was wrapped in the blanket-- and probably very cold.

God only knew how they might have come to be out here in this weather, but they obviously needed help. It looked like whoever it was was not fully covered.

Foolish.

As she got closer she could see that it was a black woman. She also quickly realized that the woman was no longer alive.

Her face, chest, and torso were completely exposed. She wanted to cover her up in the name of the woman's dignity.

But she knew the police would want to see her as she found her.

As fast as as she could she climbed back up the hill to the path and made her way to the nearest house across the street to phone the police.

Within minutes a couple of Spokane police patrol cars blocked off the road and secured the scene.

She kept looking down the hill toward the poor woman and wondered how she could possibly have ended up on that hillside, naked and in a wool blanket?

She wanted to go and cover her up.

It was going to be a long day.

People were already missing the unfortunate woman.

At the Spokane Street Motel, Yolanda had not returned from working the corners the night before. It was not unusual for her to come in at one or two or even three in the morning.

But to not come home at all? That really concerned her boyfriend, Darrell.

Yolanda had been living at the Spokane Street Motel since early in 1987. At only 26 years old, she had been employed as a nurse's aide, but she simply could not kick the drugs. Originally from Tacoma, she had two young daughters back in western Washington who were in the care of family members while she tried to get herself back together.

She was well on her way.

Her boyfriend, Darrell, was nervous about calling the police and reporting her missing. Although the police always tried to do right by the folks on Sprague, it didn't always happen.

Who was going to take it seriously when a prostitute didn't show up from a night of turning tricks?

The Spokane Street Motel manager did her best to not allow the tenants to bring tricks back to the motel. This worked to keep the people living at the motel "honest."

Sort of.

When detectives arrived at the scene of the body, they immediately noted that none of the victim's personal belongings seemed to be anywhere in the vicinity.

No clothes.

No shoes.

No purse.

They determined that she had been shot in the chest with what appeared to be a small caliber firearm— most likely a .25- or a .22-caliber weapon. There seemed to be no signs of any struggle, and there did not appear to be any defensive wounds on the victim as though she had fought back. Detectives hypothesized she probably had been caught by surprise by her attacker, killed, and then brought here and dumped.

The green wool blanket wrapped around her feet was nearly fully soaked in blood. The white floral blanket up the hill was only partially covered and probably slid off the victim as her body slid down the hill.

Within hours detectives realized that the dead body most likely belonged to a prostitute reported missing that morning, Yolanda Sapp.

Detective Nick Stanley interviewed Yolanda's boyfriend, Darrell, and the boyfriend genuinely appeared distraught.

A quality not often found in a murderous boyfriend.

Stanley did not like Darrell for the murder.

* * *

It was nearly dark outside when Clairann finally woke from her slumber. She knew she had some explaining to do, but Doug was not acting nearly as mad as she thought he would. In fact, it seemed as though he simply wanted to forget it ever happened. Much of what Doug did was odd, but Clairann found this to be very unusual, even for him.

She didn't really even know where she wanted to start.

Nickie showed up and they were talking and she seemed like she was so sincere about staying clean.

Clairann threw her face back into her pillow.

She was so ashamed and disappointed.

Staying drug free was not just something she was doing for Doug. She really wanted to stay clean for herself as well.

But at times it was so hard.

With each passing day she would stay clean, a part of her felt like she had "earned a vacation" from the grind that was being clean and sober. Even if it was just a day or two.

Cunning.

Baffling.

Powerful.

The clichés familiar with those who use Alcoholics or Narcotics Anonymous were clichés for a reason.

They were true.

As she and Nickie traded stories of how things had been for them over the past few months, the stories became more and more about what wasn't working in their lives.

More so than what was working.

Soon they were in a metaphorical bobsled racing down the Matterhorn of fear and self-doubt.

Rather than focusing on the good, they began feeding off of what was wrong in each other's lives.

It was sick

It was twisted.

Within a few hours of drinking coffee and chatting at the 24-hour cafe downtown, they were planning how they could get some cocaine and just "hang" for a few hours. It was already so late that Clairann was scared to go home, and Nickie had only been clean for a couple of days any way.

Nickie finally admitted that she had heard a rumor that Clairann was "chairing" a meeting on Tuesdays up the hill and wanted to see if it was true.

No one knew how to blow an eight ball of coke like Clairann.

And usually the dealers would trade even more if they could fuck Clairann. Her beauty was not lost on the local cocaine dealers. Nickie knew all of this when she showed up at the NA meeting.

But she had to come up with a better version of events than the hard truth. There was no point telling Doug she fucked Nickie's dealer and two of his friends. By the time she got to the third one she was actually enjoying it.

That would just make Doug mad

Somehow if she could just get the conversation started, she knew she could explain it in a way that Doug would be receptive to. Even if he wasn't, she had to remember that she had the upper hand. Doug was obsessed with her, and she knew it. It wasn't as though he was going to do anything in the end other than what she wanted him to do.

It was just easier if she made him think he had control.

All men wanted that.

She heard Doug get in the shower, so she hopped out of bed and threw on a pair of white sweat pants and a tight T-shirt that she knew Doug loved. She grabbed her hair ties and pulled her hair into as cute a pony tail as she possibly could. There would be no time for putting makeup on — but at least she could divert his attention away from it a bit.

She even thought it might be better to fuck him first, but then she thought it might come off as too contrived. She needed to appear remorseful and sullen about her poor choice.

After staring in the mirror that Doug had hung next to the bed for her for a few more seconds, she turned and went down the hallway. Doug had obviously been up long before her, as he had left the television on. He must have been on the phone as the television was muted.

She dropped herself on the couch and grabbed the remote for the television when her friend Yolanda's picture hit the news.

Holy shit.

Before she could get the sound on, the news coverage had cut away to a commercial.

Yolanda must have been taken down in a big sting or something.

Anxiously, she curled her knees up under her and turned the sound on. A few moments later, Doug emerged from the bathroom wrapped in a towel.

"You won't believe this!" Clairann hollered down the hall as Doug turned away from her and toward the bedroom, "It's Yolanda! I think she was arrested or something; she is on the news!"

The news?

Doug stopped mid-stride and turned for the living room. His towel nearly dropped from his torso as he darted down the hallway and sat beside Clairann on the sofa.

Arrested?

"*A Spokane prostitute was found dead along the banks of the Spokane River early this morning.*"

Clairann gasped in shock and covered her mouth.

"*An elderly woman out for a morning on a walk near the 4100 block of East Upriver Drive came across the grisly scene. Police were on scene most of the day and confirmed that a woman who had been living at the Spokane Street Motel and was reported missing early this morning is, in fact, the woman found along Upriver Drive. Twenty-six-year-old Yolanda Sapp, originally from the Tacoma area, was a known prostitute and drug user. Police are tight lipped about details, but according to the manager at the motel, police have interviewed the man she lived with, but no arrests have been made. Sapp apparently died from multiple gunshot wounds to her chest, and her body was dumped some time between midnight and seven a.m. this morning. Anyone with any information is asked to call (509) SUS-PECT.*"

Doug sat in silence.

The next few moments could be some of the most important in his entire life.

Clairann looked at him and sobbed.

He pulled her into his chest so she could not see his face.

This was something new.

"I can't believe it!" she started to cry, "Yolanda. Who would want— why would anyone— "

She couldn't even talk any longer; she just wanted to cry.

Her friend was gone.

Doug could hard breathe, himself.

One wrong move or response and things would be bad. He rubbed the back of his head.

"Maybe it was a bad trick?" he finally whispered.

Clairann jerked away from him.

"*A bad trick?*" she gasped, "Of course it was a bad trick. What else would it be?"

Doug just stared at her. Frozen.

"Everyone loved her, I mean, she was kind of opinionated sometimes, but she always meant well. Oh, God. Her poor daughters. They will never know her now," Clairann wiped the tears from her face.

"I just meant... just meant that it's a risky life —" Doug began.

Clairann cut him off again.

"*You think I don't know that?!!*" she yelled at him, "How dare you!"

Doug swallowed hard again.

Not yet.

"I just wish I had gotten the chance to see her. The last time I saw her was... well, at least... I wanna' say it was October?" Clairann said starting to sound normal as she was speaking.

October?

Doug nearly choked.

Why was she lying?

"I need to call Nickie. She might still be in jail though," Clairann said, rising from the couch.

Nickie?

"She was with me when I got popped last night; I don't know if she got free or if they took her, too. I never saw her after we got vamped on; she might have gotten away," Clairann's voice trailed away as she headed into the kitchen for the telephone.

She was with Nickie?

Those lying fucking whores.

He was stuck now. He didn't know if he should mention that he thought she was with Yolanda last night — but that would be monumentally stupid. But if the whores who told him Clairann had been busted with Yolanda ever told her that they had told Doug they thought Clairann had been popped with Yolanda— would Clairann wonder why he never mentioned it? That would be stranger still.

What a fucking mess.

This had not been well planned.

He slapped his hand to the side of his head.

Whenever he screwed up as a kid his mother would smack him on the side of the head. At times it nearly made him pass out. He wanted to kill her for it.

But he couldn't.

Larry would have known it was him.

He hit himself again.

Fuck.

He strained to remember who had told him she was with Yolanda. An older white woman with an attitude like she was some sort of mother hen.

He remembered her face. But that was it.

Things were already starting to spiral out of control. He had to keep ahead of the game. He was smart. Smarter than everyone— certainly smarter than a bunch of whores— or the fucking cops.

What a clusterfuck.

Nickie? She was with Nickie? Not Yolanda? And now some other whore knows.

This was going to take some work to sort out.

But he had to.

19

A Single Story Brick Warehouse

Consequence and circumstance seemed to smooth over domestic strife far more than any amount of communication could between Doug and Clairann.

Yolanda's untimely demise shielded Clairann from a barrage of questions about her relapse. From her perspective Doug simply felt the requisite kind of compassion for the death of a loved one's friend.

Doug, on the other hand, simply knew better than to even ask. Keeping the mystery surrounding her relapse also kept the inconvenient truth that he may have made a slight error hiding in the corner.

Questions neither of them wanted to ask.

But the older whore who told him Clairann was with Yolanda that night…

That bothered him.

All he could do was hope that enough time passed so the days and nights of late February would eventually blend into a single frozen memory.

Blended together like cheap Indian whiskey.

No one of character wanting to drink it.

And those who did were branded with such ill repute that no one cared what they had to say.

The snow storm and cold stretch had clearly marked the end of winter. By mid-March, spring was nearly at hand. Nothing— not cold winter, nor rains of March— ever really shut the action on Sprague down. Things ebbed and flowed during the winter months. As expected, and as desperation warranted, those who needed the action sought it as well as delivered it.

The cycle never ended.

It was no surprise that despite her couple of good months during the autumn and early winter, Clairann would fall into her old ways. Doug continued to beg her to stop the drugs and stop the whoring, but Clairann would only make it a few days and fall back into the gutters of Sprague.

At times, Doug threatened to make her leave for good, but eventually Clairann saw through it all. There was no way Doug was ever going to make her leave. There was never going to be a time that she could not show up at Doug's doorstep, whether it be 3 a.m. or 5 p.m., and Doug would not take her in his embrace, scold her for falling again, and then fuck her into a much-needed slumber.

By late March Clairann didn't even care if Doug knew that she was going to go drinking, drugging, or whoring. She, and her vagina, had assumed complete control of Doug.

He hated her friends.

He hated her enemies even more.

He hated the drugs and the whoring.

And when he found her he would forget all of her transgressions.

But he never forgot Nickie.

He Said, She Said: The Spokane River Killer

He never forgot that it was she who had taken Clairann back to Sprague Avenue that night in February.

Whatever dignity or self-respect remained was washed away whenever she would be gone for more than a couple of nights, and he would go searching for her like he always did.

On March 24, 1990, Clairann had been on a run for almost five days. He knew it was time to go get her and bring her home. Maybe this would be the time she'd finally want to stop and go back to the days of Thanksgiving and Christmas when she was clean and sober.

She had been talking about going to a meeting— more so than she normally did. She even seemed genuine about it.

But five days?

It had been storming for more than 48 hours when he jumped into the Scout and headed south toward Sprague Avenue, crossing the river on the Greene Street Bridge.

Through the darkness and the blowing rain his eyes fixated upon the huddled shapes of desperation. Street lamp after street lamp, he prayed he would see her— her beautiful long legs, her high heels, the way her purse hung from her shoulder.

Nothing.

Nothing but shadowy figures, dark shapes, and occasional drenchings of his windshield as the oncoming traffic raced down the Avenue. Up and down the side streets off of Sprague, he circled and circled.

She had to be here.

Crowded beneath the lit entry way to one of the nameless industrial parks, a crowd of women had gathered to avoid the downpour. He jerked the wheel to the left, and the Scout lunged and hopped over the four-lane divider in the middle of the road as he made a u-turn. An oncoming Volkswagen honked and swerved to avoid him.

It mattered little.

He pulled up and stopped in front of the huddled women. The raindrops were so heavy on the opposite side window that he could not even make out who they were. Of course, two of them slipped out from under the cover and into the rain to offer their services. Before they could take more than a few steps toward his side of the rig, the door creaked and groaned as he threw it open. Raindrops pelted his cheeks and his glasses quickly fogged up. He reached up and wiped his hair out of his face.

She had to be here.

"Clairann? Is Clairann here? Clairann!" he yelled toward the oncoming women and the few left under the entryway. His body bobbed and weaved as he tried to look around the onslaught of lipstick-clad sirens moving toward him as if he were on a masted schooner. The rain was hitting the asphalt so hard that the spray was dancing up and into the yellowed beams of the headlights. He could barely hear himself think.

"You can call me whatever you want, sweetie..." a woman answered him as she stepped off the sidewalk in his direction.

Her red high heels nearly disappeared into the storm water as it ripped down the trench along the curb.

He desperately tried to look around her at the women in the entryway.

"No. I'm looking for Joan! I'm looking for Joan!" he hollered back dismissively, "I'm her boyfriend... not a..."

A tall, white woman in a tight red skirt pulled her gum from her mouth and turned squarely toward Doug, "I'll be your girlfriend, honey."

It was always the same response with these stupid bitches.

Never gets old.

His disdain for their come-ons was overshadowed by their desperate need to turn a trick and get the hell back to wherever it was they would call home for the night. So much so, they hardly noticed he wasn't paying any attention to them at all.

Around the corner and a few blocks down Sprague, an ambulance siren began to wail and the blackened reflections from the rain-soaked sidewalks and dark corridors began to dance in red and blue light. For a second, everyone stopped what they were doing and stared down the alley through the dumpsters and trash piles toward the ambulance. The all-too-common sound signaled that someone was in worse shape than they were, albeit, not by much. Once the red and blue no longer bounced between the concrete barriers, the women quickly turned their attention toward Doug.

But it was too late; before they could say another word, he had climbed back into his Scout and gunned it out of the alley.

He was going to find Clairann.

No matter what.

He turned back onto Sprague Avenue, and then he saw her — standing under the outcropping at the Checkerboard Tavern, trying to stay dry from the rain.

Not Clairann.

Nickie.

*   *   *

March 25, 1990.

It was nearly 7:30 a.m.

If Gerry wanted to get a jump on the other recyclers, he was going to need to pick up the pace a little. The dumpsters just south of Sprague were new to him. He didn't even know the pick-up days, but he had overheard that not only did many of them contain troves of recyclable metal, but oftentimes used pieces and collectibles could be gathered and sold to antique shops and even pawn shops. For a "dumpster diver," the hierarchy of turning in your recovered treasures into recompense was clear and deliberate. Most dumpsters always had some recyclable metal in them, but the take was little for a lot of weight to carry.

Gerry was in his late fifties. Life had not been kind in most respects, but recycling augmented his meager disability income quite nicely.

On occasion, however, someone would discard some valuable items which could be turned over to a collector or antique shop. Items of this caliber were few and far between, but there were enough times he could remember that the allure was still there.

Rarer still were items which could actually be pawned. Finding a working electronic device, box of jewelry, or better could bring a trip to the pawn shop. A trip to the pawn shop was second only to finding actual cash or coin. It didn't happen too often, but he had heard stories. Sometimes a landlord will dump the remains of a recently evicted tenant right on the sidewalk next to the dumpster not even caring what's there. The tenant might have gone to jail or worse.

Finding boxes or furniture stacked next to a dumpster usually made for a rush to get through it. Most illegal dumping is done from the cover of darkness; if you show up too early, you might get there too soon. But if you show up too late, someone else will have sifted through the items of value already.

He could tell that most of the dumpsters had been emptied within the last 24 hours. He made a note in his notepad to remind himself for next week. It was already nearly 9:00 a.m., and the Sunday morning traffic was picking up. No one really cared about the dumpster divers, but it seemed a good idea to just avoid the inevitable confrontations with those who frowned upon the activity.

The dumpster behind the upholstery shop looked like it was brand new, and a lot of car-repair places often dumped scrap metal in them. It was very likely, given the nature of the business, that if any metal at all was to be found inside, it would be from interior car parts and not the grungy, oily stuff you got from mechanics or repair shops.

Acme Upholstery had been there for years. The single story brick warehouse had once housed an auto repair shop.

Gerry reached up to the hard plastic cover and flipped it open. With a quick leap he hopped up onto the side and gripped the edge with his hands as his feet struggled to catch traction on the angled lip of the container. He immediately realized that this dumpster, too, had been recently emptied.

What the heck are those? They look brand new.

A pink and black sneaker had caught his attention. Carefully, he adjusted his perch on the edge of the dumpster and noticed that a pair of brand new women's sneakers had been cast into the dumpster. Closer to the edge of where he was looking over, he also noticed a woman's pocketbook and some other items which looked like makeup or lipstick. With a heave he hoisted himself over the edge and dropped into the empty enclosure. His feet hit the bottom, and a loud gonging sound rang through the Sprague Avenue morning.

He picked up the pocketbook first and unzipped the pocket.

Nothing. No cash.

Gerry was not a dishonest fellow. Even if he found cash or a credit card he would return it to the owner. Most of his compatriots would not, however.

He flipped through a couple of business cards, notes, and phone numbers and found a Washington state identification card. The woman in the picture appeared to be about 30 years old and somewhat attractive. He slid the lid back into its place and continued on. The sneakers were untied and looked like they were less than a week old. He tossed them aside.

Not even he had any use for used sneakers. No matter how new they were.

He sifted through the makeup, lipstick, and other items and quickly determined there was not much of value. Tossing the pocketbook over the edge of the dumpster onto the asphalt, he jumped up to the edge and threw himself over.

He grabbed the pocketbook and continued west along Sprague. Tired and worn out, Gerry headed home to get some sleep and decided he would retrace the route again tomorrow morning.

A few miles to the northeast, the Greene Street Bridge crossed the Spokane River near Upriver Drive. Just to the southeast, the enormous parking lot of Spokane Community College sat mostly empty. It was Sunday and little if any traffic would be on the roads until church services began later in the morning.

On the south side of the river, opposite of Upriver Drive, East South Riverton Avenue curled underneath the Greene Street Bridge and turned southbound for a block until it hit Ermina Avenue and the campus for Spokane Community College. The road connected local residents who lived along the river to Greene Street and saw little if any traffic most of the day.

Under the Greene Street Bridge the road ran directly parallel with the river. A guardrail and an eight foot drop were all that separated South Riverton from the Spokane River.

It was dark and it was solitary.

As Gerry lay dozing in his recliner, the news report pulled him from where he had fallen asleep with an ice cream carton and spoon balanced on his chest.

"Good evening. A grisly discovery this morning under the Greene Street Bridge. The body of 34-year-old Nickie Lowe was discovered along the Spokane River near Spokane Community College. Police have already ruled this a homicide and are asking for your help tonight to determine the last known whereabouts of Ms. Lowe. Anyone with information about where Ms. Lowe may have been or whom she was with are asked to call the Spokane Police tip-line at (509) SUS-PECT. Police are refusing to confirm, however, if this case is related to the discovery of a body only a few blocks away along Upriver Drive just three weeks ago. In February, the body of Yolanda Sapp was discovered by a woman walking the

pedestrian trail. Both victims were known prostitutes in the Sprague Avenue district. Jim?"

The picture of the pretty brunette faded from the television screen, and Gerry felt a sense of déjà vu. He had seen her somewhere. But he wasn't exactly sure. He dove his spoon back into the ice cream container.

Where do I know her from?

Suddenly, he lifted his legs off of the foot rest and nearly threw himself and the melted ice cream onto the floor. Gerry jumped from his recliner and darted into the kitchen where he grabbed the plastic bag he had tossed on the kitchen counter after last night's route. He fished the pocketbook out and slid the identification card from its pouch.

Nickie Lowe.

When two Spokane police detectives arrived, Gerry rode with them back down to Sprague Avenue to show them the dumpster he had found the stuff in. The detectives recovered a tube of sex lubricant, some mascara, lipstick and some papers. They also found her brand new tennis shoes. It seemed as though someone had gone through the items one by one as they tossed them in the dumpster.

Privately, they knew this case was probably connected to the murder of Yolanda Sapp.

Publicly, they needed to hold back.

The bodies were recovered literally within eyesight of each other on opposite sides of the river.

Police knew Nickie and had a lot of contact with her. They knew she was hooked on dope and worked the streets regularly.

According to her mother, Diane, who had reported her missing that morning, Nickie's pimp had dropped her off around 10 p.m. near Altamont and Sprague. Nickie was supposed to meet her pimp by midnight at the Checkerboard Tavern on Sprague. When she didn't show up as planned, he called Nickie's mother in a fit of rage, thinking she was trying to rip him off.

Her body was discovered partially nude and draped over the guardrail on Riverton, directly beneath the Greene Street bridge. She had been shot once in the chest with a .22 caliber firearm. The scene looked as though someone had tried to dump her into the river from Riverton Avenue but was not strong enough or had panicked from an approaching car or headlights.

So they left her.

In the most undignified way possible.

Or maybe they had posed her.

In the most undignified way possible.

20

Brilliance Overwhelmed

The silence and tranquility of a sunrise after an enormous rainstorm can be quite striking. From darkness to light, from wetness to dry, from loudness to quiet. As the water streamed its way down the drains and gutters of the dimly-lit streets of Spokane above the river, he just stared.

Wipers right and left… right and left.

The beating of his heart in his chest nearly made his throat hurt.

It was almost 6 a.m., and he really needed a Super Big Gulp of Coke and a package of Hostess mini-chocolate donuts. They reminded him of going into the woods back in Omak and killing birds with his .22 rifle. How he and his friend would walk the ridge lines looking for starlings or robins— any living creature for that matter, and see who could kill one from the greatest distance. Once he wounded a baby starling from 70 yards. For 20 minutes he watched as the small bird fluttered in circles trying to fly with a broken wing but unable to do so.

He could have finished off the helpless creature with another shot from his 22.

But why?

If he had to suffer this world —

So should they.

How they died mattered little to him. He was cleaning up the forest so the other birds had more places to nest, more food to eat.

Or so he told himself at the time.

It wasn't just senseless killing for the sake of it. He had a reason.

A plan.

A means to an end.

When he parked the Scout alongside the house, he noticed his crotch was wet and extremely cold. As he was driving, the lid had slipped off of his Super Big Gulp, and the cold beverage had sloshed out into his lap where he had been holding it between his legs.

Fuck.

He replaced the lid and straw and slid the remaining two donuts into the package and then into the pocket of his black denim jacket.

It was time to get some sleep and go looking for her downtown near the 24-hour Cafe. She, and all of the other whores for that matter, only really hung out near Sprague after dark. The local business owners and tradespeople were willing to tolerate the bullshit, but not while commerce was being conducted.

It was an arrangement of solitude.

There would be no cleaning up of Sprague. Without the drugs and the tricks and the occasional violent outbursts, Spokane would have no soul at all.

And a city with no soul, dies.

Everyone wanted Sprague to stay just like it was, whether they would admit it or not. North Seattle had Aurora Avenue and south Seattle had Pacific Highway South. If you were going to be thought of as a burgeoning metropolis, you had to have your red-light district. Who were the rich people going to save if it were not the whores and the homeless?

Everyone was a trick.

Everyone used the whores.

Symbiosis.

Doug gently kicked the bottom of the door leading into the kitchen from the back porch. With a jolt and a shudder it popped open. Things seemed to be falling apart around the house. He dropped his keys on the counter.

The remote for the television and VCR caught his eye first.

Clairann.

Whenever she went to bed she left the remote on the top of the back of the couch.

She was home.

A quick glance around the corner and down the hallway into the bedroom confirmed it. As quietly as he could he slipped down the hall.

Gently, he pushed the door open a little further.

Her jeans were lying in a heap on the floor near her side of the bed. Next to them her tiny white panties.

Underneath the white down comforter he could make out the shape of her little frame as she lay on her side facing toward where he normally slept. Her bare arm outside the covers, as he watched, her tiny hand twitched. She drew in a quick breath and smiled in her sleep. She must have been dreaming about something as pretty as she was.

Doug smiled.

He could tell she was happy.

Whatever stories or words needed to be exchanged could wait. He just wanted to watch her sleep.

Quietly and in peace.

She was so beautiful.

Within a few minutes she rolled onto her back, and her twinkling eyes came to life.

She blinked at him.

And smiled.

"Where have you been?" she whispered and stretched her arms up over her head.

"Looking for you," he answered and stroked her hair away from where it had fallen in front of her face.

She pulled the edge of the sheet up over her breasts and pushed them together just enough to make them look even bigger.

She knew exactly what she was doing.

"I've been here since like 2 a.m. I went to a ten o'clock meeting last night and then to coffee. *I gotta get clean, again; I gotta,*" she implored.

It was exactly what Doug wanted to hear.

As tumultuous as the addict's life always is, and despite the number of times the addict will lie about their intentions with regard to getting high or getting sober — the path that leads with 'I gotta get clean' is always preferable.

No matter where it leads.

*　　*　　*

Doug had been given an opportunity.

He had to go big.

For the first time since before Thanksgiving, she had suggested she stay clean and sober. No fighting. No prodding. No begging.

This was her idea.

The longer he could keep her from any contact with her old friends in 'the life' — the better.

He tucked her back into bed and suggested she sleep for a little while longer.

Without a sound he slipped through the house and unplugged the phones. If she noticed, he would just tell her it was so she could sleep. The only way she would want to use the phone anyway was if her pager went off.

The pager.

Shit!

As he darted back into the bedroom, he arrived in just the nick of time. Underneath her jeans, her pager was buzzing incessantly.

It was a wonder she had not heard it. She had a keen ear for such things.

All the whores did.

Her pager was always a contentious issue. As the obvious lifeline between her and Sprague, whenever he tried to separate her from it, she resisted and rebelled. He had tried numerous times to get rid of it, disconnect it, or even lose it — but each time was met with stiff resistance. The more he tried — the more she asserted her right to have it. Sober or not.

Somehow he had to manipulate her into *wanting* to give it up.

That would be impossible.

Camping.

All he needed were a few days away, and the fog of confusion and untenable memories would cloak his deed.

If they were camping in the mountains, there would be no pay phones, and if he went out of the service area of the pager — she would not be prompted into calling anyone.

It was a brilliant plan.

He simply had to buy himself enough time to go buy some camping gear and get the Scout loaded up to go.

How?

He tapped the pager on the kitchen table to help him think. How could he make it so she wouldn't get any pages? He thought he could turn it off, and when she finally noticed it was off, he could just say he was trying to let her sleep. But that was what the silent mode was for.

He stopped tapping it and looked closely at the bottom of it where the battery slid out.

That's it.

As quick as the thought came to him he slipped the battery out of the pager. Without the battery, it weighed far less. She would notice that right away. He could not simply remove the battery.

Too obvious.

He needed a *dead* battery.

Of all of the times he had pondered what use there might be for a dead battery, now he had it. But he had no dead battery.

He would have to make one.

In the spare bedroom where he tinkered with his guns he pulled a couple of small strips of wire and fished through his tool box for the package of replacement taillight bulbs he had bought at the auto parts store for his Scout. With a small amount of electrical tape, he fashioned the wires onto the battery and connected them to the small light bulb.

The bulb jumped to life.

He set the contraption down on his work table and slipped out to the hallway to see that she was still sleeping.

He marveled at how well his plans always seemed to come together. At least with a dead battery, she might not notice it right away, and when she does, she will have to wait for him to return to buy more batteries for it. If he could have everything packed and ready to go by the time she awoke, then he might be able to convince her to wait until they returned from the camping trip to get new batteries. Even better, there would be no television news or any other distractions.

Her and him.

Alone.

In the woods.

Inside the closet of the spare bedroom he took inventory of the camping equipment he already had. He considered himself to be quite the survivalist, but eating bugs and building lean-to tarp shelters was probably not going to get him laid in the woods with his beloved Clairann.

Not even close.

He needed a tent and an air mattress.

And something for her to sit on around the campfire while he made her s'mores.

He pulled a small tablet from his table and began writing notes.

After diving through his closet, basement storage space, and dragging the ladder in to look in the attic, he felt he knew exactly what was needed. He glanced toward the taillight bulb attached to the battery.

It was dead.

He tore off the electrical tape and wires and tossed the battery back into the pager.

He turned it on.

Lo Bat.

Lo Bat.

Lo Bat.

The low battery warning flashed at him three times and the pager went dead.

The last thing he had to do was sneak back into the bedroom without waking her and flip the breaker in the living room that the television was plugged into. It was unlikely that there would be any news coverage on a Sunday, but there was also no sense in taking any chances with his plan.

Stick to the plan.

Sleep deprived and worn out, he jumped into his Scout and headed west toward Division Street and then down to the White Elephant Sporting Goods. The White Elephant was a landmark of sorts in Spokane. Camping equipment, guns, tents, toys— it had it all. Normally he liked the store out towards the Valley— even though the store on Division Street was right near his house. But to get to that one meant driving across the Greene Street bridge.

A prospect he would rather avoid at this point.

Inside the store he pulled his notepad from his cargo pocketed pants and pushed the cart slowly through the aisles. The gun counter near the entrance always drew him in. But today, he had to resist such indulgences. Despite his efforts, a sign indicating .22 ammo was on sale captured his interest, and he tossed a couple of 5000-round boxes into his cart. He had been promising Clairann he would show her how to shoot.

And one can never have too much ammo.

He found a great deal on a 2-person tent, and with a little help from one of the clerks, he also found a double-wide air mattress. Propane stove, propane canisters, frying pan, camp silverware, waterproof matches... Soon he had almost everything he needed.

Near the checkout counter he stopped to browse through the collection of maps. He had not yet fully decide where he wanted to go and wasn't quite sure if he wanted to go back toward Omak and Okanogan, where he was more familiar with the area, or if he wanted to venture out into his newly adopted surroundings. He really wanted to go explore Idaho, but the conditions of his probation forbid him from exiting the State of Washington without prior approval from both his state community supervision officer and his federal probation officer.

After a short conversation with the same clerk who had helped him find the double air mattress, he decided to head toward Mt. Spokane. The area was just across the border from Idaho, and if he traveled clear around the other side, it was highly unlikely that her pager would still have service. It was perfect.

He corralled the bags of goods into his arms and packed them neatly into the back of the Scout.

The last thing he needed to do was stop at the grocery store to get food for three or four days. His brilliance overwhelmed him when he decided he would also buy new batteries for the pager, and when she noticed the battery was dead, he could tell her that he already had batteries, but that they were packed away with the camping stuff and he could get them out once they got to their camping spot.

His superior intellect was daunting at the very least.

He even decided he would quietly try and pack her clothes before he awoke her so that he could simply sweep her off of her feet and into the Scout.

It was the little details that mattered.

Next to his house he pulled the emergency brake and turned the engine off. He sat for a second to gather himself; he had garnered his second wind despite his near 36 hours without sleep. But there was no need to be hasty.

He unlocked the back porch door and, as had become his habit, kicked the bottom of the door to pop it open. He was first going to sort the groceries and then pack her clothes.

On the couch he noticed the television remote had been disassembled, and the cover holding the batteries was lying loose next to it.

Shit.

His face began to turn red.

She had pulled the batteries from the remote and put one into her pager?

He dropped the bag of groceries and darted into the hallway. The bedroom door was open, and Clairann was gone.

He found a note on the bed.

Something happened to my friend Nickie. Meeting friends at the 24-hour cafe downtown. Come down when you get this. Where did you go? Love, C.

21

Lace Ruffles So Perfectly White

He lifted the note up to his face so he could read it again. This was not how it was supposed to happen.

The 24-hour cafe?

He let out a long sigh. He just needed to think for a minute.

What should he do?

What could he do?

She had to have known that he didn't take too kindly to Nickie. She was the one who Clairann always seemed to be getting in trouble with.

He knew that.

And she knew that he knew it.

If he pretended he felt bad that Nickie was dead, she might find his remorse to be completely disinguous and therefore suspect.

But if he didn't appear distraught that Clairann's friend had been murdered, he just looked like an asshole.

Fuck.

There was no way to win this one. But what'd he expect?

He looked at the note again:

"Something happened to my friend Nickie. Meeting friends at the 24-hour cafe downtown. Come down when you get this. Where did you go? Love, C."

"*Something happened?*" She must know Nickie has been murdered. But what if she didn't know it was murder yet? And he did?

This was getting so fucking complicated.

He put the groceries he had bought for the camping trip into the refrigerator and pantry.

Maybe she would still want to go?

Outside the weather had turned a little nasty. March was unpredictable in the Inland Empire, and a day that started sunny and clear could end very differently. The clouds rolling in from the west were dark and foreboding.

It was going to rain.

He could smell it.

A quick whiff of air rushed down the street as he jumped into the Scout to head downtown. The dust and trash swirled upwards in a fury and then were gone. A paper napkin and hot dog wrapper floated gently back to the ground as he heard thunder in the distance.

Downtown Spokane was not very busy for a Sunday afternoon. It never was. Finding a parking spot close to the 24-hour cafe was easy. When he opened the door to the Scout a gust of wind nearly pulled it from his grasp. The rains had not yet come, but the wind seemed to have picked up quite a bit.

Through the glass bay windows of the cafe he could see a small group of women gathered around the big horseshoe-shaped booth in the corner near the bathroom foyer. He began to sweat just a little.

What if they knew?

Just as a precaution he looked around to see if it looked like a set-up. Were the cops going to come in and get him right now?

Even he knew he was being paranoid.

Just as he pulled one of the glass double doors open, the first raindrops of the storm pelted his forehead.

He had just barely made it.

Slowly, he sauntered toward the table where Clairann and her friends were sitting.

Oh fuck.

The whore who had mistakenly told him that Clairann had been arrested with Yolanda was sitting right next to Clairann.

This was fucked.

He thought he might turn around before anyone saw him enter and just pretend like he hadn't got the note until later.

Something.

But his legs kept walking him toward the table as if they were not under his control any longer. Before he could wrestle his faculties back from his undermined will, the decision had been made for him.

"Doug!" Clairann cried and pushed her way out of the booth through her friend. Two other women and an older gentleman were engrossed in conversation and grief beside Clairann, but they paid no attention to Doug's arrival.

She reached her arms out to hug him. At least he had one hurdle cleared so far.

"What happened?" he asked as they embraced.

Clairann pulled back, and he could see she had been crying a lot.

"Nickie," she said somberly, "somebody fucking killed her."

She froze and started to sob.

Doug pulled her into his arms again.

"They won't say it, but we think there is some kind of freak or something running around out there. She was found directly across from where they found Yolanda," she painfully struggled to reveal.

Clairann's friend slid further into the booth and finally looked up.

"Hey," she said as jovially as the occasion would allow, "I know you."

She recognized him.

Shit.

He had to play it cool. He had been in situations like this before, well, not exactly like this, but he had been in stressful situations, and he just had to keep things calm and collected. There was no need to say anything quick-witted or hasty. Every word he said needed to be deliberate and well thought out.

Or shit would go south.

Fast.

If she never brings it up, he certainly wasn't going to. But that might look suspicious as well.

He took a couple of deep breaths.

Clairann slid in and Doug followed suit.

"This is Kathy. Everyone calls her Wiggy," Clairann continued, "You guys know each other?"

Doug swallowed so hard he thought the lump in his throat was going to rip open and bleed. He nearly choked.

"Yeah, I seen him around a few times. With you," Kathy answered and looked at Doug disapprovingly.

"Aren't you the guy that tries to keep her locked up at home all the time?" Kathy continued sarcastically.

Clairann elbowed her in the ribs.

"I'm just kiddin,' I'm just kiddin'" Kathy joked and smiled at Doug.

"What do you mean 'they won't say' about Nickie— and Yolanda?" Doug asked as innocently as he could muster.

Before Clairann could answer, the waitress interrupted, and Doug ordered a coffee and some hash browns.

"The cops! They won't say it— but word is that whoever killed Yolanda probably killed Nickie too," Clairann answered.

"Why do they think that?" Doug quizzed.

He noticed Kathy just stared at him.

"Same gun or something or type of gun. They were found so close together— that kind of stuff," Clairann answered.

With each passing question, Doug felt more and more at ease. It seemed he was going to get through this.

"Hell, they are probably going to think Clairann did it 'cause she was with them both the night they was killed. You remember—" Kathy pointed at Doug, "that night I seen you and you was asking where Clairann was, and I thought she had gone to jail with Yolanda."

Doug felt like he had been daggered in the chest. He didn't even want to look at Clairann to see her reaction, but he had to.

"You what?" Clairann asked and glared at Doug.

"No, you said she… said she was with Nickie— or no— somebody— was it *Yolanda?*" was the best Doug could muster.

Clairann looked shocked.

"Hell yes I thought it was Yolanda. Remember— you heard me 'cause you asked about her street name, Marilyn. Remember?" Kathy shot back.

He was not ready for that but had better have an answer quick.

"Whether it was Yolanda or Nickie or whoever—" Clairann tried to dampen the obvious.

"No— I said it was Yolanda— he heard me—" Kathy argued.

Doug just sat.

His blood boiled.

"Well, whatever— it doesn't matter. That's what the cops think— but they won't say," Clairann continued.

Clairann's entire demeanor had shifted.

She didn't know what to think.

Doug?

He Said, She Said: The Spokane River Killer

No fucking way.

Clairann excused herself to go to the restroom. Kathy introduced Doug to the two other women and the man they were with, but their names or faces did not even register.

He had to sort this out.

"Somebody's killin' girls," Kathy said and looked at Doug, "we all better be careful, that's all I'm sayin.' That's all I'm sayin.'"

Doug could sense where Kathy's mind was headed. He felt he had no choice but to make an enemy of her quick. If she began running her mouth about him, and he could deflect its efficacy with claims to how she hated him— it was his only option.

"I'm not worried," he began.

His entire voice and demeanor changed.

"If someone were a threat to me or to Clairann, I'd fucking kill them. No ifs, ands, or buts. I'd gun them down right fucking quick."

Kathy was no stranger to tough talking men. This little weasel, however, was no tough man. But something went off in her head that she needed to back the fuck off from this guy.

Something that nearly made her sick to her stomach.

But Kathy was no pushover. She hadn't made it this far by ever being pushed around. If someone wanted to get rude with her, she was able to dump it right back at them.

"Oh yeah? You say it like you've killed people before, Doug," she whipped back in his face.

"When I was involved with the Aryans— the Brotherhood— you know," Doug retorted.

Kathy wanted to laugh in his face.

"Were you a hitman, Doug?" she said sarcastically.

"You know," Doug repeated himself, "You know."

"I think you're full of shit," Kathy said flippantly.

"Just sayin' — if someone hurts Clairann— in any way."

"What are you going to kill me?" Kathy laughed.

She could tell Doug was a big talker.

But something still felt wrong.

She didn't know what it was.

Clairann came back to the table and could sense the awkwardness between her friend Wiggy and Doug. It had been another long day and she could see no point in fanning the flames of discontent between them.

"Perhaps we should get home?" she asked Doug.

The couple said their goodbyes and paid the bill.

Something about the downtown streets didn't feel like spring at all. Doug unlocked the passenger door to the Scout and Clairann climbed in. Her feet were wet from stepping in the gutter by accident.

"How come you never mentioned Yolanda that night?" she asked after sitting in silence for nearly five minutes.

Doug already knew by the tone of her questioning all he had to do was provide some sort of plausible denial and she would let it go.

"I don't even remember. Maybe she mentioned Yolanda-- I don't know. The whole thing is just stupid," he answered.

"It's just weird. That's all," she replied.

"Look. What? Do you think I killed Yolanda? And Nickie? Is that it?"

"No, of course not. But it's—"

"They— you— all of you— live a life that is— that exposes you guys to this shit. What did they think would happen? The drugs? The Johns? All of it isn't any good. You of all people know this! Maybe this should be a wake-up call or something?"

"I know— you're right—"

"But blame *me* – *right?* I have been the only one who has been there for you all of the time. You come to my house— our house— whenever you want. I cook for you. I clean for you. I take you in. I love you! But it's me? Right? It's me? It's not possible it might just be a bad lifestyle? Whores. Whores. Whores!!"

Doug was visibly upset.

But his calculations were correct.

Clairann never brought it up again.

If she had any doubts or reservations, they were mired in her inability to get clean and stay clean.

Yolanda's death and Nickie's death had a profound effect on her. But nothing was going to scare her straight.

For more than two weeks Clairann bounced around Sprague Avenue. One day she would be at an NA meeting and the next she would be doing lines and smoking weed with men she did not know. She would go home to Doug, and he would take her in, give her a bath, and a good night's sleep.

She would fuck him better than he had ever had.

And she would leave again.

It wasn't Yolanda.

And it wasn't Nickie.

But Sprague still had its hold on her. Nothing was prying her from its grip.

On May 15, 1990, Clairann was arrested again. But by now, Doug had spent all of the money from the court-ordered gun sale. All he had was his Social Security income and whatever he could muster through his small-time hustling.

She implored him to come and get her.

She even told him to call Wiggy and borrow the money. She would do it; she would do it for her, Clairann begged.

* * *

Wiggy cupped the pipe in her hands to block the wind. Nothing made turning tricks easier than smoking a little dope before the action on the strip heated up.

"So this guy..." Kathy began, struggling not to exhale, "this guy... that... that Clairann," she stopped and blew the smoke out of her mouth, "that Clairann has been fuckin' living off of since last summer. He's a fuckin' weirdo—"

"They're all fuckin' weirdos, come on!" her friend Shannon laughed as she reloaded the pipe.

"No. I mean— really fuckin'... like... out there, and shit," Wiggy continued.

Shannon pulled a small lighter from her purse, looked around the corner and started to take a hit.

Wiggy leaned back against the wall and folded her arms.

"He thinks he's gonna' save Clairann or some shit," Wiggy said.

Shannon kept inhaling on the pipe.

Wiggy laughed out loud.

"Like he's got somethin' Clairann wants, ya' know?"

Shannon nodded and blew out a giant cloud of smoke.

"He even told me to quit hangin' out with her. That he was hit man for the Aryan Nation," Wiggy laughed.

"Do you think he whacked Yolanda and Nickie?" Shannon asked.

"Fuck no! He's a punk. Some little wiry lookin' dude. I hope Clairann loses him soon, though. Every time we gonna' catch some shit— he wants her to 'think about what she's doin'' or some other bullshit. And then one time— he wanted to fuck me! I mean— he is just a fucking weirdo."

Shannon looked in the glass window to see how her hair looked and thanked Wiggy for smokin' her out. Shannon stepped onto the sidewalk and headed east down Sprague Avenue. Wiggy headed the opposite direction. Before too long she heard a whistle and turned to look.

Well, speak of the devil.

At 7:30 p.m. on May 15, 1990, the body of 38-year-old Kathleen Brisbois (Wiggy) was found in a gravel pullout near the Trent Avenue train trestle a few miles east of Spokane. The Trent Avenue trestle crossed the Spokane River. A few hundred feet below where she was found, the dirty waters lapped and boiled their way toward the city.

He Said, She Said: The Spokane River Killer

Kathleen Brisbois had been shot in the arm, shot in the chest, and in the head with a .22. Her clothes were tossed in a pile. A blood trail led from the gravel road to where her body was discovered. It was obvious she had been in some sort of physical fight. Her head was covered in bruises and lacerations. Clumps of hair and dried blood were everywhere around the crime scene.

Whoever had killed Wiggy had faced quite a battle.

Based on her defensive wounds, she likely took a gunshot through her hand and continued to fight until her assailant finally got one in her chest. Once she went down, the final shot in her head was probably to make sure the tiny woman didn't rise from her injuries and keep fighting.

She had kicked, screamed, and clawed back.

She had wanted to live.

No matter what life had dealt her up to that very moment in time.

Kathleen Brisbois fought viciously to live.

And she nearly did.

The fight she put up would be instrumental in bringing her killer to justice.

Eventually.

Because she had been found outside of the city limits of Spokane, her case was handled by detectives from Spokane County. Even so, they were familiar with the murders of Yolanda and Nickie. Because they knew Kathleen's history of prostitution and drug use, they quickly surmised that all three women may have suffered from the same hand or hands.

Ballistic evidence eventually confirmed that the women were killed with the same gun. However, the conclusion was not solid enough to ever be used as evidence.

But the cops knew.

* * *

Clairann had been gone for more than two months.
And this time he knew it was for good.
No note.
No goodbye.
Nothing.

He had searched all the usual haunts and talked to everyone he knew or who had known her on the strip.

No one was talking.

Carefully, he slipped the snapshot from the gondola ride into the frame and secured the glass over the top. It was perfect. He could see in her eyes how much she loved him. She had been clean for over a week when they took that picture.

Clean.

When her mind was not clouded from drugs and drinking and those... those fucking whores- then she knows that she loves him.

But those fucking whores.

Always nagging at her to go out with them. Always trying to ply her away from him. Why can't they see that she wants to be with him and not them? Why can't they just let go of her? It's what she really- *what she really* wants- when she's not drugging and workin' the strip at least. If it wasn't for them always stopping by the house whenever they feel like it and begging her, begging her to just spend a few hours or even a few minutes away from him. The only reason she gives in is because she has such a huge heart and truly understands why they do what they do.

She was the most kind and beautiful woman he had ever known.

He set the picture on top of the end table and slipped toward the bedroom. Inside the closet he pulled out the cardboard shoe box and lifted the lid off. He reached inside and slipped a pair of her white lace panties out and caressed his cheek with them. A few weeks earlier, when he washed the dried blood from them, he took great care to only wash the crotch area and not to remove the scent of her perfume.

He closed his eyes and took a deep breath.

Once again they were holding hands at Riverfront Park as they walked along the path to the gondola. His heart began to race faster as he pictured her in those cut-off Levis. Her tan legs and the way her loose-fitting pink top bared her shoulder. He remembered how special he felt that she had curled her hair and not worn her "working" makeup but kept it subtle and classy. She had even worn chartreuse hoops in her ears that matched her high heels. For the first time in his life he was walking and holding hands with the prettiest woman in the park.

Drawing in a deep breath through his nose, he cupped the panties in his hands and pressed them to his face.

God, they smelled so good.

Nothing was as soft or as comforting.

He wanted to stay in that moment forever.

He pulled them away from his face and untangled them. The lace ruffles so perfectly white. The silvery sheen of the silk where it covered her vagina made him think of that first time he slipped his hands around them and slid them across her hips and down her thighs.

How surprisingly soft the narrow strip of hair above her vagina was. How smooth her freshly shaven legs felt on the back of his hands. He wanted her so badly. He craved her, desperately. He would do anything for her. Anything she wanted if she would just be his girl again.

But Clairann was gone.

Forever.

Jon Keehner

Part III:

As The Bodies Pile Up

22

Princess

After the murder of Kathleen Brisbois was officially connected to Yolanda Sapp and Nickie Lowe, a task force was formed between Spokane City and Spokane County. The task force was led by the Spokane Major Crimes Unit.

The investigators began interviewing anybody and everybody who would be willing to talk with them. In a police interview in Yakima, Washington, Shannon Zielinski, who had left Spokane out of fear for her life, described a man whom Kathleen Brisbois had a "weird feeling about" before she was killed-- he owned a small red car and claimed to be a "hit man."

This was as close as they would get.

Representatives from the Task Force eventually met with the Green River Task Force. The FBI behavioral analysis teams even became involved. Rumors were rampant that the notorious Green River Killer who had been highly active in the south Seattle area between 1982 and 1987 might have moved into the Spokane area or had been released from prison recently, explaining the gap in killing between 1987 and 1990.

But speculation was all the Task Force was able to come up with.

Within a year, the task force was disbanded.

Evidence from the three murders remained locked away in a locker in downtown Spokane.

Some of it was even destroyed by mistake.

But women kept on dying.

On May 12, 1992, a 19-year-old woman by the name of Sherry Palmer was found dead near Bill Gulch Road and Mt. Spokane Drive, a few miles to the northeast of Spokane. She was shot with a small caliber pistol several times in the chest and had a plastic grocery bag placed over her head when her body was discovered. She was last seen May 1, 1992, leaving Al's Motel on Division Street. The public wondered if Sherry's murder was related to the 1990 murders. Spokane County detectives, for reasons they did not disclose, did not believe the murders were related.

Doug settled in to as much of a routine as he could. Clairann was gone for good, and he continued to seek comfort and companionship from the women of Sprague Avenue. It had become clear to him that he offered something that some of these women may want, albeit at quite a cost.

By 1994, Doug was no longer under community supervision or on any kind of probation. Most of his civil rights had now been restored although he was a convicted felon, and therefore it was illegal for him to possess any firearms or ammunition.

This mattered little.

Without the threat of probation violations or community supervision conditions, Doug was no longer required to attend mental health counseling. No one monitored or reported whether he maintained his medication regimen. He was free, like any other citizen, to choose his own medical treatments.

He indicated to people who knew him at the time that he wanted to return to Omak. He felt he had resolved things with his mother well enough and preferred to be able to spend his money on things other than rent, namely— guns. He decided to make peace with Okanogan Mental Health and hoped they would write a letter to the Judge in order to help him restore his right to possess firearms.

Not a chance in hell.

In fact, staff working there at the time considered obtaining restraining orders against him should he return to Okanogan County. The last thing anyone wanted was for Doug Perry to end up back on Pogue Flat with his firearms rights restored, without mental health counseling, and off of his medications.

Doug was incensed.

On June 20, 1994, a mentally ill, recently discharged airman named Dean Mellberg took a MAK-90 semi-automatic rifle and a 75-round drum magazine and killed four people at Fairchild Air Force Base only a few miles west of Spokane.

The tragedy drew international attention.

As Doug's frustration with Okanogan Mental Health reached the boiling point, he suggested that the reason he was unable to return to Omak and possess firearms was completely their fault and that the same thing that happened at Fairchild Air Force base might just happen to them.

Two days later, the ATF raided his house and discovered 22 rifles, 11 handguns, and thousands of rounds of ammunition. Nearly a dozen cats had to be removed by animal rescue. Once again, his failure to keep his ridiculous grandiosity to himself had backfired.

Sometimes his plans worked.

Sometimes they landed him in jail.

This time the federal judge was not going to be so forgiving.

In an interview with the Spokesman-Review on July 2, 1994, Doug tried to justify his outbursts with his obsession for guns:

"I picked up dog dung, mowed lawns, and even pulled tricks on East Sprague as a male prostitute for extra money to buy my guns. People probably think I'm crazy, but I just wanted to fit in and be left alone with my family."

"Everybody needs a purpose in life and mine is guns."

In September he plead guilty, and on December 14, 1994, he was sentenced to almost three years in prison. On January 12, 1995, Doug was transported to the Federal Correctional Institution in Sheridan, Oregon. If he managed to receive all of the potential reductions in his sentence for "good behavior," then he would be released on October 31, 1997.

Two and a half years in the rainy forests of northwestern Oregon.

How lovely.

Not surprisingly, Doug's awkward appearance and stunted social mannerisms kept him in constant turmoil. Other inmates teased and belittled him endlessly. He kept quiet and to himself. Doug was nothing if not a survivor. On occasion he would befriend a short-timer or a rookie corrections officer, but his relationships, much like they were on the outside, were meaningless.

More than 400 miles to the northeast, life on Sprague Avenue wasn't getting any easier for the prostitutes he had come to know either.

Doug's former acquaintance, Shannon Zielinski, who had alluded to police some years earlier that she knew who killed her friends in 1990, was found dead by two young boys who had just gotten off their school bus on June 14, 1996. Her body was badly decomposed, but investigators were able to determine that she had died from a single small-caliber gunshot wound to the head. She was found in a rural area 12 miles to the northeast of downtown near Holcomb Road and Mount Spokane Drive. Four years earlier, a few hundred yards away, the body of Sherry Palmer had been discovered by a hiker in 1992.

And just like Sherry, Shannon was also found with a white plastic grocery bag covering her head.

Odd.

Doug had the best (but probably most uncomfortable) alibi one could hope for.

He was in prison.

Halfway between the two dump sites, a lone tavern sat along the highway. Presumably a "stopover" for travelers on the highway toward Mt. Spokane, another five or six miles up the road. A perfect place to dump a body where the killer might think investigators would just chalk up the slaying to a night of violence and inebriation stemming from the tavern's remote location.

A little more than a year later, JoAnn Flores was found dead on November 7, 1996, from a single small-caliber gunshot to the head. Unlike Sherry Palmer and Shannon Zielinski, Flores was discovered inside the city limits, near the 200 block of West Riverside Avenue.

Less than a block from Sprague Avenue.

And less than a mile from the Spokane River.

Doug was 350 miles to the southeast.

Locked in a prison cell.

The similarities between the Flores murder and the murders of Sapp, Lowe, and Brisbois seemed obvious to the public. But police were less than convinced.

Whores had a tough life.

Everyone knew that.

But this was Spokane.

Police would need evidence of a connection— otherwise they had nothing more to offer on the subject.

But things were starting to heat up. Some members of the law enforcement community felt that politics was keeping this investigation from going where it needed to go. Others felt that alarming the public unnecessarily and tarnishing the reputation of the city and surrounding communities would not serve them well in the public eye. From here, residents could turn up their noses at cities like Seattle, 275 miles across the state to the west. Spokane didn't have the kinds of problems you found in cities like Seattle. Spokane was different.

Better.

Just peace, beauty, and tranquility.

But on a hot August morning in 1997, that was all about to change.

The vileness and stench of Sprague Avenue was going to force itself upon the suburbs and rural farming communities of Spokane forever. And like Seattle, and all of the other big cities in the world, the whores were going to bear the brunt of it.

Late August in downtown Spokane is always scorching hot. The concrete buildings, iron bridges, and trashy overpasses along Sprague Avenue do nothing to alleviate the uncomfortable and often unbearable heat. Even the regular Johns seem to avoid trolling the Avenue for $40 worth of their favorite entertainment. Across the Spokane River to the northeast of the city, cool breezes roll off of nearby Mt. Spokane, and although it is only a few miles from downtown, the northeast corridor of Spokane County is an entirely different world.

Scenic mixed forest, mountain views, and hayfields.

Modern ramblers situated on 5- or 10-acre lots with outbuildings full of ATVs and late-model cars.

The slower pace and beauty of the area almost redefined what a suburb should be. There were no whores, drug dealers, or panhandlers maneuvering for hard-earned dollars.

Just respectability and clarity of purpose.

On August 26, 1997, a pair of workers were performing some field maintenance on a hay bailer. As a mild summer breeze began to float back and forth across the hayfield, the fetor of decaying flesh swam beside them. At first, the pair thought it was a dead deer hit by a car near the corner of Forker and Judkins roads, just off of the Mt. Spokane Park Drive. However, as anyone who has ever experienced the malodorous misfortune of a rotting human body can attest, there is no smell quite like it in the world. It did not take long before the workers investigated the source of the stench, and discovered human remains.

The remains were so severely decomposed that the police investigators believed they were more than a week old.

The corner of Forker and Judkins roads was less than 5 miles from where Shannon Zielinski and Sherry Palmer had been discovered earlier.

Publicly, police would not reveal the possibility of a serial killer for months, but with the close proximity to the Palmer and Zielinski dump sites, investigators privately wondered if they might have a serial killer cleansing the streets of Spokane.

Hours earlier, a man looking for aluminum cans in a lot behind 1800 East Springfield within the Spokane city limits couldn't help but notice a foul odor permeating the hot, dusty morning in the weeded alleyway cutting through the center of the Sprague Avenue industrial district.

It wasn't uncommon for a dog or possum to get hit by one of the many freight trains rolling through Spokane day and night and crawl a few blocks towards Sprague before succumbing and beginning its well-deserved journey back to the ashes and dust.

As the man struggled to push his cart over a small dirt berm designed to keep car traffic from cutting through the lot on a small, narrow trail, he discovered the body of a young Latino woman. Drag marks and blood stains indicated she had not been there very long.

Without a doubt, he could see that she had been shot in the back of the head.

Jon Keehner

The body discovered near Forker and Judkins fell under the jurisdiction of the Spokane County Sheriff's Department; the remains dumped near East Springfield Avenue fell under the jurisdiction of the City of Spokane.

Within days, police identified the body found near Forker and Judkins as 16-year-old Jennifer Joseph. She had been working as a prostitute for more than a year with arrests for solicitation in San Francisco, California, and Salem, Oregon. Her father, John Joseph, lived across the state in the Tacoma suburb of Spanaway. He explained that Jennifer did not adjust to the continuous moving around the world as a military child.

Clearly.

The other body was identified as 20-year-old Heather Hernandez. She was also a known prostitute who floated around among Idaho, California, and Arizona turning tricks to survive. She was born in Phoenix, Arizona, but other than a marriage certificate to a man named Bladimir Hernandez and a high school diploma, very little was known about her. The newspapers even characterized her as a "transient" rather than a "prostitute."

At least for a couple of a days.

Police detectives told the public that they did not have any evidence to connect the two murders. Members of the press and people working in the community disagreed. Social workers, clergy, and concerned citizens did everything they could to mount public pressure on the Spokane Police and Spokane Sheriff's Department. But later that evening, on August 31, every channel on television began showing images of the Eiffel Tower, a narrow two-lane tunnel in Paris, and a mangled Mercedes-Benz. Princess Dianna had been killed in a car wreck in Paris, France.

The whores on Sprague Avenue had little chance against a Princess.

They had little chance against anything.

And Doug was still in prison.

23

Advanced States of Decomposition

By late September of 1997, Doug was counting down the days to his release.

Halloween.

How fitting.

As the sun rose up over the Spokane River on the morning of October 22, 1997, crews cleaning an intake pipe of the Post Street Dam made a sickening discovery— a body entangled in the grating designed to keep debris from the spillway. The woman was eventually identified as Teresalynn Asmussen, a 22-year-old mother with a history of drug arrests and prostitution. Her head had been smashed in with a blunt object, and she was dumped in the river. Police noted the similar background to Yolanda Sapp, Nickie Lowe, Kathleen Brisbois, Sherry Palmer, Shannon Zielinski, JoAnne Flores, Heather Hernandez, and Jennifer Joseph, but the manner in which the women died led police to believe they were not connected.

The public, however, was not as easily convinced.

Nine women.

Drugs.

Prostitution.

Violence.

On October 31, 1997, Doug was unceremoniously released from prison. After an eight-hour bus ride, he was back in Spokane hoping to reconnect with his beloved whores on Sprague.

And how beloved they were, these soiled doves.

On November 1, 1997, the day after Doug was released from prison, a 41-year-old mother of two young sons, Sunny Oster, who had been living in a motel known for drug dealing and prostitution in the Lakewood area of Tacoma, almost 300 miles to the southwest of Spokane, had been reported missing. Earlier, in September, she had finally agreed to travel to Spokane to enter a drug rehabilitation program. The shy and quiet Sunny mostly kept to herself and rarely let much be known about her life circumstances to those around her. She completed the program on October 31 and was reported missing the very next day.

On November 6, 1997, the Spokesman-Review reported that skeletal remains were found near the Hangman Valley Golf Course just a few miles southwest of Spokane. Hangman Creek meandered through the partially wooded, upscale residential development. A man walking his dog became curious when, each evening, the dog disappeared into the same brushy area. After a few nights of repeated behavior, the man followed the dog and discovered the remains.

Eight days later, dental records revealed the remains belonged to a known prostitute and drug addict, Darla Sue Scott.

She had probably been dead for days, maybe even weeks.

No one had even bothered to report her missing.

She was 29 years old.

Darla Sue had been shot once in the head with a small caliber pistol, and a white plastic bag had been placed over her head.

Just like Sherry Palmer.

Just like Shannon Zielinski.

Doug had been out of jail for exactly one week.

Someone was killing women with ties to Sprague Avenue.

And it wasn't Doug.

For two weeks he had been staying at a motel just off of Sprague Avenue.

It was cheap.

And familiar.

Doug regularly read the newspaper in hopes of renting a new house, finding deals on used guns, and discovering new opportunities to hustle.

On November 14, 1997, an article caught his eye:

"3 Sought in Prostitute Slayings — Women May Help Solve Series of Killings."

The article begged for information on three missing women and implied they may have had ties to prostitution on Sprague Avenue. Lonna Marie Hughes had been missing since October 27; Shawn Johnson was reported missing on October 29; and Laurie Ann Wason went missing on November 3.

Welcome back to Spokane my love.

Doug was shocked at what he read.

He had talked about killing prostitutes while he was in prison and let his feelings be known to all who would listen.

Whores were lying, no-good pieces of shit.

Had someone taken it upon themselves to do it?

He stared intently at the pictures wondering if he recognized any of them. Their given names were worthless.

Everyone on Sprague had a street name that they went by. The next day it got even worse. Public outrage at the slayings prompted Spokane County and the City of Spokane to consider forming another task force to solve the murders.

Now they were going to put a task force together?

He started to tremble.

Shit.

He thought all this was behind him. But a task force? Every time his thoughts tried to move forward he kept coming back to it. The government was bad enough on its own. But now an organized force whose task it was to find the killer of those whores? Doug looked up from the newspaper to see if anyone was watching or looked out of the ordinary. A kid on a skateboard slid by, staring at the long-haired guy with the big glasses.

Doug tried to ignore him and folded the newspaper in half and kept reading. Within seconds he dropped the paper and stared as the kid disappeared out of sight.

He wasn't sure if he should be worried or not. His instincts told him he had better get ready—always be ready. But part of him figured if the police thought that all the killings were tied together then this could work to his advantage.

If they were killed by the same person, it couldn't have been him. He was in prison when three of them were killed.

Toward the end of the article he realized that the police did not necessarily believe the three killings from 1990 were tied to the most recent ones.

There must be something they aren't saying.

Fuck!

If the police were putting a task force together it might not be long before the trail led to him.

But he had been in prison.

This was perfect.

And fucked at the same time.

Obviously somebody was killing whores, and obviously the police would think it was all the same guy.

And obviously he had an alibi.

It couldn't have been him.

*   *   *

Within a few weeks, living out of the shitbox motel was starting to wear on his tranquility. Every time he stood paralyzed before the door to his room, fumbling with the key, the old canker sore that managed the motel stared disapprovingly through her living room window right at him.

It wasn't as though she were an innocent onlooker.

Her delicate sensibilities had been scorched years earlier when, on her 36th wedding anniversary, her husband jumped in front of a freight train a few blocks from where she and Doug now awkwardly pretended not to see each other. Her family in Ogden knew full well of her propensity to make grown men seek their own destruction rather than continue to listen to her perpetual flood of angry bullshit.

They wanted nothing to do with her.

So, after her husband removed himself from her reign of agony and terror, years earlier when Sprague Avenue held greater promise, she sold their home and bought the lovely 18-unit lodgings.

Now she monitored the comings and goings of her overnight guests.

He threw down the bag full of Penthouse and Hustler magazines he had bought at the 7-11 convenience store down the street and pulled out the newspaper from under his arm.

Each time he opened the paper to prowl the classifieds for estate sales where might be able to replenish his gun collection without attracting any attention, the stories of missing and dead whores jarred darkened memories he could not bury.

No matter how deeply he dug the grave.

But today, his attention was fixed to one of the estate sales. Not for the guns, but because a small home where an elderly woman had died months earlier was listed by her heirs who were willing to carry the contract on the house with a small down payment.

He knew the neighborhood well.

The tiny salt box house on Empire Avenue in north Spokane was only a few blocks from where he had been renting on Dalton before he had gone to prison. The estate was asking $25000 for the house with $5000 down. While in prison, his social security checks continued to fill his bank account. He would take a small amount of money each month and place it in his prison account so he could buy things, but he had managed to amass nearly $8000 by the time he was released. Best of all, Sprague Avenue was less than a 10-minute drive down the hill.

On November 25, 1997, Doug drove two hours south of Spokane to Lewiston, Idaho, with a cashier's check for $5000 and signed the papers to purchase the house.

It was going to be perfect

Just him and his family of guns.

Quaint.

Four days later, on November 29, 34-year-old Linda Maybin was reported missing by social worker Lynn Everson who had not seen her in over a week. With all of the media attention surrounding dead prostitutes, Lynn Everson had been watching over them, as much as she possibly could, for years. Linda was a known crack addict and prostitute who had spent time over the previous few years circulating among the cities of Ellensburg, Cheney, Seattle, and Spokane.

A week before Christmas, on December 18, 1997, the body of Shawn Johnson, who had been missing since October 29 and was one of the women mentioned often in news reports about the dead and missing prostitutes, was discovered at the 11400 block of South Hangman Valley Road— only a few hundred yards away from where the body of Darla Sue Scott had been found a little more than a month earlier. Shawn had been killed by a gunshot wound to the head and also had a white plastic bag on her head.

Two days later, the newspaper reported that the police may suspect a serial killer may have dumped the bodies near Hangman Creek.

A serial killer.

Yolanda Sapp, Nickie Lowe, Kathleen Brisbois, Sherry Palmer, Shannon Zielinski, JoAnne Flores, Heather Hernandez, Jennifer Joseph, Teresalyn Asmussen, Darla Sue Scott, and now Shawn Johnson.

11 women.

On December 23, 1997, the Spokesman-Review reported that a task force had been formed to focus on the murders. There were four detectives assigned to solve these murders.

Spokane's serial killer was receiving international attention.

Amateur sleuths around the world began to believe that the notorious Green River Killer had moved east to Spokane, 275 miles from Seattle.

And was killing again.

Doug just hoped that whoever was doing it would get blamed for Yolanda, Nickie, and Kathleen. But if they didn't catch someone soon, he knew it would not be long before they came to see him.

It was only a matter of time.

He knew too many whores, too many pimps, and too many people on Sprague.

On December 26, 1997, the body of 31-year-old Laurie Ann Wason, who had been missing since November 3, was discovered by a jogger in a gravel pit near 14th and Carnahan in Spokane.

The gravel pit at 14th and Carnahan was nearly smack dab in the middle of a residential district south of the Spokane River and on the east end of Spokane's South Hill. Trails and ATV paths had evolved over the years, and the pit became a dirty, impromptu park of sorts.

Nearly 18 hours later when they removed the body from where it had been partially buried, police discovered another body— 39-year-old Shawn McClenahan, who had been missing a little more than a week. McClenahan was last seen leaving her brother-in-law's house in a blue van with another woman. Both bodies were in advanced states of decomposition, with gunshot wounds to the head and white plastic bags over their heads.

Laurie Ann Wason had been missing since early November, and Shawn McClenahan had been seen a little more than a week ago.

Police were befuddled.

Had the killer moved Laurie Ann Wason's body from somewhere else (Hangman Valley) and dumped it on top of Shawn McClenahan whom he had just killed? If so, was he trying to keep Laurie Ann Wason from being discovered by choosing a new dump site?

Why?

Bodies had been dumped along the Spokane River.

Bodies were dumped near Mt. Spokane.

Bodies had been dumped in Spokane's industrial district.

Bodies had been dumped on the way to Mt. Spokane.

Bodies were dumped near Hangman Creek.

Bodies had been dumped on the east end of the South Hill.

The bodies of dead prostitutes were piling up everywhere.

On January 9, 1998, Doug was awakened from a nap on his couch.

"Good morning, sir. Are you Douglas Perry? I wondered if I might ask you about some women you might know or have known from Sprague Avenue. Is this a good time?"

24
A Gender Psychosis Disorder

On January 9, 1998, Steve Sines questioned Doug about missing girls, dead prostitutes, and his relationships and knowledge of their friends and associates. He notes that unnamed inmates had told prison staff that Perry talked about "saving prostitutes" from the streets, and some of these inmates believed that he had killed prostitutes before.

Doug was terrified.

He thought the man was there to solicit Doug's help when, in fact, he was trying to pin the murder of them dirty whores on him?

Doug quickly showed Sines his prison intake and outtake paperwork. Doug had been in federal prison in Oregon between January of 1995 and October 31, 1997.

If all of these murders were tied together, and Doug continuously suggested that they must be, then he couldn't *possibly* have done it.

Sines was not so easily convinced.

He pressed further.

This was not what Doug had expected — how could he possibly have killed these women from prison?

Sines pointed out that four of the women either went missing or their bodies turned up during the week Doug returned home from prison.

Was someone trying to welcome him home, perhaps?

As the conversation turned, Doug, who by now had a lot of experience with police detectives, politely informed Mr. Sines that if he wanted to question him any further, Doug was more than willing to help find whoever was behind killing ALL of these whores, but he had an appointment he needed to get to.

This wasn't going to be as easy as he thought.

Three weeks later, on January 30, 1998, police announced that 24-year-old Melinda Mercer, whose body was discovered December 7, 1997, outside of Tacoma, Washington, with a white plastic bag over her head, was likely a victim of the Spokane serial killer. She had died from a small-caliber gunshot wound to the head.

Now Tacoma was connected?

Tacoma was 280 miles to the west.

Immediately, police considered the obvious possibility of a military connection, as McChord Air Force Base was just a few miles south of Tacoma, and Fairchild Air Force Base was only a few miles west of Spokane.

On February 8, 1998, the decomposing body of Sunny Oster was found along Graham Road in rural Spokane County by a man and his wife who were out walking their dog. She had been reported missing the day after Doug was released from prison.

It had now been over three months.

Police did not immediately reveal the location where the body was discovered to the public — they just said they had found another body. The lack of scavenging on the body and the advanced decomposition indicated that she was probably buried somewhere and then exhumed and dumped here by the killer or accomplices.

Directly in the middle of farm country, the farmers and residents confirmed what was mostly common knowledge about the area— predators and scavengers were everywhere. If her body had been dumped there when she was killed in November, there would either have been nothing left of her, or some evidence of scavenging.

There was nothing.

It was very possible she had been dumped near the Hangman Valley dump site or some other dump site, but whoever was killing them eventually wanted them to be discovered.

Instead, his beautiful creations were rotting into the Spokane landscape.

Quietly.

Unnoticed.

And now the police were finding them, and they weren't even telling the press and the media where they were.

This was not going to work.

It was time to give the police a little message about who was the smart one in this relationship.

Who had the brains?

What better way to tell the police that they are fools than stage a body on April Fool's Day?

On April 1, 1998, the body of 34-year-old Linda Maybin was found at the gravel pit on 14th and Carnahan. Her body was dumped literally where the forensic truck had been parked during the forensic sweep of the Wason and McLenahan dump site. It would have been impossible for Maybin's body to have been there in late December and not have been noticed.

Maybin had been dead since November.

Where had her body been stored?

He Said, She Said: The Spokane River Killer

During the first week of July, on July 7, 1998, a transient discovered the body of 47-year-old Michelyn Derning at 200 North Crestline Street. She had been shot in the head and had a white plastic bag on her head.

Police had thought the serial killer had maybe left or been incarcerated on other charges since he had not killed for quite a while. But this new death invigorated the police in the Sprague red-light district to really get moving.

He (or she) was toying with them now.

Sixteen potentially connected murdered women.

Doug could do nothing but watch while someone killed his whores.

He knew they probably deserved it.

He just didn't want to take the fall for it.

It had been more than six months since that investigator had tried to pin all of this on him. The papers claimed that the task force was growing by the week, and they were narrowing down the list of suspects.

They were going to get their man.

By Wednesday, July 22, 1998, Doug was tired of hiding in his house like a hermit. He wanted, *needed,* some companionship. Clairann had awakened a beast within him and sparked his masculinity.

Cruising Sprague for some company had become somewhat more complicated since the inception of that damn task force, but as long as he only made one loop he probably wouldn't get flagged and pulled over by the patrols. He headed east on Empire and turned right when he hit Market Street. Eventually he made his way down to the Greene Street Bridge.

A wry smile crept across his face.

For a second, his blood began to tingle.

Once he hit Sprague Avenue he took a right and the hunt was on. Summer nights were usually easy. But all this talk of a serial killer was really putting a damper on activities.

He slowed down as he approached Altamont, crossed Napa Street, and passed the Checkerboard Tavern. On Helena he took a right to loop around on Riverside.

No one?

He crept down Riverside until he got back to Altamont and headed back toward Sprague.

Within seconds a Spokane patrol car pulled right up on his rear bumper and turned on its lights.

Fuck.

Doug sat as upright and as still as he could. He knew better than to bring any of his firearms with him out on Sprague as that would surely send him back to prison.

That had been well established.

Doug rolled down his window as the officer approached.

The patrolman took his license and registration but Doug refused to carry the mandated insurance on his vehicles. It wasn't the government's job to see that he was financially protected in the event of an accident or unforeseen occurrence.

The officer returned and handed Doug back his driver's license and his registration.

"So, you don't have proof of insurance, but I am going to give you a break tonight on that one. Are you out here trolling tonight?" the officer began.

Doug was irritated.

"What? Because I couldn't be looking for an address or something?" he retorted back at the officer.

"Look, sir, you pulled around the loop; this area has signs and is under heavy patrol for prostitution activity. But if you were looking for an address — what address? Maybe I can help?" the officer replied sarcastically.

He knew Doug wasn't looking for an address.

"So why don't you explain to me why you think I was trolling?" Doug fired back.

"It's pretty simple. Middle-aged, white male —"

"So if I were weren't a middle-aged— " Doug cut him off.

The officer fired right back, "Exactly; it is men who are out here trolling. Not middle-aged white women. Most of those out here have nothing to do with it. Or are trying to help..."

Doug drifted into a dazed fog.

He heard not another word.

Somehow he returned to his house. Finally, he had come up with a plan to end all of the bullshit harassment from the cops.

He knew it wouldn't happen fast— nor would it be cheap.

But he had a plan.

*   *   *

On September 24, 1998, police in Kitsap County revealed that the murder of Patricia Barnes, 61, whose body was found August 25, 1995, off Peacock Hill Road some 10 miles northwest of Tacoma, Washington, was the work of the Spokane serial killer. Law enforcement agencies all across Washington and the neighboring states of Oregon and Idaho were scouring missing persons' reports and unsolved homicides going back decades for possible connections.

As it stood, the City of Spokane, Spokane County, Pierce County, and now Kitsap County were all running active investigations.

But the bodies quit turning up.

Had he been incarcerated? Had he moved on? Had he stopped?

Not likely, according to the FBI Behavioral Analysis teams.

Serial killers just don't stop. They might go through cooling-off periods, but they never just stop.

Killing is like a drug to them.

One with no cure or treatment.

On December 31, 1998, Doug decided to treat himself to a little New Year's Eve party. At the corner of Pacific and Cowley he picked up a prostitute named Valerie. Normally he would have simply conducted business in the car and slipped in to a cheap motel for a quickie.

But tonight was going to be special.

He offered to take her to his house, which typically included a higher payout. Valerie enthusiastically agreed.

Once inside his house, Valerie started to get a little nervous. By now most of the working women on Sprague were extremely careful. With the stream of endless bodies being discovered finally drying up, it must have been working. But Doug had guns, knives, ammunition, and even electronic stun guns all over the house.

Doug tried to reassure her that he wouldn't hurt her, because "he liked her." Valerie assumed this meant that if he didn't like her, he would have harmed her. Rather than risk raising his ire, she went along with it and gave him some of the best sex he had ever had. Despite his pleading to the contrary, Valerie insisted he return her to where he had picked her up.

As soon as she was safely back on Sprague Avenue, she called the police.

Doug, who was counting on having companionship all evening, continued to loop Sprague trolling for another prostitute. As Valerie was providing a statement to police, Doug drove right by in his newly-acquired teal blue Geo Metro.

Once again police pulled him over and berated him about all of the dead whores.

This was the final straw.

It was never going to end.

He agreed to let them search the Geo rather than wait hours and hours while a search warrant was secured. He knew he had nothing of interest in the car, because he had just bought it. As police searched, they discovered legal papers that stated Doug "...has a gender psychosis disorder which makes him not like females." The officer asked Doug why he was in the area, and Doug said he liked trying to help get prostitutes off of the streets.

His intentions seemed pure.

His method seemed highly questionable.

A week later, on January 8, 1999, the murder of Connie LaFontaine-Ellis was officially connected to the Spokane serial killer. Her body was discovered near rural Tacoma on October 13, 1998. She was shot in the head and had a white plastic bag over her head. She had lived on the Spokane Indian Reservation but had moved to Tacoma five years earlier. She traveled between Spokane and Tacoma a lot and was rumored to have known Kathleen Brisbois.

Although police never officially connected them, agencies across the western United States and even in Europe suspected this killer may have killed dozens and dozens of women all around the globe.

The Green River Killer was eliminated as a possible connection. Washington State had two of the most prolific serial killers in history.

And neither one of them had been caught.

In June of 1999, Doug finally accepted that his counselors were not going to go along with his plan.

The State of Washington wouldn't pay for it.

The Federal Government wouldn't pay for it.

He had no choice but to take out a second mortgage on his house for $10,000.

With no suspects or arrests, law enforcement is forced to start re-evaluating previously held beliefs about the cases. Some believe the 1990 and more recent killings might be related as the women were all killed with small caliber handguns. Others in the department adamantly maintain that they are not related. The public is not offered any explanation, as the disclosure of confidential information might jeopardize the case.

It is possible, some hypothesize, that the killer was evolving and had learned from the Sapp, Lowe, and Brisbois murders. Thus, the white bags over their heads may have been to minimize blood or tissue evidence being left in whatever the killer was using to transport them to the dump sites. The dump sites themselves may have been evolving away from the downtown area and toward rural areas, because the killer might have been coming close to getting caught. Kathleen Brisbois had only been dead an hour or so when she was discovered.

That might have been enough to scare him away from killing until he killed Sherry Palmer in 1992. Maybe something went wrong with her and he waited again until Shannon Zielinski in 1996. Maybe he was killing elsewhere the whole time and only came to Spokane occasionally?

The questions and public furor over the dead whores was reaching a fever pitch. Mark Fuhrman, a retired Los Angeles detective who had become somewhat famous for his role in the O.J. Simpson murders a few years earlier, had retired to the north Idaho area and spent a lot of time investigating the murders with a local radio host. He was extremely critical of the Spokane Task Force, and his consternation was well known among the rank and file of the Spokane police.

In the autumn of 1999 the police revealed that they had a working DNA profile of a man whose DNA was found on and inside many of the victims. They knew if they eventually caught a suspect they would be able to link him to most of the deaths.

They did not simply wait for a suspect to be apprehended. They tried matching the DNA to many suspects. In an odd and intriguing case, a man from the Lewiston, Idaho, and Clarkston, Washington, area who had been a person of interest in killings there from the 1970s and

1980s agreed to provide his DNA to Spokane County under the agreement that the DNA he provided was destroyed immediately after the tests were performed and not used or compared in any other cases. Recently, the case involving the deaths of the five people in the late '70s and early '80s has received renewed attention from the police and the media in the Lewis Clark Valley.

In January of 2000, Doug finally put his plan in motion. He traveled halfway around the globe to Thailand where he was able to have gender reassignment surgery.

Doug Perry was no more.

In March of 2000, Doug officially changed his name to Donna Rebecca Perry.

He was now she.

No one would give two shits about a lady trying to help prostitutes. No one would bother her ever again about them dead whores.

Her plan had finally worked.

They were never going to catch the killer anyway.

Never.

Less than a month later, on April 18, 2000, Robert Yates was arrested at 6:30 a.m. and charged with murder in the first degree in the death of an unnamed prostitute. Yates was a 47-year-old married father of five. He had been a helicopter pilot for the US Army for 18 years and was currently a Warrant Officer for the Washington State National Guard assigned to the 185th Airborne Battalion out of Ft. Lewis, Washington. A few miles from Tacoma, Washington. He had no previous criminal convictions. He grew up on Whidbey Island an hour north of Seattle, Washington.

Donna was convinced that Yates would be convicted of doing all the whores— she told everyone who would listen how she was convinced they were all killed by the same person. They will never find her now. This Yates guy was going to take the heat for all of it.

Her brilliance, once again, had overwhelmed her adversaries. First it was Deputy Johnson, then it was them stupid whores who kept trying to get between her and Clairann…

Clairann.

She sighed.

Now she had bested the Spokane Task Force.

Fuck them.

In October of 2000, Yates confessed and pleaded guilty to multiple murders — but he was not in the area during the 1990 murders or the murder of Sherry Palmer in 1992.

Yates takes and passes a lie-detector test.

Although police and prosecutors suspect Yates is not telling them everything — they believe Yates did not do the 1990 or Palmer murders.

The murders of Yolanda Sapp, Nickie Lowe, Kathleen Brisbois, and other missing women remain unsolved.

25
Unencumbered By Her Past

How is it fucking possible?

All of those damned dead whores and they believe that guy didn't kill the other three?

Donna was beside herself.

At least the continuous harassment on Sprague would finally stop.

Life moved on.

And so did death.

Her mother, Ruth, died in California on September 30, 2001. Good riddance as far as Donna was concerned. She hated her mother like she hated those whores.

A month later, on November 30, 2001, an arrest was made in the Green River killings. Police all over Washington,

Oregon, and Idaho begin to scramble to see if Gary Ridgway could be tied to any of their unsolved prostitute homicides.

The media attention surrounding the Yates case wound down very quickly. Most of the uninformed or ill-informed public felt that the police just didn't have the evidence they needed to get Yates on the 1990 murders, and the only reason they were not going after him was simply to save the county money.

As far as the public was concerned, Sprague Avenue had been saved. Everyone could go back to $20 blow jobs, $40 thigh fucks, and free condoms from the AIDS-awareness lady near the church.

A fun-filled fuck-fest.

It got even more joyous in Spokane when prosecutors across the state in Pierce County announced that although Robert Yates had struck a deal with Spokane County to plead guilty and avoid the death penalty, Pierce County was not a party to that action, and, therefore, they were free to pursue the death penalty for the murders of Melinda Mercer and Connie Ellis. In September of 2002, Yates was convicted of their murders and sentenced to die by lethal injection.

As of this writing, he is still on death row. His latest appeal claims he was mentally ill, a necrophiliac, and therefore unable to control his murderous urges.

Donna's brother, Larry, who had so severely abused Doug when he was a child, died a couple of months later on December 1, 2002.

The only family Donna had left was her sister in California.

And they hadn't spoken in years.

After a thorough investigation of Green River Killer Gary Ridgeway and his eventual confession to 48 murders of prostitutes on the west side of the Cascade Mountains, the 1990 murders officially remained unsolved.

The monkey remained.

He Said, She Said: The Spokane River Killer

In 2005, Detectives Mark Burbridge and Jim Dresback were assigned the cold case. Other than reviewing the files, there was not a lot they could do.

By 2008, all federal inmates were required to submit their DNA profiles to CODIS (Combined DNA Index System). Law enforcement agencies across the nation who had been sitting on cold cases for years scrambled to get DNA samples analyzed, profiles constructed, and results fed into the system. The forensics lab in Washington had been consistently pushing and plodding its way through the backlog of cases. In many cases, samples were given a low priority due to the quality of the sample or the age of the case. Other cases were held back because the samples appeared so small it was possible the sample might have been consumed during the analysis. This could have been a disaster if the case was solved, but the DNA sample was no longer available for defense analysis or further scrutiny.

In the back of the Spokane County evidence room, fingernail clippings taken from Kathleen Brisbois sat untouched for nearly 20 years. Based on the evidence at the crime scene, it was clear that whoever had attacked and killed her had probably suffered some sort of injury themselves. Clumps of hair and dried blood, coupled with scuff and drag marks, led detectives to believe that one hell of a brawl had gone on there in the moments before Kathleen was finally subdued, shot, and killed.

Advances in DNA technology allowed forensic scientists to create genetic profiles from samples so small that even five years earlier may not have been possible without consuming the sample. The 1990 murders had been designated for another look— and with the new CODIS requirements— it seemed the potential to nab a suspect was strong enough that it was worth the risk to attempt to process the samples and try to develop a DNA profile to enter into the CODIS system.

In 2009, Detective Dresback gathered what evidence he felt appropriate and sent it in to the Washington State Crime Lab.

It was a Hail Mary at best.

By the end of the year, the Crime Lab informed Detective Dresback that the lab was able to develop a DNA profile for whoever Kathleen Brisbois sank her nails into on that warm, early spring evening in May of 1990. Although the DNA profile could only help identify the person if a match to compare it to was found, one thing they now knew for sure, although they were not at all surprised, was that they were looking for a man.

Donna, of course, had no knowledge about what was going on with that case. All she knew was that it was still open. But she felt relatively at ease about it.

No one was looking for an old lady in her mid-fifties.

By 2001, she had settled into a fairly predictable routine. Most of the neighborhood knew who she was and that she had a sordid past, but no one seemed to care much. As long as you left her alone, the neighbors claimed, she seemed to leave you alone.

At least by now she had learned that much.

In the summer of 2011, Spokanimal, an animal rescue entity in Spokane, obtained a court order and removed dozens of cats from her home. On November 14, 2011, she had been served with a notice that the City of Spokane was going to attach a permanent notice to the title of her home if she did not clean up the fecal matter and contaminated areas of the house.

How dare they.

Why can't they just leave her and her cats and her guns alone?

Once again the government just couldn't let her alone.

Once again they had to get their mitts on everything she did.

But at nearly 60 years old, she had become much wiser and more subdued. Rather than fight the order on principle or in court, she simply chose to ignore it.

And like she always seemed to do with her guns...

She simply continued to amass more cats.

She figured she had about six months before the City would try and do anything. And as always when she felt threatened, she turned to her guns.

In her bedroom closet she stared at the arsenal she had amassed and sighed. Adding to her ammo collection always seemed to be a good way to alleviate some stress. Nothing gave her as much comfort as a few more rounds of ammo and maybe a new magazine for her pistol.

It was March 14, 2012.

Her Social Security direct deposit had been done on the prior Thursday, and now that the bills were paid, maybe a little shopping at the White Elephant wouldn't hurt.

Outside it was cloudy, but the spring was warming up enough that she knew winter's grip had finally loosened for good. She turned east on Empire from her house and made a right turn onto Crestline. The neighborhood felt comfortable to her in a lot of ways. She had lived here over twenty-three years save for her short stint in prison.

But that was Doug.

This was *Donna*.

She turned east on Trent and headed along the river toward the Spokane Valley. Every gun shop around Division Street knew about her. They knew she was not allowed to purchase or handle any firearms. She wished they would just mind their own business, but she knew they wouldn't. At least out in the Valley she could do her thing unencumbered by her past.

The White Elephant Sporting Goods Store had been a familiar place since she wandered into the one on Division Street so many years ago to take Clairann camping.

She wondered how different things might be if she had just taken all of the batteries in the house that fit in that damn pager.

The White Elephant store out in Spokane Valley was one of the more popular stores in the entire area — guns, ammo, sporting goods, paramilitary clothing — even children's toys. Just like the Division store, it had it all. Everyone seemed to mind their business there. They had better things to do. No one would bother an old lady.

Even if she did have too many cats.

Donna crossed I-90 at Sullivan and headed up the hill.

The parking lot at the White Elephant Sporting Goods store didn't seem to be too full. But parking there was always a pain in the ass. Thank God her little Geo Metro was easy to park. These asshole men in their 4x4 trucks with camouflage trim and their window decals of antlered bucks were always so condescending. If they knew she was a transgender woman, they would laugh and mock her.

Everyone did.

Everyone laughed at the obvious man who dressed, acted, and sort of resembled a woman.

Fuck them.

For a minute she sat in the seat of her little car with her hands affixed to the worn-out steering wheel. The seat had lost most of its padding and a metal spring jabbed through the vinyl and poked into her leg.

She was used to it and didn't seem to care. Pain was just a part of life.

Sprague Avenue had changed little since she first arrived 23 years earlier. It was still noisy, dirty, crowded, and sick. No one ever looked happy on Sprague. And why should they?

She stared across the parking lot and beyond Sprague Avenue towards Mount Spokane in the distance. The top of the mountain was still covered in snow. The smoke from a yard fire drifted through the windows of the little car and reminded her of the orchard back in Omak. She held her hand up in front of her face and blocked out the view below the horizon so all she could see was the mountain in the distance.

She smiled.

Then she moved her hand upward so she could see nothing but the busy street in front of her. Back and forth she moved her hand, playing a little game with herself. A couple of young men on skateboards dashed suddenly in front of her and laughed at her while pointing.

Let one of those assholes run into me in my orchard.

But those days were gone. She didn't want any trouble.

Men were pigs.

As she stared outward toward the north, her little car filled with pitch black smoke from the exhaust of a giant Ford diesel truck as the driver accelerated to turn out of the parking lot onto Sprague.

Asshole.

She nearly choked.

But it snapped her out of her daydream. She threw the door open and climbed out of the little car. She turned deliberately back toward the door of the Metro and locked it with her key. With a snap she pulled up on the door handle to verify it was locked.

Inside the store she grabbed a basket and wandered aimlessly down the aisles.

It was so nice, she thought, not having men always trying to bump into her like they did when she was Doug. His long-haired ponytail, thick glasses, and awkward appearance always seemed to draw them to him.

But now, everyone tried to get out of the little old lady's way.

Near the back corner of the store in the clearance aisle, she found a couple of magazines that would fit her pistol.

They were exactly what she needed.

The ammo was kept up behind the front counter.

Patiently she waited behind a couple of other customers and finally garnered six 50-round boxes of 9mm ammo. Oddly, an older fellow who looked like he worked there seemed to be taking video of her with his smartphone.

Everyone laugh at the freak, right?

What an asshole.

A few minutes after she pulled her little Geo Metro out onto Sprague Avenue and headed west, for old time's sake, she got pulled over by a Spokane Police Officer.

Some things will never change she laughed.

She knew that when they saw she was just a little old lady on her way back home from the White Elephant that they would probably apologize and send her on her way.

But as was the common thread and theme of her pitiful existence over the previous 60 years, that was not going to be the case.

Inside the White Elephant, a retired police officer who had worked the Sprague Avenue beat recognized Donna as Doug and knew she or he was not supposed to be in possession of firearms or ammunition.

Without any hesitation at all he phoned the active-duty police.

Shortly thereafter agents from the ATF raided her home at 2006 E. Empire Avenue. And to their surprise, they discovered dozens of firearms and thousands of rounds of ammo.

Donna, once again, was arrested for possessing firearms and placed in federal custody. A few months later, in August of 2012, as required by law, she was swabbed and her DNA profile was entered into CODIS.

While searching the house, one of the ATF agents noticed that a closet in the back corner of one of the bedrooms had been 'painted' shut. Agents gained entry to the closet but found no firearms or ammunition.

Just boxes.

Of women's panties.

26

Fingernail Clippings and a Vaginal Smear

On September 14, 2012, Washington State Patrol Scientist Mariah Low informed Detective Dresback that the lab got a "hit" on the DNA in the Kathleen Brisbois case. The DNA match from CODIS matched a woman who was in a federal prison in Texas.

A woman? How was that possible?

There was no mistake.

The DNA match, she told Detective Dresback, was from a woman who was arrested in Spokane on gun possession charges in March of that same year. She had undergone gender reassignment surgery in 2000.

Her name was Donna Rebecca Perry aka Douglas Robert Perry, originally from Omak, Washington.

Dresback was tickled.

This was a 22-year-old triple homicide.

He knew that the case would not be easy — he had a lot of work to do.

But he knew they FINALLY had their man.

Or in this case, *woman.*

A quick investigation into Ms. Perry's past revealed that she has significant ties to Spokane and that she had been living there since August of 1988 when she, as Douglas Perry, struck a plea deal with the Feds on some explosives charges.

In fact, illegal possession of guns and firearms was something not unfamiliar to her. Douglas Perry had been busted for it in 1994 and served time in a federal prison for that also.

More importantly, she appeared to be popping up all over the "radar screen" when it came to connections with Sprague Avenue and prostitution. She had been arrested for soliciting only six months before Yolanda Sapp was found dead along Upriver Drive on a cold February morning.

For weeks Dresback and his cold-case partner, Mark Burbridge, dug into Donna aka Douglas Perry. The further they dug, the more convinced they were they had the right guy.

Or gal.

On October 17, 2012, Donna was transferred from federal custody to the Spokane County jail. She was awaiting resolution of her federal case, but Dresback and Burbridge needed to "tune her up" prior to questioning her, and keeping her in Spokane County provided easier access to her.

They had some pretty strong evidence that Doug had been in contact with Kathleen Brisbois in her final hours. But anyone with a 6th-grade education could explain how the DNA got under a whore's fingernails.

He had sex with her and she liked it.

Lab work tying Perry to the murders of Yolanda Sapp and Nickie Lowe might take months or even longer. They needed to get her talking and trip her up if they were going to make a case. On November 15, 2012, the Spokane detectives interviewed Donna Perry.

And trip her up they did.

At one point in the interview, Detective Burbridge reminded Donna that "…people who kill multiple people over periods of time generally don't stop killing." Burbridge then asked Donna why the killing stopped, and her reply was that "Douglas didn't stop; Donna stopped it!"

There it was.

A week later the Spokane police inform the media that Donna, aka Douglas, Perry is a person of interest in the 1990 murder of three prostitutes.

The words eventually became so popular in the media that reporters were characterizing her response as the "Transgender Defense"— whereby the person was not responsible for crimes they might have committed when they were a different gender.

Worse, the media and public were eating it up.

Media outlets even went as far as to claim that it was going to be the trial of the century and revolutionize transgenderism.

Debate raged.

Donna— Doug— whatever you choose to call this person at this point— *never claimed to be using the 'transgender defense.'* It was nothing more than media sensationalism.

On December 14, 2012, Donna was sentenced to 27 months in federal prison for the gun charges. On the same day, detectives processed the old International Scout that Doug owned during the time of the 1990 murders.

They find a .22 shell in it.

None of the previous owners ever owned a .22.

As the investigation continued, the Washington State Crime Lab continued to process the forensic evidence in the case. Techniques and procedures which hadn't even been invented in 1990 were put to use. There was no hurry as Donna was going to be in prison until at least early 2014.

Nearly a year later, on October 31, 2013, Detectives recommend three counts of first-degree murder. It has been exactly 16 years since Doug was released from prison during the Yates string of murders.

On January 14, 2014, the following affidavit is filed with the Spokane County Clerk:

Statement of Investigating Officer
Affidavit of Facts

<u>Count #1 - Yolanda Sapp Murder</u>

On 2/22/1990 Yolanda A. Sapp, BF, 1/10/64, was found nude, halfway down a steep River near 4100 E. Upriver Drive in Spokane, Washington. Ms. Sapp had a green blanket wrapped around her feet. On the river bank above was a white floral patterned blanket with blood on it. This blood was later identified as Ms. Sapp's. The body recovery scene was processed by SPD detectives and Forensic Unit (FU) personnel. All evidence was collected and placed into police property. The body of Ms. Sapp was taken to Holy Family Hospital for autopsy.

Forensic Pathologist Dr. George Lindholm conducted an autopsy on Ms. Sapp and found she had three small caliber gunshot wounds to the chest which completely penetrated her body. Ms. Sapp's cause of death was determined to be gunshot wound and the manner of death was homicide.

SPD Detective Nick Stanley interviewed Ms. Sapp's boyfriend, Darrell Thomas. Mr. Thomas told Detective Stanley that Ms. Sapp was a prostitute and routinely worked the street corners near Sprague and Spokane St. Mr. Thomas said he last saw Ms. Sapp on 2/21/1990 at approximately 11pm. Ms. Sapp said she was going out to prostitute and earn money. Mr. Thomas last saw Ms. Sapp walking towards Sprague and Spokane St.

SPD Detective Mark Burbridge was assigned Ms. Sapp's homicide after SCSO Detective Jim Dresback obtained a CODIS match to DNA in the Kathleen Brisbois homicide. Detective Burbridge reviewed Ms. Sapp's homicide. After reviewing the case, Detective Burbridge believed the blankets dumped on the hillside with Ms. Sapp had a high probability of belonging to the suspect. Detective Burbridge has been a police officer for 25 years and during that time worked in the Special Investigations Unit. One of the Special Investigations Unit's responsibilities is the investigation of prostitution in Spokane. Detective Burbridge has never encountered a street level working prostitute who carried blankets with her. Detective Burbridge checked property and found the green blanket had long ago been destroyed by property, but the white floral blanket still was secured as evidence. Detective Burbridge submitted the white floral blanket for DNA testing.

<u>Count #2 - Nickie Lowe Murder</u>

On 3/25/1990 Nickie I. Lowe, WF, 6/20/55 was found deceased under the Greene St. Overpass at 3200 E. South Riverton in Spokane, Washington. Ms. Lowe was partially nude, draped over the guardrail next to the road. Spokane Police Detectives and FU personnel processed the scene and collected evidence. Ms. Lowe's body was removed from the scene and taken to Holy Family Hospital for autopsy.

Ms. Lowe was known to the Spokane Police Department as a drug user and a street level prostitute.

Forensic pathologist Dr. George Lindholm conducted an autopsy on Ms. Lowe. Ms. Lowe died as the result of a single gunshot wound to the chest. The projectile was recovered from Ms. Lowe's first lumbar vertebra and later identified as a .22 caliber bullet. The cause of death was determined to be gunshot wound and the manner of death was homicide.

Gerald Burchfield was checking the dumpster behind Royal Upholstery for aluminum cans, at 1st/Spokane St., City and County of Spokane, State of Washington, on 3/25/1990 at approximately 0800 hours. Mr. Burchfield noted the dumpster was mostly empty except for some clothing, paperwork and other assorted items. Mr. Burchfield found a red woman's pocketbook among the items. Mr. Burchfield took that pocketbook home. Mr. Burchfield opened the pocketbook when he got home and noted several items with the name Nickie Lowe on them. Mr. Burchfield was watching the news when he saw a story about Ms. Lowe being a homicide victim. Mr. Burchfield called the Spokane Police.

SPD Detective Ron Graves and Bruce Nelson responded to Mr. Burchfield's residence and collected the red pocketbook. Mr. Burchfield showed the detectives where the dumpster was located that contained the additional items. Detectives Graves and Nelson collected as evidence from the dumpster a black/white sweater, pair of blue tennis shoes, one tube of sterile sexual lubricant, one hypodermic syringe, paperwork, eye drops, beer and pop bottles, green plastic lighter, blue Bic pen, matchbook and a blue notepad with writing. The above items were found piled together in the otherwise empty dumpster giving the impression that all these items were dumped together. These items were placed on the property book and then submitted to the Forensic Unit for fingerprinting. Fingerprints were developed on several items to include the tube of sterile sexual lubricant. These fingerprints were never identified to an individual.

SPD Detective Burbridge reviewed the case and asked the Forensic Unit to compare the unidentified fingerprints to Donna R. Perry, WF, 2/26/52, aka Douglas R. Perry, WM, 2/26/52.

Forensic Specialist Kristin Storment subsequently identified fingerprints on the tube of sterile sexual lubricant as belonging to Donna R. Perry, WF, 2/26/52, aka Douglas R. Perry, WM, 2/26/52.

He Said, She Said: The Spokane River Killer

Count #3 - Kathleen Brisbois Murder

On 5/15/1990 Kathleen Brisbois' nude body was found on the west riverbank of the Spokane River between Trent and Pines overpass and the Burlington Northern Railroad trestle in what is now Spokane Valley, Washington. S. Brisbois was a known prostitute and drug user. Spokane County Sheriff Detectives and FU processed the scene and collected evidence. The immediate area above where Ms. Brisbois' body was found appeared to be the scene of a significant fight. There were clothing items spread about, drops of blood and clumps of hair that covered dozens of feet and seemed to lead to the edge directly above the area of the riverbank where the body was found.

Ms. Brisbois' body was removed to Holy Family Hospital where Forensic Pathologist Dr. George Lindholm conducted an autopsy. The autopsy showed that Ms. Brisbois sustained several blows to her head causing skull fracture(s) and she had three broken ribs. Ms. Brisbois also had three gunshot wounds including one to her head, one to her chest and one to her right arm. All three of these gunshot wounds were found to be close contact gunshot wounds. The gunshot wounds were found to have been made by a .22 caliber firearm. Among items collected from the body of Ms. Brisbois at the autopsy was fingernail clippings and a vaginal smear.

The three above murders were investigated as a series of murders due to the close time frame of their occurrence and similar MO. All three were shot with small caliber firearms, all three bodies were found on the Spokane river bank, two of them were found nude and the third was partially undressed, all three victims worked as prostitutes in the Spokane area and all three worked the street on east Sprague. On 06/08/1990 Spokane PD Det. J. Peterson wrote a report about an interview he had with Shannon Zielinski in Yakima, Washington. Det. Peterson interviewed Ms. Zielinski on 06/05/1990 because she reportedly one of the last people to see Kathleen Brisbois alive. During that interview, Det. Peterson asked

Ms. Zielinski if Kathy Brisbois had talked about anyone Brisbois dated who was strange. Ms. Zielinski said there was one guy who Brisbois told her about. This guy drove a small red car and claimed to be a hit man. Your affiant knows that Donna Perry had an apparent affinity for small Geo Metro cars and had at least four of them parked at her house when she was arrested in 2012. Your affiant has also learned that Perry told Chero Everson of FMC Carswell Prison that he was a contract killer.

All three of these murder cases went cold and were eventually assigned and reassigned to various detectives.

Det. Dresback was eventually assigned the Brisbois murder as an unsolved case and he submitted several items for additional DNA testing including the aforementioned fingernail clippings.

On 06/17/09 WSP Scientist Mariah Low called Det. Dresback and informed him that she had developed a full amle profile from under the left middle fingernail of Ms. Brisbois and she would be entering that profile into the Combined DNA Indexing System (CODIS).

On 09/14/12/ Det. Dresback received a call from Mariah Low that they got a "hit" from CODIS on the profile from the fingernail of Ms. Brisbois. This profile matched Douglas R. Perry. WM 02/26/1952.

Douglas/Donna Perry Background

Det. Dresback obtained an NCIC II history on Douglas/Donna Perry. The following are entries from that inquiry that are pertinent to this investigation and do not include all of Perry's criminal arrests:

08-07-1974 Second Degree Assault (Disposition not received) in Okanogan County, Washington

03-16-1979 Firearms/Dangerous Weapons Violation (Guilty) in Okanogan County

03-07-1986 Second Degree Assault (Disposition not received) in Okanogan County

05-15-1987 Reckless Endangerment (Guilty) and (Aiming or Discharging Firearm (Dismissed) in Okanogan County

04-26-1988 Simple Assault/DV (Guilty) in Okanogan County

He was arrested by Spokane PD on 8-13-1989 for Patronizing a Prostitute.

In addition to the above state charges, Perry was arrested by the Federal Government in 1988 for possessing a pipe bomb and in 1994 for Unlawful possession of Firearms and Possession of Ammunition. During this 1988 arrest, there were 49 firearms and 20,000 rounds of ammunition seized from him by the ATF. This included 22 handguns and 27 rifles. Perry is currently in Federal Custody for an Unlawful Possession of Firearms and Possession of Ammunition from an arrest on 3/14/12. When Perry was arrested in 1988, numerous firearms and rounds of ammunition were seized from him which included .22 caliber handguns. When Perry was arrested in 1994, numerous firearms and rounds of ammunition were seized from him. This included at least one .22 caliber handgun and a couple .22 caliber rifles collected during the search of Douglas Perry's residence at 544 E. Dalton in Spokane, Washington. These firearms were subsequently disposed of by the property room in August of 1995 on the authorization of ATF Special Agent Layne Hearst.

Other investigation into Douglas Perry's background showed that on 01/09/1998 Steve Sales (Criminal Investigator) provided information that Douglas R. Perry had been in prison in Oregon from 1/12/95 to 10/31/97. Unnamed inmates told prison staff that Perry used to talk to inmates about taking prostitutes home and feeding them. These unnamed inmates claimed Perry acted very strange and they believe he may be involved in prostitute murders.

On 07/22/98, Spokane PD Officer Hager stopped Douglas Perry on a traffic stop at Sprague and Helena. Perry had been circling the area of Sprague and Napa. He was hostile and was wearing a knife with a 4" blade and a stun gun on his belt. Perry denied any prostitution activity but Off. Hager noted an arrest in 1989 for Patronizing a Prostitute.

On 12/31/98, Douglas Perry picked up prostitute (Valerie Katrell, wf dob: 11/16/74) at Pacific and Cowley and took her to an address he gave as 2007 E. Empire. She saw a lot of guns, knives and a cross-bow in that house. He told her not to worry, he wasn't going to hurt her because he liked her. They had sex and he drove her back to 1st and Cowley. She called the police who were taking a statement from her when she pointed to a green/blue Chevy GEO and said "that's him." SPD Officers Hager and Collins stopped the GEO and identified Douglas Perry as the driver and the person who took Vallerie Katrell to the E. Empire address. A consent search of his vehicle revealed "...attorney papers which said that Douglas R. Perry had a gender psychosis disorder where he does not like females." There were other papers found in the vehicle showing the proper steps for getting a sex change. Perry had two knives and a stun gun on him when he was patted down. Perry told the officers that the reason he was in the area was because he wanted to help prostitutes get off the street.

In early 2000, Douglas Perry went to Bangkok, Thailand whee he received gender reassignment surgery and became Donna R. Perry.

During the early 1990's Perry's girlfriend was a Spokane prostitute named Clairann Gallaway who was living with him. A check of Ms. Gallaway's criminal history shows she was booked at the Spokane County Jail on 2/21/1990 and 05/15/1990. These two booking dates are about the same as the dates that the bodies of

Yolanda Sapp (02/22/1990) and Kathy Brisbois (05/15/1990) were found.

On 03/14/12, the Bureau of Alcohol, Tobacco and Firearms arrested Donna Perry for Unlawful Possession of Firearms and Possession of Ammunition. ATF executed a search warrant on Donna Perry's current residence, 2006 E. Empire in Spokane, Washington. During the search of the residence, ATF recovered more firearms and ammunition.

DONNA PERRY INTERVIEW

On 11/15/12 Detectives Burbridge and Dresback interviewed Donna Perry. Perry denied having murdered anyone. Perry did say she took prostitutes home for sex but was careful to do it when Clairann Gallaway was not there. Perry said she was driving a 1968 International Scout in the late 1980s and early 1990s but she has since sold it. During this interview, we showed Perry thirteen individual photographs one at a time including photographs of Yolanda Sapp, Nickie Lowe, Kathy Brisbois and Clairann Gallaway. These photographs were all booking photographs of known prostitutes during the early to mid-1990s. Except for the photo of Clairann Gallaway, Perry denied recognizing, knowing or having any contact with any of the other 12 women. Perry made a point of explaining that she did not date black girls. Perry said that when she had sex with prostitutes there was no violence so no one would be injured or bleeding.

Det. Burbridge told Perry that people who kill multiple people over periods of time don't stop killing. He asked Perry why the killings stopped, she said, "Douglas didn't stop. Donna stopped it." Perry said that since the sex change, she is paranoid and emotional but won't hurt anybody. As this was discussed further, Perry said, "I'm not going to admit I killed anybody. I didn't. Donna has killed nobody." Det. Burbridge said, "Doug did." To which Donna replied, "I don't know if Doug did or not it was 20 years ago and I have no idea whether he did or didn't." When Det. Dresback asked

Perry how she reconciles what Douglas did, she said she doesn't, "...I walked away from it." When Det. Dresback pointed at the photos of Brisbois and Lowe, Perry said, "I did not kill those two people." Det. Burbridge interjected, "Doug did" to which Perry replied, "No, Doug didn't do it, as far as I know, Doug didn't kill those people." Perry stated that she had a sex change operation as a "...permanent way to control any violence" and explained that when one goes from a male to a female there is "... a very great downturn in violence." Perry said that part of the problem in Doug's life was that Doug was acting like a woman and getting called on the carpet for it but after the sex change, it all fits together.

Det. Dresback obtained a reference DNA sample from Donna Perry using a buccal swab. This reference sample was subsequently submitted to the WSP Lab to be checked against the original DNA evidence from the scenes.

Det. Lyle Johnston located Perry's 1969 International Scout which was parked in Richard Crawfords's yard at 2313 Mockingbird Ln in Woodland, WA. Det. Johnston determined that Perry sold the International Scout to Danny Moller in Spokane, WA who sold it to Robert U. Hodgins in Cle Elum, WA who in turn sold it to Richard Crawford.

On 12/14/12 Det. Dresback and Det. Johnston were present when WSP Crime Lab Scientist Stephen Greenwood processed the International Scout at the WSP Crime Lab in Vancouver, WA. The search of the Scout was pursuant to a search warrant signed in Spokane Superior Court. The Scout in question was a 1969, 2dr international Scout. Det. Dresback found a .22 caliber cartridge under the front passenger floor mat of the Scout. This .22 caliber cartridge was obviously old and had some corrosion on it. It was taken as evidence because the caliber matched the victim's wounds and bullets recovered from the victims.

Det. Johnston contacted the three people who owned the Scout after Perry to ask about the presence of the .22 cartridge. None of them recalled ever owning a .22 caliber firearm.

WSP Scientist Lorraine Heath compared the profile obtained from the fingernail clipping of Ms. Brisbois to the reference DNA sample from Douglas/Donna Perry and found they matched. Ms. Heath's report states, "The combined estimated probability of selecting an unrelated individual at random from the U.S. Population with a matching DNA and Y-STR profile is 1 in 790 sextillion."

Ms. Heath's report also compared Perry's reference sample to the Y-STR DNA typing profile obtained from the vaginal smear of Ms. Brisbois. Ms. Heath reported that "This Y-STR profile has been observed 7364 times in the U.S. Y-STR database and is not expected to occur more frequently than 1 in 3 male individuals in the U.S. population."

Lorraine Heath identified DNA on the white floral blanket found with the body of Yolanda Sapp using the YSTR method. This DNA was consistent with Donna R. Perry, WF, 2/26/52, aka Douglas R. Perry. The YSTR DNA which was identified has been observed one time in the U.S. YSTR database and is not expected to occur more frequently than 1 in 330 male individuals in the US male population.

CHERO EVERSON INTERVIEW AT CARSWELL

On 06/19/13 - Det. Dresback and Det. Burbridge interviewed Chero Everson in an office at FMC Carswell in Ft. Worth, Texas. Ms. Everson was a cell mate of Donna Perry who had been sentenced to 18 months in Federal Prison for Unlawful Possession of Firearms. According to Ms. Everson, Perry took a liking to Ms. Everson and talked to Ms. Everson about her (Perry's) past. Perry claimed to Ms. Everson that she was a contract killer and had a tremendous knowledge of guns. Perry told Ms. Everson that Perry had killed nine prostitutes while "just taking care of business." Perry told Ms. Everson that Perry had gender reassignment surgery in Thailand and Perry claimed to be a sociopath. Perry explained to Ms. Everson that the reason Perry killed these women *was because Perry couldn't breed and the women had the ability have children and they were wasting it being "pond scum." Ms. Everson said Perry claimed that she didn't bury the women she killed she just shot them dead and it was someone else's job to bury them. Perry further told Ms. Everson that she killed these women in the Washington area and "Spokane was hot." Perry told Ms. Everson that the police destroyed some of Perry's guns including some evidence used in the killings.*

This affidavit was prepared by Detective Dresback.

Donna aka Douglas Perry was booked into Spokane County Jail on March 14, 2014 on three counts of murder.
Those fucking whores.

27
Yolanda, Nickie and Kathleen

On March 17, 2014, Donna refused to show up in court, because the docket had listed the court date as belonging to a Douglas R. Perry. Under Washington law, she was, legally, no longer referred to as Douglas Perry. The courts admitted their mistake and corrected the information. Once again, however, the mainstream media went nuts with the entire "transgender" issue.

From the NY Daily News on March 19, 2014:

Transgender woman held in prostitutes' murder blames male alter ego, Douglas
They at least got one of them.
A transgender woman accused of killing three prostitutes in 1990 says it wasn't her who killed them but her violent male alter ego, Douglas.
The head-spinning defense given by Donna Perry of Spokane, Wash., comes after her arrest in the shooting deaths of Yolanda

Sapp, Kathleen Brisbois and Nickie Lowe, whose bodies were found naked along the Spokane River.

The 62-year-old, who underwent gender reassignment surgery in 2000, allegedly told police in 2012 that her decision to change from Douglas to Donna was done in part "as a permanent way to control violence," KXLY reported.

Despite being linked to the murders through DNA evidence, according to an arrest affidavit, Perry has argued her innocence.

In an interview with detectives in 2012, she allegedly said that she didn't know what Douglas Perry may have done.

"I'm not going to admit I killed anybody, I didn't. Donna has killed nobody," she said.

She argues Douglas Perry is an entirely different person and the crimes were been committed 20 years ago − too long for her to remember.

When detectives asked her why the murders stopped, she allegedly replied: "Douglas didn't stop. Donna stopped it."

Adding to the confusion, during her bond hearing on Tuesday, her defense attorney claimed she was unable to meet with the defendant because jailhouse records have her listed as Douglas Perry.

"They say she's not here because they have her listed under her prior name," defense attorney Anna Nordtvedt said, according to Spokesman.com.

Her bail was set at $1 million.

The story was written by Nina Golgowski and typified how ridiculous the media perception was becoming.

As is always the case in a trial of this nature, Donna was evaluated for mental competency. She was found competent to stand trial and aid in her own defense. After a number of delays, the case was set to be tried in September of 2016.

On September 14, 2016, rumors swirled that one of Donna's attorneys might have acted unethically, because they had access to Robert Yates's files, and by attempting to use Yates to raise reasonable doubt in this case— they would in turn be putting Yates's plea deal in trouble.

A monumental conflict of interest.

Three of Donna's attorneys withdrew, and the trial was delayed again until June of 2017.

When the trial finally started in June of 2017, the prosecution retold their story linking the three women's deaths. They all knew each other and died in similar manners, their bodies dumped like trash along the Spokane River.

Nude and with no consideration for their dignity.

They all died from small caliber gunshot wounds to the chest.

Doug Perry's DNA was found on a blood-soaked blanket only a few feet from where Yolanda Sapp's body was discovered.

Otherwise her body was completely naked when a woman walking a popular trail along the Spokane River found Yolanda's body on a cold February morning.

Prosecutors described how a partial fingerprint was matched to Doug Perry. The print was recovered from Nickie Lowe's belongings that had been dumped in a dumpster off of Sprague Avenue. The items in the dumpster were discovered, along with Nickie Lowe's tennis shoes and pocketbook with her ID inside, only hours after her body was found nude and draped over a guardrail under the Greene Street Bridge— not more than a couple of hundred yards from where Yolanda Sapp had been discovered.

The prosecution then described how Kathleen Brisbois had been discovered along the Spokane River near the Trent Avenue trestle. She had fought for her life. She wanted to live. She had sustained multiple defense wounds, having been shot in the arm, the chest, and then finished off in the head.

She scraped and clawed and fought and screamed.

Whoever was trying to kill her ended up leaving their DNA under her fingernails.

It is what people do when being attacked.

They scratch.

Prosecutors pointed out that Doug had the kinds of weapons that were used in the killings in his possession on multiple occasions.

He knew how they worked, and he knew how to get them.

He had threatened to kill people before.

In fact, while in prison for her most recent gun charges, Donna had told another inmate that she had killed whores.

She killed them and left them to be buried by someone who cared about them.

He said.

She said.

Detectives Burbridge and Dresback detailed how Donna admitted that the killing wasn't stopped by Doug; it was stopped by her. They even highlighted how they had found ammo similar to what was used to kill Yolanda, Nickie, and Kathleen in the vehicle Doug owned at the time.

When it was all said and done, even the defense probably knew that the jury was convinced. Trying to refute the evidence on a case-by-case basis would only solidify its validity even more. They had to try to sideswipe the jury by using a common tactic of "the defense rests" without presenting any evidence. The idea is that the jury might be swayed into believing the "burden of proof" has not been met. Hopefully, at least from the defense's perspective, the jury thinks they will look like fools if they convict.

If the defense is so confident, they must be not guilty, right?

Without offering any evidence, the defense did exactly that.

In closing, defense Attorney Brian Whitaker argued that the threshold of reasonable doubt was not overcome in this case. He pointed out that prosecutors never really pinned down a motive for the killings. In fact, the motive changed as the prosecution saw fit. There was little physical evidence that proved Doug Perry killed any of these women.

Sure, he might have had lots of interactions with them. *He knew them.*

But nothing the prosecution brought forward proved he, or she, killed anyone.

The entire interrogation of Donna Perry, he argued, was nothing more than a technique used to get confessions from innocent people when the evidence doesn't support the conclusion.

With a pill bottle in hand, her defense attorney made a bizarre last ditch metaphorical attempt to raise reasonable doubt. He held a bottle of Tylenol in his hand and equated the threshold of reasonable doubt to opening a 30-year-old bottle of Tylenol— *you better be damn sure.*

"You have to be really confident before you break into that old bottle of Tylenol," he claimed.

The jury deliberated for a few hours.

Donna was found guilty of first-degree murder on all three counts.

Like nearly everything in his life he attempted to do, Doug's grandiose scheme had failed miserably.

He would likely spend the rest of his life in prison.

As a woman.

During her pre-sentencing evaluation, Donna, once again, just like she did when she was Doug Perry, begged and pleaded to go to Eastern State Mental Hospital. Victims' family members implored the court to give her the maximum sentence allowable by law as she now has more access to abuse women since her gender reassignment.

Donna herself had little to say when asked about her conviction, "I have nothing to say about it. It wouldn't do me any good. Hear no evil, see no evil, speak no evil."

Prosecutors, however, made the most compelling argument of all— and it wasn't really even an argument. The court, they reiterated, had no choice under the law but to sentence Donna to a life sentence without the possibility of parole for each victim, "*As a result of the jury finding that there was more than one victim and each murder was part of the same common scheme or plan, this court has no discretion and must sentence the defendant to life in prison without the possibility of parole on each count."*

On July 24, 2017, the judge did exactly that.

Donna Rebecca Perry, aka Douglas Robert Perry, will spend the rest of his and/or her life behind bars.

With no possibility of parole.

As of this writing, the 1992 murder of Sherry Palmer still remains unsolved.

28
Final Thoughts

When this case first came to my attention, I wanted to avoid becoming another whining writer who fanatically proclaimed that we seem to have more respect for the dogshit we pick up from our neatly manicured lawns than we have for the women who occupy Sprague Avenue. Rants about how Sprague is really our fault and we are the problem. Maybe if we all just loved each other a little bit more, right?

Horseshit.

When whores get killed, the first thing we wonder is if it's a serial killer. Part of us wants it be. We want those predators out there.

Feeding.

Feeding on somebody besides us.

And when they are killing whores they seem to be satiated.

Most of the public starts to believe that the only way whores get killed is by serial killers. If there are no serial killers going around, then the whores must be OK, right?

Oh, and, quit calling them whores.

When I set about putting "pen to paper," I had endeavored to remain as respectful to the victims as I possibly could without watering down their stories.

These victims were human beings. They left behind loved ones. They had hopes and dreams beyond the latrine that is Sprague Avenue. In most of the articles or media coverage of this case, these women were relabeled as "prostitutes" within the first 20 seconds of any coverage.

What a simple way to communicate to the listener. What are they really saying?

Obviously there is no need to panic — the killer is only killing whores.

Obviously, the prostitute probably did something to deserve her fate.

Obviously, this doesn't concern any of us — let the police care about it.

I wanted and attempted to interview family members. I remembered when Rich, my stepfather, was killed and how the press and media tried to interview my mother and me.

It sucked.

I tried my best to find the right time, but based on my experience of living through the murder of my stepfather — there never is a right time.

When my stepfather was murdered on the west side of the state of Washington (13 days before Kathleen Brisbois), everyone seemed to care about a young, rich, white guy who was a real estate broker.

Everyone wanted to help.

Three women are murdered in Spokane?

Well, they were prostitutes.

"Sports and weather, next..."

And then it dawned on me. The victim's story is not mine to tell. Sure, I gathered what info I could and even spoke with a few family members of the victims. All I spoke to were wonderful human beings. The stories of their loved ones are theirs.

Not mine.

Consistent with all of my books, I try to write about cases in which I am connected in some, even miniscule, way. In this case, I did have a strangely unique personal connection.

As many of my readers know from past books, as a young man I had my own bouts with alcoholism and drug abuse. Thankfully, I have been free from those demons for more than 25 years now. A large part of that freedom is owed to Alcoholics Anonymous (A.A.). I spent a fair share of my time in and around A.A. halls throughout the Seattle area as a young man. At one point, I ran across a gal who had birthed twins fathered by one of my friends. And no, recovering, twenty-something alcoholics don't always marry each other when they conceive. Sometimes they hate each other and battle over child support and visitation schedules.

Well, this particular gal I knew through A.A., who prefers to be referred to by only her first name, Christy, had relapsed and had been turning tricks in Spokane in the mid- to-late '90s. I had not seen her or interacted with her in almost eight years — and I certainly doubt she would even remember who I was. But she told another friend a story of how she was turning a trick in the back of a guy's van, and he couldn't get it up, so he was getting irritated. According to her, he hit her "so fucking hard she saw stars." He then dumped her out of the back of the van and left. When she awoke he was gone. Over a year later she had sobered up and was driving her Ford Ranger to Seattle to visit friends. Along Interstate 90, while traversing Snoqualmie Pass, she was involved in a major car accident. At the hospital, she was given an X-Ray of her head, and one of the hospital staff asked Christy why she did not tell them that she had bullet fragments in her head.

She had no idea they were there and did not recall ever being shot.

By this time, Yates had been arrested, and she started to recall the date she had been in the van where she thought she had been punched.

Eventually, she identified Yates as her assailant, and bullet fragments removed from her head matched the weapon used to kill many of his victims.

She was the only victim of Yates known to have survived.

I attempted to track her down for an interview through the mutual friends we have but was unsuccessful.

Of course, everyone wanted to criticize the Spokane County and City of Spokane Police forces for "not doing a good job." Sure, they could have caught Yates sooner had they known they were looking for a white Corvette instead of a white Camaro— but all in all— after the shit went down— the Spokane area detectives had done a pretty damn good job of knowing which murders were related to which.

Is Sherry Palmer one of Doug's victims?

I don't know— police don't seem to think so.

When everyone was saying they all HAD to be connected, and then it turned out they weren't— did critics of the local Spokane law enforcement community publish apologies and retractions in the local media?

Fuck no.

When the Spokane Police detectives got called on the carpet by Mark Fuhrman in his book, "Murder in Spokane" (available on Amazon— you're welcome, Mark), did he send them any notes of apology? Maybe he did.

Thankfully, based on my experience in dealing with detectives like John Hinds, who tracked down the man who killed my step-dad in less than two weeks (see: *Murder Myself, Murder I am*), or Detective Tedd Betts, who continued to dig into the murder of Linda McNeely while every media outlet continued to run the narrative that Linda McNeely had "asked her husband to kill her" (see: *For She Knows Not What She Does*)— when that CLEARLY was never the case, I have never been in the position of having to criticize detectives.

But this case was nearly 22 years old.

Every detective that worked the murders of Yolanda Sapp, Nickie Lowe, and Kathleen Brisbois worked them with passion and a sense of duty.

In the end, detectives Mark Burbridge and Jim Dresback made these cases.

By the time they went to trial, evidence was more than 27 years old.

Through every delay and every defense team tactic hoping that a critical witness would die or another piece of evidence would get lost or destroyed, the Spokane County Prosecutor's Office stayed the course.

With blood from an old wool blanket, half a fingerprint from a tube of KY jelly, and DNA from under Kathleen Brisbois's fingernails— combined with the brilliant interrogation of Donna Perry by Dresback and Burbridge— the Spokane law enforcement community ripped the monkey from their metaphorical backs.

This case was a no-win from the start.

But they won it.

All of Spokane law enforcement are owed a big thank you from many of the press and media.

But it won't come.

Nor will any of them expect it.

They will keep doing their jobs.

But as one who has had family members murdered, known men who have murdered others, and watched from the outside like so many of us do— thank you Detectives.

Thank you.

One cannot discount the piss and vinegar that must have been in the soul of Kathleen Brisbois. I suspect Yolanda and Nickie had no idea what was coming— but Kathleen took her final moments and collected evidence under her fingernails.

Her will to live brought Doug Perry to justice.

And yes, I say *Doug Perry*.

Donna Perry is no more than a little coward's way to hide from what was done.

And it didn't work.

This case is no more about transgenderism than Charles Manson was about movie fans.

One final note.

Clairann.

Clairann Gallaway passed away before the publishing of this book. Shortly after the murder of Kathleen Brisbois, she disappeared off the grid COMPLETELY. No prostitution, no drugs, no thefts. No criminal convictions of any kind. She may have known or at least suspected what happened back in the spring of 1990, but like many women who suffer from as severe a mental illness as she did, no one could possibly blame her for how she responded.

She ran.

And she ran far.

By the time she resurfaced, the wagons had been circled around her pretty tightly by her family. My impressions of her are based on conversations with women who claimed to have known her when she lived in Spokane and Sequim, Washington. Whether my writing has done her justice or not, I hope she, and her family, are at peace.

She seemed like a dandy gal.

He Said, She Said: The Spokane River Killer

Jon Keehner

Pacific Northwest True Crime Series

Book #1:
"Murder Myself, Murder I Am."

Book #2:
"For She Knows Not What She Does"

He Said, She Said: The Spokane River Killer

Get e-mail updates of my future books with sneak peeks and SPECIAL offers not available anywhere else!

http://jonkeehner.com/subscribe/

Connect with me:

Facebook
https://www.facebook.com/Drjonkeehner

Pinterest
http://www.pinterest.com/jonkeehner/

Google +
https://plus.google.com/u/0/110543336429732283420/about

JonKeehner.com
http://jonkeehner.com/

E-Mail
corvuslatrans@gmail.com

He Said, She Said: The Spokane River Killer

The Snake River Killer

A cold case is not a closed case!
PLEASE HELP

From top left:
Kristina Nelson, Christina White

From bottom left:
Kristin David, Stephen Pearsall, Brandy Miller

Jon Keehner

On April 28, 1979, 12 year old Christina White disappeared while attending the Asotin County fair a few miles south of Clarkston, Washington in rural southeastern Washington state.

In 1981, University of Idaho student Kristen David was last seen alive before riding her bike from Moscow, Idaho 30 miles south toward Lewiston, Idaho. Her headless torso and leg were discovered along the Snake River 8 days later. Police believe the same killer is responsible for both victims.

On September 12, 1982, 35 year old Stephen Pearsall was dropped off by a friend at the Lewiston Civic Theater, where he was employed as a janitor, to practice with his clarinet. He was never seen again.

That same night, September 12, 1982, 18 year old Brandy Miller and her 21 year old step-sister Kristina Nelson also disappeared. Their bodies were discovered 2 years later near Kendrick, Idaho— 27 miles away.

With the advent of DNA testing technology that was not available in 1982, the Kristin David and Brandy Miller cases have recently been re-opened.

Anyone who may have information regarding this case is asked to contact the Lewiston Police at the number below. Cold cases are NOT closed cases.

PLEASE HELP BRING ANSWERS TO THE VICTIMS FAMILIES.

ANY INFO PLEASE CONTACT:

Lewiston Police Department's Investigation Section
(208) 746-0171

He Said, She Said: The Spokane River Killer

Acknowledgments

This book would not have possible without the dedication, motivation, and hard work of my editor, Nancy Teppler, or as I like to call her, Nan. She made me laugh when I needed it, kept me grounded when I started to wander, and most of all, she taught me how to properly respect my readers. Thank you, Nan!

In addition, this book would not have been possible were it not for the tireless work of Spokane County and City of Spokane detectives, prosecuting attorneys, and forensic analysis teams.

A special thank you to my beta readers, Amy and Nadine, who suffered through endless iterations of edited and non-edited chapters and sections. Their feedback was vital.

Thank you to my wife and three sons who have suffered the laborious task of watching me dive headfirst into the deep, dark, and maddening world of murder. They have indulged my multiple-year obsession with three (now four) dead women whom I never knew.

And finally, to Dexter-- the best writing partner I could ever ask for, he helped me write my Master's Thesis, my Ph.D. dissertation, three other books, and three scientific journal articles. Without him, I would surely have failed, and been overrun with mice.

He Said, She Said: The Spokane River Killer

Jon Keehner

Made in the USA
Lexington, KY
02 November 2017